# EDISTO ISLAND
## 1663 TO 1860

# EDISTO ISLAND

## 1663 TO 1860

### WILD EDEN TO COTTON ARISTOCRACY

CHARLES SPENCER

Charleston · London

History
PRESS

Published by The History Press
Charleston, SC 29403
www.historypress.net

Copyright © 2008 by Charles Spencer
All rights reserved

*Front cover images:* Photograph by Henry P. Moore, courtesy of New Hampshire Historical Society.
*Back cover image:* Photographs courtesy of Edisto Island Historic Preservation Society (top) and Richard D. Porcher (bottom).

First published 2008

Manufactured in the United Kingdom

ISBN 978.1.59629.184.3

Library of Congress CIP data applied for.

*To the memory of*
*Mary Murray Spencer*
*who started me early on local history.*

*And to*
*Sheila Lane Beardsley*
*who believed I could write it.*

# CONTENTS

# CONTENTS

# PREFACE

O ne book or another about Edisto Island has been writing itself in the back of my mind for at least thirty years, while I labored in Washington and traveled on five continents on the taxpayers' business. For me, Edisto is that place that each of us holds as an anchor deep inside, the place one's thoughts return to at odd moments in Cairo, Quito or Anaheim, as if to reassure oneself that this, too, shall pass, that you'll get through it somehow, and some things will always be there, will never change. (Would it were so.)

The opportunity and the need for this book came together in a conversation with Sheila Beardsley, founding curator of the Edisto Island Historic Preservation Society (EIHPS), on Edisto Beach in 2000. I recognized my opportunity because my family's nest was empty, as a retiree my time was my own and I no longer needed to work for a living. Sheila talked about the serious need for a full-length, documented history of the island and the beach. For some time she had been on the lookout for a qualified researcher, perhaps a graduate student, who would write the book and get a thesis out of it. Would I help her find such a person?

Well, did she think *I* could do it? *Of course*, she thought I could do it. And the rest is (you guessed it) history.

The intellectual and financial sponsorship of this project by EIHPS was critical. The society recruited volunteer researchers, opened private archives and enlisted the help of scholars and librarians who expedited the work. Large sums of the society's money, contributed by enthusiastic members and friends, were used to reimburse me for out-of-pocket research expenses I never could have afforded otherwise. I am very grateful for this help, and I deeply regret the frustration I caused successive presidents and staff of EIHPS as the project's completion stretched on from three years, to four, to five and now to six. I can only plead good intentions and inexperience, never before having undertaken a book-length project for publication. I hope the result will serve the purposes that Sheila first had in mind.

From the outset I made clear that any history I wrote would deal explicitly and frankly with slavery and racism; this was not going to be just about the plantation owners. I intended to relate, as factually as I could, the story of *all* communities whose histories are inextricably intertwined on our beloved island. EIHPS, to its credit, said it would have it no other way. I have worked hard to do that. I hope that both white and African American Edistonians, their descendants and their friends and relatives in the "Edisto diaspora" will find here a deeper understanding of their shared history, a deeper appreciation of the unique contributions of each community to the fragile fabric we call Edisto. I am more convinced than ever that each community has produced admirable legacies, remarkable leaders, courageous heroes and creative men and women who deserve our respect. As one reminder of the huge disparity between the power and wealth of the white and black races on Edisto during much of its history, the term "Golden Age" always appears in quotation marks in this book.

This book, as it happens, turned out to be two books. My manuscript (essentially finished in January 2005) was far longer than any commercial or academic publisher would normally issue for what is, after all, a local history. Would I be willing to cut it down almost by half? I would not. I was tired of working on it by then, and the full manuscript satisfied my obligation to EIHPS. I was ready to give up on publication and get my life back. Then The History Press generously offered to publish it in two volumes, and here it is. I am very grateful to them for that decision. Without The History Press, this book very likely would not have found an audience larger than those who already were acquainted with Edisto Island and familiar with EIHPS.

Even with two volumes, a large chunk of my research did not fit. I transcribed several long sets of documents about Edisto Island and its people, African American and white, that I thought would be useful to readers who wanted to pursue further research on a specific family, place or event. I carefully edited and reformatted several other document sets, already transcribed by others, to maximize their accuracy and accessibility and to supply context and identifications. All these original documents, some 150 pages in all, I hoped to append to these books. But we had to leave them out to hold the books to a commercially viable length. Instead, EIHPS has arranged to issue those supplemental papers as a separate volume called *Documents on Edisto Island History*. It will be available in printed or digital format. For further information, visit the EIHPS website, www.edistomuseum.com, or write to them at 8123 Chisolm Plantation Road, Edisto Island, SC 29438.

This book disappoints me in one major respect. The African American community on Edisto Island does not make a significant enough appearance in my book, especially in the twentieth-century chapters. I believe I have discovered and used enough published and archival material on Edisto's African Americans in the eighteenth and nineteenth centuries to begin to make their experience "come alive" for those who do not share their history and to try to balance the treatment of the white community up to about 1900. To continue to build that balance through the twentieth century would have required extensive interviews with African American family historians and community leaders living today. That did not happen. I think I understand why. Still, it is a serious shortcoming of this book, which is most evident in volume two. The African American families and their lives on Edisto Island, especially in the twentieth century, is a story yet to be told systematically and in depth. I sincerely hope that someone will take up the task soon. We all need to hear it.

# ACKNOWLEDGEMENTS

I gratefully acknowledge the contributions of several persons who know a lot and care a lot about Edisto's history, and whose generous help is reflected in this final product:

JACK BOINEAU made available his amazing ten-year collection of Edisto Island maps and plantation plats, and helped me for days at a time to piece together the mosaic of early land history.

DAVID LYBRAND made available to me his now-completed master map of Edisto plantations in the 1850s (Chapter 7), and was always available for me to consult with when I was stuck.

NORMA ARMSTRONG repeatedly located needed materials in Charleston libraries, archives and land records when I was five hundred miles away in Virginia and discovered holes in my data set.

RICHARD PORCHER generously sent me whole chapters of *The Story of Sea Island Cotton* while it was still in manuscript, to save me the effort of parallel research on its history and production.

STEPHANIE SPENCER edited my final manuscript of both volumes, and formatted them to the publisher's specifications, while working a full-time job. Greater love hath no daughter.

BETTY MURRAY BRYAN gave me free use of a vacation cottage on Edisto Island, at any time and for any length of time, for four years, as a base of operations for in-state research. What can I say?

Several published authors gave me moral support and reassurance when I most needed it. First and foremost was SHEILA BEARDSLEY, as noted above. Another was NICK LINDSAY. And another was HARVEY TEAL. If they think you can do it, who are you to doubt yourself?

The research for this book has been a true community effort. Dozens of persons responded to my appeals and gave me copies of privately held documents, or steered me to valuable sources of which I was unaware, or both. They include:

# Acknowledgements

Bill Albergotti
Peter Andrews
Arthur Bailey
Billy and Pinckney Bailey
Bob Baynard
Jack Boineau
Gary Brightwell
Patrick and Rhoda Butler
Fran Cardwell
Amy Connor
Bill Cooper
John Culbertson
Jane Darby
Sarah Fick
Mary Floyd
Lewis Frampton
Elaine Freeman
P.C. Grimball
Waring Hills
Yates Hazlehurst
Frances Horsley
Gordon Houston
Alice and Harry Hutson
Florence Kizer
Chuck Klotzberger
Jim Lawson
Nick and Dubose Lindsay

David Lybrand
Clara Mackenzie
Robert Mackintosh
Pat Martin
Jane McCollum
Linda McLain
Terry Meggett
Marion Mitchell
Chick Morrison
Marion Norwood
Olaf Otto
Nancy Peeples
Ted Pockman
Jann Poston
Gary Rake
Pam Santo
Ben Skardon
Bud Skidmore
Daniel Spencer
Stephanie Spencer
Dottie Thomas
Lish Thompson
Mary Townsend
Reggie Washington
Budge Weidman
Curtis Worthington

I have no doubt that errors have crept in despite all the help I received. The errors are all mine.

My Murray cousins on Edisto Island—Gerry and Okie, Jim and Linda—took me into their homes and their families whenever I was around, no questions asked. There is no better way to relax from the grind than to "hang out" with family—and eat delicious seafood. Thanks, you all.

Finally, Lucy Norman Spencer endured seven years of marriage to a novice author who bit off more than he imagined. She stood by me longer than I deserved, and I am very grateful for her support.

CHAPTER 1.

# EDISTO BEFORE COLONIZATION

## The Land

"Sea island" is both a cultural and a geographic term. Most of this book is about the human cultures that have evolved on one of the sea islands over the last three hundred years. In this chapter, however, we use "sea island" in its narrower sense: a unique landform that occurs in the United States only on the Southeast coast. The sea islands stretch along the coasts of South Carolina, Georgia and Florida from James Island, at Charleston, to Amelia Island, near Jacksonville. Edisto Island nestles near the upper end of this 180-mile swath of coastline; its side nearest Charleston is barely 20 air miles from Charleston Harbor. (See Figure 1)

Edisto is one of the largest sea islands. With seventy square miles of land above mean high tide, it is about the size of the District of Columbia, and is second only to its neighbor, Johns Island, among the sea islands.[1]

Like most of the sea islands, what we consider to be Edisto Island is really a composite of many islands, large and small, connected by bridges and causeways, assembled by nature into a giant jigsaw puzzle. (See Figure 2) The high land areas are filled out by extensive salt marshes, which are both physically and culturally part of Edisto. This composite island is defined by deep water boundaries: the Atlantic Ocean on the southeast, the North Edisto River on the northeast, the Dawhoo River on the north and the South Edisto River on the west. Together, the high land and marshes of Edisto Island form an irregular rectangle about twelve miles long and ten miles wide.

Edisto Island proper ("Big Edisto") is by far the largest piece of "Edisto Island." Little Edisto Island, Jehossee Island, Edisto Beach, Edingsville Beach, Botany Bay Island, Bailey Island and Scanawah Island are other large pieces of the composite. Dozens of smaller islands, from many acres down to a fraction of an acre, complete the mosaic of Edisto Island. Some of the smaller constituent islands will be noted, as appropriate, in succeeding chapters.

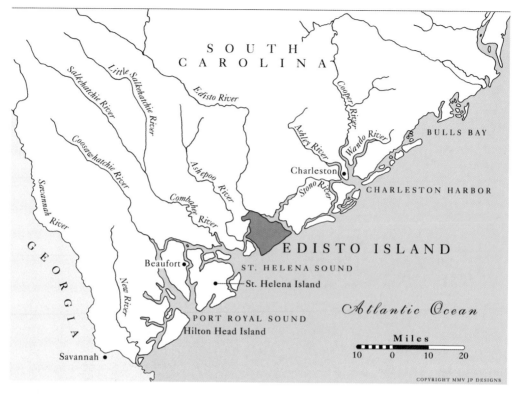

Figure 1. Location of Edisto Island, South Carolina. *Adapted, with permission, from Kovacik and Winberry, 1987.*

## An Erosion-Remnant Island

Edisto Island—the entire composite except for its barrier island beaches—is an erosion-remnant island that once was part of the mainland.[2]

For most of the last 130 million years, the Atlantic Ocean lapped against the Piedmont at what is now the fall line, near Columbia. During those millions of years, rivers flowing out of the mountains and the Piedmont deposited submerged strata of sediments far out to sea. Then, about 170,000 years ago, when the earth cooled, gigantic ice caps and glaciers formed, and sea levels began falling worldwide.

The formerly submerged sediments became the coastal plain and the continental shelf of South Carolina. The coastal plain now contained rivers and streams that drained rainfall into the ocean. By about sixteen thousand years ago, the great North American ice sheet extended south of the Great Lakes; the ocean level was more than three hundred feet lower than today;[3] the coastline was fifty miles out at the edge of the continental shelf; Edisto Island was just part of the coastal plain; and Edisto Beach did not yet exist.

The final event in the creation of Edisto Island came about when the earth started warming again. Continental ice sheets started melting and sea levels began rising. Until

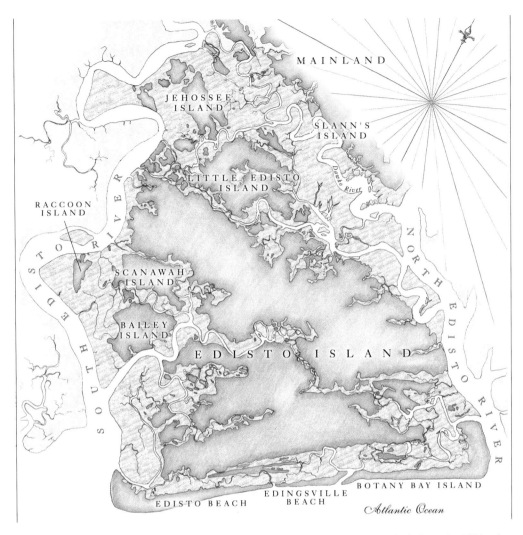

Figure 2. Edisto Island is a natural composite of many smaller islands. Topography is from the 1850s; the modern beaches have different shapes.

about five thousand years ago, the seas rose steadily; then they stopped. As the Atlantic Ocean rose, it flooded the outer coastal plain and reached the present coastline. The plain on this part of the coast was characterized by river mouths every ten to thirty miles, cutting through low ridges or hills that ran parallel to the coast. Behind these hills, smaller rivers and streams drained into the larger rivers. As the sea rose, it first flooded the river mouths, making large sounds and tidal estuaries (St. Helena Sound and North Edisto River), then flooded the smaller streams behind the hills (Bohicket and St. Pierre's Creeks, Dawhoo and Stono Rivers). The ocean completely flooded not just river- and streambeds, but their entire valleys. The irregular landmasses now cut off from the mainland (and from each other) by tidal rivers and creeks are the erosion-remnant islands we call sea islands.

# Edisto's Barrier Islands

Edisto Beach came into being in a way totally different from Edisto Island, and geologically the beach is much younger than the island.

As the sea level rose between sixteen thousand and five thousand years ago, waves beating on the headlands between the river mouths may have eroded the shorelines and created sand spits parallel with the coast. Over time, the sand spits apparently became substantial barrier islands, separated from the coast by narrow bays. As the sea continued to rise, the coastline retreated and the sand spits or barrier islands tended to retreat with it, by means of the over-wash of waves during storms. When the coastline stabilized at approximately its present location, many of these barrier islands, including Edisto Beach, also stabilized, and the narrow bay behind Edisto Beach became a marsh. (See Figure 2 and Figure 3) Meanwhile, the barrier island grew seaward by the accretion of sand, which formed successive low ridges parallel to the beach, with shallow depressions or swales between them. This is the typical topography of a beach-ridge barrier island.

Today Edisto Beach measures 4.4 miles from Jeremy Inlet to the South Edisto River and contains about 920 acres of high land. Botany Bay Island, at the mouth of the North Edisto River, is also a beach-ridge barrier island, though much smaller than it was in quite recent history. It is 1.2 miles long and comprises 260 acres of high land.[4] (See Figure 3)

At the same time that Edisto Beach and Botany Bay Island were created, and by the same process, Edingsville Beach and Botany Beach took shape in front of Edisto Island. It is very likely, in fact, that these four beaches were formed as a single barrier island just a few thousand years ago.

Subsequent natural forces have divided, redivided and recombined the one barrier island into several. Successive maps (Figure 3), covering just the three-hundred-odd years since the arrival of European cartographers, document the breathtaking fluidity of Edisto's barrier islands.

In 1696 there were three barrier islands. Frampton's and Jeremy Inlets were already in place. Edisto Beach was the thinnest of the three beaches. In 1786 there were four barrier islands. Edisto Beach had taken much the shape it has today, but it was two beaches, not one, separated by an inlet approximately where a lagoon remains today, behind the main boulevard. By 1825 that inlet had "healed," and again there were only three barrier islands. From the 1876 map we know that all three barrier islands had extensive forested dunes (see below, "Maritime Forest Community"), and Edingsville was a thriving summer resort. But successive hurricanes took their toll, and by 1918 Edingsville Beach and much of Botany Bay Island were reduced to a narrow strand with no dune ridges, while Edisto Beach was clearly gaining width to seaward.[5] Hurricane Gracie in 1959 cut a new inlet through Botany Bay Island to Townsend Creek,[6] so again—for the present—there are four barrier islands in front of Edisto Island.

The northernmost corner of the old Botany Bay Island remains a high beach-ridge barrier island, with roads and houses. But the longest part of it (now called just Botany Beach) is, like its neighbor, Edingsville Beach, a classic "thin, retreating" barrier island. And the northeastern end of Edisto Beach, which is part of the state park, also has all

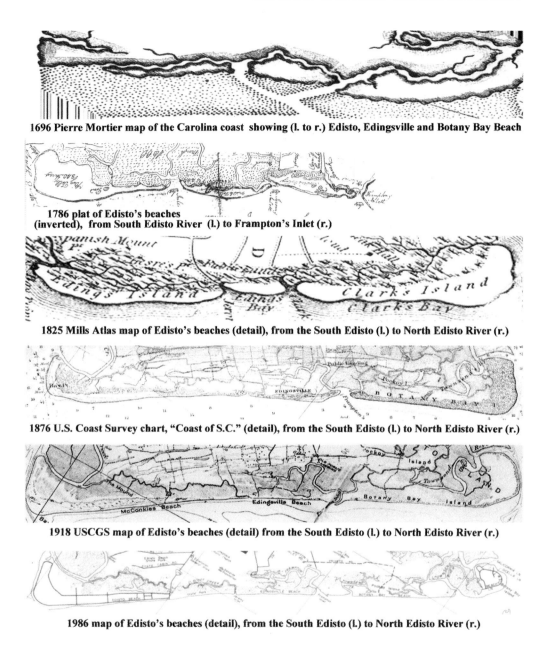

**1696 Pierre Mortier map of the Carolina coast showing (l. to r.) Edisto, Edingsville and Botany Bay Beach**

**1786 plat of Edisto's beaches
(inverted), from South Edisto River (l.) to Frampton's Inlet (r.)**

**1825 Mills Atlas map of Edisto's beaches (detail), from the South Edisto (l.) to North Edisto River (r.)**

**1876 U.S. Coast Survey chart, "Coast of S.C." (detail), from the South Edisto (l.) to North Edisto River (r.)**

**1918 USCGS map of Edisto's beaches (detail) from the South Edisto (l.) to North Edisto River (r.)**

**1986 map of Edisto's beaches (detail), from the South Edisto (l.) to North Edisto River (r.)**

Figure 3. The evolution of Edisto's beaches from 1696 to 1986.

the earmarks of a thin, retreating barrier island, though at this writing it is still connected to the robust western end of the barrier island.

Ocean currents parallel to the coast have carried away the beaches' sands for many years, wearing them thin from front to back, while depositing those sands elsewhere along the coast. Meanwhile, summer hurricanes and winter storms have attacked the beaches frontally, flattening their dunes and destroying their plants, shrubs and trees.

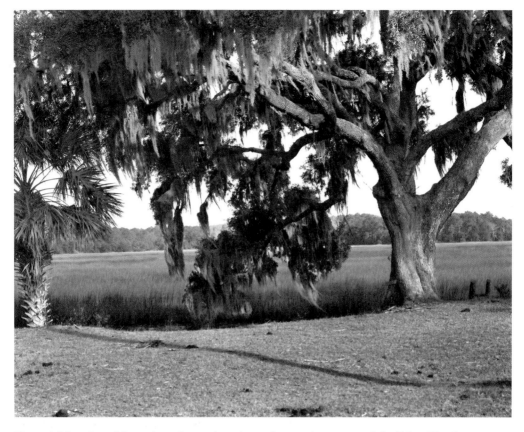

Figure 4. Moss-draped live oaks and extensive salt marshes are the essence of the Edisto Island environment. *Photo courtesy of Julia Cart.*

At some point storm surges washed completely over the islands, carrying sand from the front and depositing it behind. Edingsville and Botany Beaches, and the northeast end of Edisto Beach, are still moving landward today. They progressively cover the live marsh behind them and expose ruined marsh and shell beds on their front sides. That is why they are "thin, retreating" barrier islands.

## Edisto's Marshes

At least a quarter of the total area we call Edisto Island is not land but rather is salt marsh. Huge areas between the sandy barrier islands and the main island, and between the island and its three boundary rivers, are marshland (Figure 2). Additional marshes line the rivers and creeks that penetrate deep into the high land of the island and between its constituent islands. There are places on Edisto—for example, looking south from Bailey Island toward Edisto Beach—where there is an unobstructed view across more than three miles of marsh. Similarly, a viewer atop the main bridge onto Edisto

Island, looking either east toward the North Edisto River or west toward the South Edisto River, sees little but tidal rivers and marshes for at least five miles. Where did these vast marshes come from?

As the rising sea reached the present coastline and stabilized there, it flooded the river mouths and coastal stream valleys. Erosion from the newly formed sea islands and the adjacent coastal plain then began to fill the flooded river and creek valleys with sediment. Wherever these deposits built a sand or mud bank that was exposed at low tide, marsh grasses began to grow. As the grasses took root on the flats, they accelerated the process by slowing the tidal currents, allowing more sediment to settle out. Over the eons, marshes grew to fill all the gaps between high land, except for the self-scouring tidal channels, which deliver the ocean waters to the marshes and return them, nutrient-enriched, to the ocean, twice a day.

A single species, smooth cordgrass (*Spartina alterniflora* Loisel.), fills Edisto's salt marshes for mile after mile of green in the summer and brown in the winter. *Spartina* marsh is, in fact, the "dominant marine wetland in the coastal zone of South Carolina, comprising approximately 150,000 acres."[7] It is fast growing, and the sea island marshes are renowned for their biological productivity. As individual stems of grass die and decompose, the detritus is eaten by tiny organisms at the base of the estuarine food chain. Large rafts of dead marsh are often seen floating on the tides, which carry them to shore, higher into the marsh islands or out to sea, where they continue to decompose and serve the same purpose. Smooth cordgrass marshes serve several valuable functions besides being part of the food chain. Their spreading rhizomes stabilize the mudflats. Their stems filter the rainwater runoff from adjacent higher land, adding sediment to the mudflats while allowing the fresh water to rejoin the ocean. They dissipate wave energy during storms, thereby moderating shoreline erosion. They remove organic wastes from the tidal waters. And they offer habitat for many species of birds, animals and aquatic life.[8]

## A Major Black-water River

The North Edisto River that borders Edisto Island on the northeast and the Dawhoo River that separates Edisto Island from the mainland on the north are both fairly short saltwater estuaries, created by ocean flooding of ancient local drainage streambeds. But the South Edisto River that borders Edisto Island on the west side is different. It too is a flooded ancient river mouth, but it is also a significant freshwater river (called simply the Edisto) that rises far away in the sand hills of the coastal plain.

The Edisto River's south and north forks rise, respectively, in Edgefield County and Saluda County, more than one hundred miles from Edisto Beach, and they come together in the coastal plain near Orangeburg (Figure 1). Many of the Edisto River's tributary streams drain from inland hardwood swamps, where tannic acid turns the clear water a dark brown that looks black from above. For that reason, the Edisto and several other coastal plain rivers are classed as black-water rivers, to distinguish them from brown-water rivers, such as the Santee and the Savannah, which rise in the mountains and the Piedmont and carry substantial loads of light brown silt and clay.

The significance of these facts for Edisto is that of all the waters surrounding the island, the South Edisto is the only one that has a "salt point" where the fresh water meets the salt, and a brackish zone below that, where the two waters gradually mix. Moreover, the salt point moves dramatically with the tides: when the tide rises, the river "inhales" salty seawater miles inland, to the vicinity of Jehossee Island; when the tide ebbs, the temporary backup of fresh water flushes much of the salt water back out to sea, and the brackish zone is near the river's mouth. The difference in salt content between high and low tide can be tasted in the South Edisto, near the mouth of St. Pierre's Creek. This phenomenon had important consequences for agriculture and aquaculture on greater Edisto Island all through its history (Chapter 4).

# Edisto's Climate and Landscape

Edisto, and much of South Carolina, falls within a climate zone geographers call humid subtropical, which simply means bordering a tropical zone. Humid subtropical climates have long, warm summers, cool winters and precipitation in all seasons. Other places on the globe with a climate similar to coastal South Carolina include Tokyo, Japan, and Buenos Aires, Argentina.[9]

Warm humid summers, mild short winters and abundant rainfall spaced throughout the year combine to create a very long growing season on Edisto: 280 days on the landward side of the island and 290 days on the sea side. This was a critical factor in the phenomenal success of sea-island cotton on Edisto (Chapter 4).

Sea islands like Edisto were covered with dense forests when the Atlantic Ocean rose and converted them into erosion-remnant islands about five thousand years ago. The climax forest on the higher elevations of Edisto Island was an oak-hickory forest. The Indians who were living on the island in the 1600s had left the forests largely intact. But European planters, with African labor, changed all that. Within a century after their arrival, the original forests were virtually gone and forgotten. Experts have searched for remnants of the original climax forest on the sea islands, but have found almost none.[10] Second-growth forest covers much of Edisto today. The first tree to reseed itself on abandoned agricultural land is the loblolly pine. Later, a mixed pine and hardwood forest appears, except along creek banks, which produce a dense, second-growth maritime forest.

Both in the forest and in the open, the live oaks of Edisto Island are festooned with generous gray beards of Spanish moss (Figure 4), a rootless epiphyte that takes its moisture and nourishment directly from the humid air and does no harm to its host.[11] Spanish moss is highly selective of its hosts: it prefers live oaks, and will live on certain other hardwood trees, but will never choose a palmetto, pine or cedar. The sight of Spanish moss is so much a part of the aesthetic experience of the Carolina sea islands that it has become emblematic of this ecosystem.

Another type of forest that may have covered substantial areas of Edisto Island in prehistoric times is the longleaf pine "flatwoods," which like a flat terrain with sandy soil and a high water table. The existence of these forests on Edisto Island well into historic times is clearly indicated by the planters' use of the term "pine barren." One

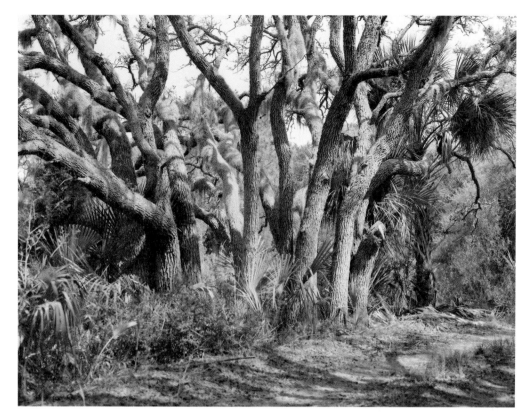

Figure 5. A second-growth maritime forest on Edisto Island. *Photo courtesy of Julia Cart.*

large cotton plantation on Edisto Island was actually named Pine Barren (Chapter 7), and parts of it almost certainly were cleared from longleaf pine flatwoods.[12]

Freshwater swamps also occur on Edisto Island, and are known to have been much more extensive in colonial times than today because many were drained and clear-cut for planting in the 1800s. Small, vestigial but persistent swamps survive today at Cypress Bottom, near the St. Paul's District Fire Station; at Tibbs Swamp, near Red House Road; and undoubtedly at other places on the island. The characteristic canopy trees of these swamps, as elsewhere, are bald cypress and tupelo gum. A great variety of shrubs and herbaceous plants also inhabit Edisto's swamps.[13]

Beach-ridge barrier islands like Edisto Beach are home to at least five distinct natural plant communities, in addition to whatever humans have planted there. The five are, from ocean side landward, the beach community, the coastal dune community, the maritime shrub community, the maritime forest community and the salt shrub community. Each is described in detail in standard reference books.[14]

Like the hardwood climax forest that existed on higher parts of Edisto Island, experts say that there is no original growth maritime forest anywhere on Edisto Beach or, for that matter, on the South Carolina coast.[15] Logging on the beaches of the South Atlantic also goes all the way back to the 1700s, when live oak was harvested to build sailing

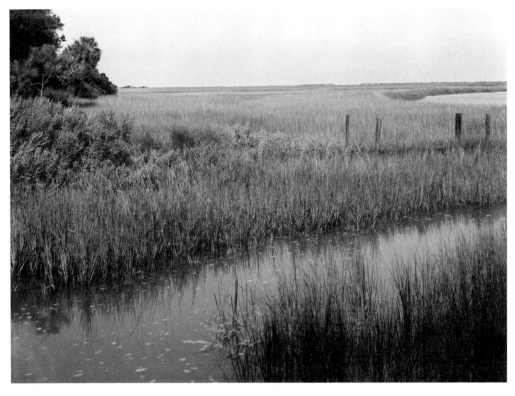

Figure 6. A salt shrub community on Edisto Island. *Photo courtesy of Julia Cart.*

vessels. The curved junctions of live oak trunk and branch were particularly prized for the ribs and knees of ship frames. As wooden shipbuilding waned in the 1800s, timber companies harvested pine and cedar from beaches like Edisto for other uses.

What we see today in the woods of Edisto Beach is all second-growth maritime forest, although the experts say the mix of species is quite similar to the original growth (Figure 5). The last systematic logging on Edisto Beach probably came in the 1920s, so most of the trees here today are younger than 100 years. This surprises many people, to whom today's large live oaks appear ancient. But live oak grows fast, and most are still quite young. Its normal lifespan in the coastal habitat is about 350 years.[16]

A rare variant of the maritime forest, called maritime shell forest, grows on top of ancient shell mounds and middens and comprises several trees and shrubs that love high-calcium soils. This community is found at only a few places along the South Carolina coast. A clear example stands on the high shell mound and the midden of Pig Island (also called Fig Island), isolated in the marshes of the North Edisto River (Figure 7). These shell deposits are the accumulated residue of hundreds or thousands of annual oyster and clam harvests by Native Americans. The site is protected by the South Carolina Heritage Trust and is not open to the public. Another site where botanists have documented the maritime shell forest is on and near the Indian mound at Edisto Beach State Park, also a protected site. This unique mini-ecosystem was only identified and studied in the late twentieth century, and its best documentation is by South Carolina botanists Richard Porcher and Patrick McMillan.[17]

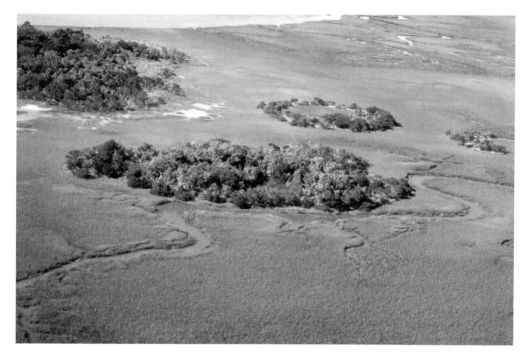

Figure 7. Edisto's Pig Island shell complex, near Ocella Creek, includes all three basic types of Native American shell deposits: shell mound (center), shell ring (top center) and shell midden (left). *Photo courtesy of Richard D. Porcher.*

## Edisto's Animal and Bird Life

From about 120,000 down to about 15,000 years ago, while Edisto was still part of the coastal plain, many faunal species that are now extinct lived and died here, and their bones fossilized in the freshwater swamps. Some of those freshwater swamps later became salt marshes when the ocean rose to its present level about 5,000 years ago.

Today, some of Edisto's beaches are considered particularly rich fossil-hunting territory. Hurricanes and winter storms that erode the strands of Edisto's thin, retreating beaches regularly expose areas that once were swamp and, more recently, marsh. Some of the more spectacular finds have been the remains of mastodons and mammoths, saber-toothed tigers and tapirs.[18]

By the time Edisto became an erosion-remnant island, about five thousand years ago, it was heavily populated by a wide range of modern animals and birds. All of the mammals, marsupials, reptiles, amphibians, birds and invertebrates that we know today were here then, in abundance. They coexisted, however, with several species that retreated long ago as the growing human population pushed them into shrunken habitats elsewhere. Species now missing, but once common, include the gray wolf, black bear, panther, wildcat and mink. Edisto's abundant marine life and land animals were important resources for the earliest people who lived here, and those that remained into more recent times continued to be central to Edistonians' diets.

Other modern species never inhabited Edisto. For instance, beavers were common in freshwater streams of the nearby mainland, but not on the sea islands. Herds of elk and bison roamed the uplands of South Carolina, but not the coast.[19] The alligator is an interesting case. It was abundant on Edisto Island both in prehistory and in recorded history. As late as 1842 a South Carolina naturalist wrote that it ranged the coastal areas of North and South Carolina, Georgia, Florida and along the Gulf Coast to New Orleans.[20] But by the early twentieth century the alligator had been hunted virtually to extinction in South Carolina. Then, under federal protection, it spread north again from Florida and is today well established—indeed, abundant—on Edisto Island and Edisto Beach.

# The Earliest Humans in South Carolina

Before the people now called Indians settled on Edisto Island, people whose names we do not know roamed South Carolina, and perhaps Edisto, for thousands of years.[21] Scholars divide pre-Columbian occupation of South Carolina into five "horizons": the Pre-Projectile Point, the Paleo-Indian, the Archaic, the Woodland and the Mississippian Horizons. It appears from the artifacts they left that each had a more complex material culture than the one that preceded it. Only in the last period, the Mississippian Horizon, does the physical evidence clearly show conflicts and mass movements or migrations of different ethnic groups into and out of South Carolina. And at the end of the Mississippian Horizon, things got even more complicated, due to the presence of peoples from across the ocean.

The earliest people arrived in what is now South Carolina perhaps fifteen thousand years ago. The climate was colder than today, but there were definite seasons. The ocean was far lower, and the coastline was fifty miles farther east than it is today. Edisto was not an island then, but part of a coastal plain with both grasslands and forests of pine and fir. People then lived in small, mobile groups and mostly ate gathered plants and some small animals.

Beginning about ten thousand years ago, a warmer climate began that produced rising oceans, hardwood forests and a more varied flora and fauna. Identifiable occupation sites in South Carolina are more numerous from this time period, both in the Piedmont and the coastal plain, and they are usually on high ground overlooking rivers, swamps or marshes. There is evidence that, during this period (five thousand to thirty-five hundred years ago), Early Archaic people harvested shellfish and, over time, deposited the shell rings, mounds and middens (trash heaps) at Edisto's Pig Island and other places on the sea islands, into the Woodland period. Archaic Indians apparently lived here in the winters and springs but went inland to hunt deer each fall.

In the Late Archaic, perhaps thirty-five hundred to three thousand years ago, these Indians also made the earliest known, thick-walled pottery in South Carolina, which was discarded in middens on the coast, including those on Edisto Island. Late Archaic people also seem to have started some plant domestication in South Carolina, probably of species native to the Carolinas, like sunflower and sumpweed.

Woodland Indians replaced the Archaic cultures about three thousand years ago, bringing agricultural intensification and diversification. Food plants such as gourds, squash and maize (corn), domesticated in central Mexico about seven thousand years ago, had spread north and eastward very gradually, perhaps reaching South Carolina about two thousand years ago. Woodland people also were the first to stalk and kill large game from a safe distance with bow and arrow.

## The Indians of First European Contact

Finally, five major cultural groups, each with a single language, evolved from the Woodland Indians and were in South Carolina during the Mississippian period, that is, between fifteen hundred and three hundred years ago. The five groups were the Mississippian, the Siouan, the Iroquoian, the Algonquian and the Muskhogean Indians, and all five groups were present during the first European contacts. The first four groups had no direct impact on Edisto Island, but are shown with their principal constituent tribes on the map below (Figure 8).

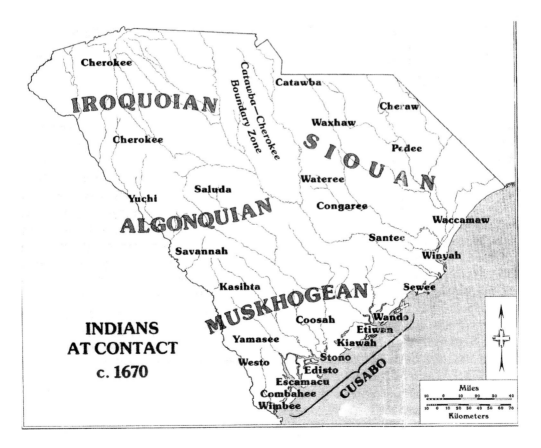

Figure 8. Location of Indian groups in South Carolina at European contact. *Reproduced with permission from Kovacik and Winberry, 1987.*

The fifth major group, the Muskhogean, was related to the Creeks of Alabama and Georgia. The South Carolina branch of Muskhogean was called Cusabo and occupied the sea islands and coastal plain from the Ashley River to the Savannah River. Cusabo was a collective name for many small tribes who could understand each other's dialects. The Edisto was one of the Cusabo tribes. Some of the others were the Wando, Etiwan, Kiawah, Stono, Escamacu, Combahee, Wimbee, Coosah (Kusso, Coosaw), Westo and Yemassee.

## How the Edisto Indians Lived

The Edisto Indians apparently lived entirely on Edisto Island at the time of European contact, and numbered, at most, a few hundred people.[22] The Edisto lived a peaceful and largely sedentary life on the island, but traded with Indians from the uplands, bartering pearls, shells and other goods from the salt marshes for things not available on the coast, such as stone to make points. They planted corn, squash and other vegetables in gardens scattered throughout the woods, to supplement their diet of fish, shellfish, game, wild berries, fruits and nuts. Their relatively small population was easily supported on the lush and productive island.

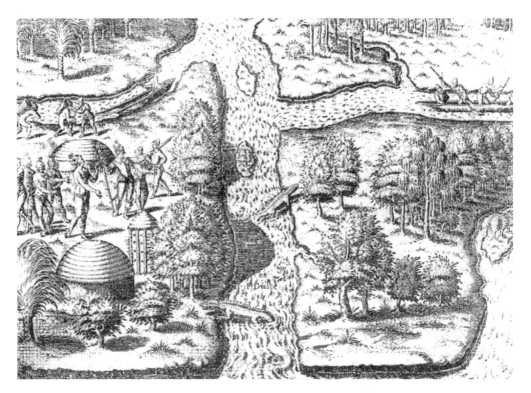

Figure 9. Cusabo Indians selling food to French settlers near Port Royal about 1562. Note the round dwellings, dugout canoes, alligators and palmettos. *Engraving from* Narrative of Le Moyne, *courtesy of South Caroliniana Library.*

Chronicles of early European explorers on the Carolina coast give us some insights into the culture of the Edisto. Their houses were circular and made of poles, sticks and bark, probably chinked with moss and mud, called wattle and daub. For temporary shelters they built small lean-tos or "booths" of poles, branches and palmetto fronds.[23] The main village of the Edisto had one large ceremonial house and several smaller houses, but most of the people actually lived next to their vegetable gardens, scattered throughout the forests, all over the island.[24] In front of the ceremonial house, the Indians had a public recreation area used by the men in the shape of a long walk flanked by tall trees. Here they competed in a kind of bowling competition, two men at a time, with a stone ball and six-foot sticks, and kept score with beads. Nearby was a smaller shaded playground set aside for children's games.[25]

The Edisto had a hierarchical social structure, headed by a cacique (pronounced ka-SEE-kay), a term that the Spanish borrowed from Indians living in Mexico at that time. Under him were several lesser leaders (the English called them captains), and then the rest of the people. Women apparently played a prominent public role among the Edisto.[26]

The exact location of the Edisto Indian village has not been determined, but it clearly lay on the sea side of the island, about four miles southwest of Point of Pines, probably in the vicinity of what is today Highway 174 between Edingsville Beach Road and Oyster Factory Road. It apparently did not face a river or marsh. Instead, it stood on the edge of a forest, fronting south and east on a large open meadow or grassland.[27]

## A Spanish Missionary among the Edisto in 1570

A hundred years before the English finally founded a successful colony at Charles Towne, Spain and France were bitterly contesting control of what became the entire Southeastern United States. One small chapter of that contest was a Spanish Catholic mission to the Orista (Edisto) Indians in 1570.[28]

The first Spanish governor of La Florida, Pedro Menendez de Aviles, hoped that Catholic missionaries could convert the coastal Indians to Christianity, making it easier for his Spanish settlements to survive. The recently founded Jesuit order in Spain responded to Don Pedro's appeals, and one of the most intrepid and creative missionaries was Father Juan Rogel, a native of Pamplona. He was among the first to arrive (in 1566) and one of the last to give up (in 1572).

Father Rogel spent the year 1567–68 among the Calusa Indians of Florida's Gulf Coast, but had little success. He returned to the colonial capital, now located at Santa Elena (Parris Island, South Carolina), and in 1569 he was reassigned to the Orista (Edisto). He was very optimistic about converting them because their culture was already similar to his view of a "Christian" lifestyle: they were monogamous, had stable families and "were not contaminated by sins such as incest, cruelty, and thievery. They interacted with one another with truth, peace and simplicity."

After six months Father Rogel could speak the language of the Edisto Indians and had their attention in regular lessons on Christianity. But in the fall the people dispersed to their scattered family farms for the harvest, and stayed there all winter, coming together only for festivals every two months. Father Rogel preached at the festivals, but they laughed at him. He tried to convince them to change their lifestyle, to plant larger gardens at the main village so they could stay together all year and attend his school. But they would not change their ways. Father Rogel gave up and left Edisto in December 1570. He wrote to his superiors that the only way he could foresee success in converting the coastal Indians to Christianity was to somehow "make them" settle down and live in one place the whole year.

That advice was, perhaps, prophetic in a way Father Rogel never intended, for when the Edisto Indians were induced to "settle down" a hundred years later, they rapidly disappeared as a recognizable cultural group.

## English Explorers Visit Edisto in the 1660s

Between 1660 and 1670 the English Proprietors of Carolina Colony (Chapter 2) made several efforts to collect better information and to arouse interest in the economic potential of their lands, from North Carolina to Florida. Both Virginia and New England were going concerns by then, and the Proprietors were competing at home for venture capital and willing volunteers. As part of their promotion, they sent officers to explore the Southeastern coast, take extensive notes and publish their travelogues in England. Several important documents came of these efforts, and two of them in particular provide more information on the Edisto Indians at the time of contact.

Captain William Hilton sailed for the Proprietors from Barbados in 1663. He spent some days among the Indians at Port Royal, who were part of the Cusabo (Muskhogean) language group and therefore related to the Edisto. He found them friendly, interested in trade and able to speak some Spanish. Their houses, large and small, were covered with palmetto fronds. They ate corn, pumpkin, melons, grapes, figs, peaches, wild game and fish. They cleared land for gardens using stone axes and fire. They had no iron tools, but they had pottery and wove baskets and mats.[29]

When Hilton departed Port Royal he took along a young man named Shadoo, who turned out to be an Edisto Indian. Apparently he went willingly. Shadoo went to Barbados, learned English and a great deal more about European ways and somehow returned to Edisto Island within three years.[30]

The next English explorer to meet the Edisto was Robert Sandford. The governor of a struggling English settlement in what is today North Carolina ordered him to sail south and look for a better location for their capital. In the summer of 1666, Sandford visited both Port Royal and the harbor at the mouth of the Ashley River, but the part that interests us here is the nine days he spent at Edisto Island. On June 22 he sailed into the North Edisto, took two Indian guides aboard, landed on Wadmalaw Island and claimed all the surrounding land for King Charles and the Proprietors. The next day he used a small boat to penetrate far up the creeks and rivers that opened off the North Edisto. Then things really got interesting.[31]

On the third day Sandford anchored at the main landing on the west side of the North Edisto—probably Point of Pines—to trade with the Indians. There he met Shadoo, now a captain of the Edisto, who urged the Englishmen to visit their village overnight. Sandford agreed to allow four of his gentlemen to go, keeping several Indians as guests aboard the ship as security.

When his men returned the next morning with glowing reports of the Edisto hospitality and the beauty of the island, Sandford decided to go himself, with a guard of armed soldiers. They were received by the cacique, who was "an old man of a large stature and bone," with his wife seated beside him in their circular statehouse. Men, women and children crowded into the house to see the unusual events. Gifts and

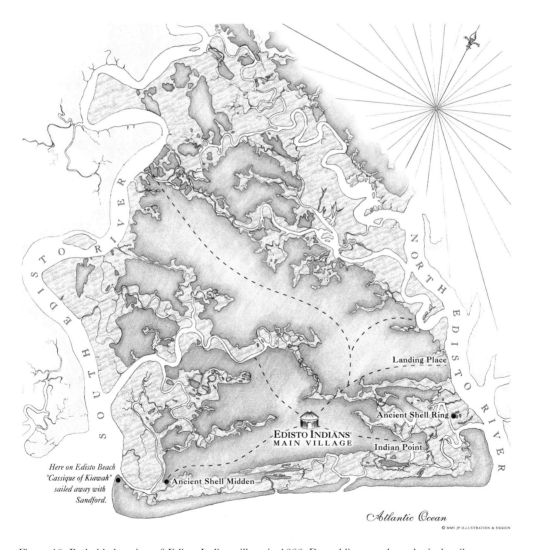

Figure 10. Probable location of Edisto Indian village in 1666. Dotted lines are hypothetical trails. "Landing Place" is inferred from Sandford's narrative. "Indian Point" was named on a 1749 plat.

speeches of friendship probably were exchanged with Shadoo translating, and then the Englishmen walked back to their ship, followed by "a great troope" of Indians. The cacique himself escorted them back and spent the night aboard the ship without a bodyguard, completely at ease.

Next, Sandford decided to try to circumnavigate Edisto Island, to have a look at the river on the other side of the island. The Indians told him they did it all the time in their dugout canoes. Sandford was in a small coastal sloop of fifteen tons with a crew of only twenty men, and he made it, but not as easily as he expected. "The river being narrow and variously winding"—a good description of the Dawhoo—the breezes were undependable and they had to tow the sloop with a rowboat much of the way. They anchored at night for safety, and careened the sloop on a sandbank for two low tides to caulk some leaks, so the passage from the North Edisto to the South Edisto and down to the ocean again actually took four days. Sandford judged it could have been done in a small boat with sails and oars in about twelve hours.

Sandford was still not through with the Indians. At the mouth of the South Edisto he "went a shoare on the East point of the entrance" (clearly, Bay Point on Edisto Beach), and there he found a party of Indians, including Shadoo, who had come to watch him sail away. They discussed the local geography and the names of various rivers, for Sandford's report. Then he returned to his sloop to depart for Port Royal, taking with him a Kiawah Indian, for Sandford had also agreed to accept their cacique's hospitality on the banks of the Ashley River on his way back to North Carolina. But before they could sail away, a mighty summer thunderstorm came over them from the southwest, with winds so violent that the sloop almost dragged its anchor. Thus Sandford experienced the best and worst of Edisto Island in one week in the summer of 1666.

And thus did a chance meeting take place on Edisto Beach that almost certainly led to Sandford's recommending, and the Proprietors' eventually agreeing, to move the capital of Carolina to the place where the Ashley and Cooper Rivers form a harbor with "a broad deep entrance."

## The Decline of the Edisto Indians after 1670

Not only the Edisto, but all the Indians of South Carolina started a disastrous decline both in numbers and in cultural vitality as soon as the English settled at Charles Towne in 1670. The coastal Indians were the first to feel the impact. Within thirteen years, Edisto Island and several other tribal lands were traded to the English (see Chapter 2), converting the small, peaceful Cusabo tribes of the coast into settlement Indians. Some individual Indians were enslaved in the early years. Some were the victims of violence by the settlers.

But the greatest devastation was wrought by diseases introduced unintentionally by the Europeans and Africans, for which the Indians had no natural immunity. Measles, chickenpox, scarlet fever and venereal diseases took their toll, but the greatest killer was smallpox. As populations declined, families weakened, food production dropped and the ceremonial and social traditions of the tribes could not be sustained.[32]

There had only been about fifteen thousand Indians in all of South Carolina in 1600, and by 1715 there were probably only half that many, and that included the Cherokee and Catawba of the interior, who were insulated by distance from Charleston in the first few decades of settlement.[33] Declines among coastal Indians were much more precipitous. By 1700 several of the small coastal tribes were close to extinction. By 1775 the Edisto were no more as a tribe, and there were few visible remnants of any of the original people of the South Carolina coast.[34]

## The Edisto Indians Today

A group who call themselves Edisto Indians are one of four communities of Native Americans still living in South Carolina today. The largest group is the Catawba, centered in York County and numbering 1,300 persons in the 1980 census. Next are the Pee Dee Indians of Marlboro, Marion and Dillon Counties. The Edisto of Dorchester and Colleton Counties are third in size, with about 660 people in 1980. Last are the Santee, with about 250 people living in Orangeburg County. Of these four groups, only the Catawba have obtained tribal status under federal law, and none have state recognition.[35] There is also a mixed-race people called Brass Ankles in South Carolina, but little reliable research has been published on them. A few are believed to have lived on Edisto Island in the twentieth century.[36]

Today's "Edisto" live mainly in two communities straddling the Edisto River about twenty miles inland from Edisto Island. Part of them live near Four Hole Swamp in the southwestern corner of Dorchester County, and the other part in the Creeltown community of eastern Colleton County, near Cottageville. The tribe has applied for, but not received, recognition by the state of South Carolina. They live on privately owned lands, not on a reservation.[37]

This Indian community has actually moved several times over the past 250 years, but has always stayed near the Edisto River. A few lived on Edisto Island in the twentieth century; there was an Indian school with sixteen children in the 1940s. Their surnames were Davidson, Russel and Mucklevaney. After a decade or two, most of those people moved again, this time to Four Hole and Creeltown. Researchers in the late 1980s believed that perhaps one or two Indians were still living on Edisto Island at that time.[38]

By their own account, however, these people are not descendants of the Edisto who lived on Edisto Island in the 1600s. They legally adopted that tribal name in 1975 because they lived near the Edisto River; whites had called them Edisto for many generations and it was simpler to adopt the name than to ignore it. But their true heritage, clearly spelled out in documents as well as oral tradition since the 1700s, is Kusso-Natchez. They represent a merger of the last two tribal remnants in the South Carolina Lowcountry, neither of which was Edisto. The Kusso (see "Coosah" on the map, Figure 8) were a Muskhogean-speaking tribe, hence related to the Edisto. The Natchez were Mississippian mound builders who had been driven out of their homeland in what is now Mississippi by Choctaw, and this band had found its way to South Carolina after 1731. Stressed by rapidly spreading European and African settlements in Carolina, the two tribes merged in the 1740s and have lived as one and stayed on the lower Edisto ever since.[39]

Thus, there apparently are no people left anywhere who descended from the original Edisto Indians. For all practical purposes—or, for that matter, symbolic or spiritual purposes—the Indians of old Edisto Island unfortunately are no more.

## CHAPTER 2

# EDISTO'S EUROPEANS

Almost two centuries passed between Christopher Columbus's first landfall in the Bahamas in 1492 and the first European settler clearing land for a farm on Edisto Island in 1683. In that time, Spain, France and England clashed repeatedly for control of the Southeastern coast of North America. Each planted colonies in what are now Virginia, North Carolina, South Carolina, Georgia and Florida, only to see the settlers give up and return home, or die of starvation and disease. Each also attacked the settlements of the others, and raided their shipping along this coast. By the mid-1600s, Spain was firmly entrenched in Florida, and England had a permanent colony going in Virginia, but there were no Europeans in between. It was a political vacuum, and empires abhor a vacuum.[40]

## The Carolina Colony

In the early 1660s the pace of events on the Southeast coast began to accelerate. England's Barbados colony, only forty years old, was rich and booming, but had run out of land to develop. Wealthy sugar planters were looking for new lands to settle. Florida and the Caribbean islands were already fully claimed and occupied by Spain, France, England and others. The Atlantic Coast between Virginia and Florida seemed their natural next step. The economic and social structure of the future Carolina colony would be decisively shaped by this early interest of successful English planters from Barbados, and by the subsequent migration to Carolina of excess white artisans and managers and African-descent slaves from Barbados.[41]

A major event in 1660 in England reopened the door to European settlement in Carolina. England's parliament ended Oliver Cromwell's eleven-year rule and restored the heir, Charles II, to the throne. King Charles surrounded himself with people who had been loyal to the crown during the Protectorate, and rewarded eight of them with a monopoly on colonization of the territory between Virginia and Florida. In 1663 they became the Lords Proprietors of the Carolina colony. They got to work immediately to encourage any and all who might be willing to settle there, expecting hefty profits on a small investment in ships and supplies.[42]

The Carolina Proprietors hoped at first to attract Englishmen from well-established colonies in Virginia and New England to move south. A small group of New Englanders had in fact settled in 1662 on the Cape Fear River in North Carolina, but had given up and returned north after six months. The governor of Virginia, Sir William Berkeley, was a friend of the Carolina Proprietors, but probably was not anxious for any of his settlers to move south either. Thus the Barbadian planters were England's best hope to settle Carolina, and the Proprietors in turn encouraged them.

A Barbadian group sent Sir William Hilton in 1663 to explore the Carolina coast. His report, published in 1664, painted Carolina as a land of opportunity. In 1665 two companies of Barbadians jointly established Charles Towne on the Cape Fear River, near present-day Wilmington, North Carolina. It lasted for two years before the colonists, discouraged, returned to Barbados. Before they left, their leaders sent Robert Sandford south in 1666 in a small ship to gather more details on the coast between Cape Fear and Florida, and he also reported back in glowing terms. His report contained the first English description of Edisto Island and its Indians. (Both Hilton's and Sandford's voyages are described in more detail in Chapter 1.)

In 1668 the Carolina Proprietors decided to take direct action. They would fund, sponsor and dispatch settlers directly from England. Anthony Lord Ashley, earl of Shaftesbury, assumed charge as executive and three ships sailed in 1669, stopping en route to pick up more settlers in Ireland and Barbados. They arrived on the Carolina coast early in 1670. They had intended to build their town at Port Royal, but were blown off course and landed instead at Bull's Bay, where the cacique of the Kiawah Indians reminded them, again, that the ideal site was on the Ashley River at Albemarle Point. They sailed back, inspected the place and agreed. And so Charles Towne came to be where it is (Figure 1).

Charles Towne had its struggles, but it grew steadily. The 130 men and women in the first group in 1670 came prepared to work the land, and they fed themselves. More settlers continued to arrive, especially from Barbados. By 1690 a majority of the whites in Carolina were English Barbadians. In the early years Carolina also drew English settlers from Jamaica, Antigua, St. Christopher's and Nevis. The English from England were a decided minority. Soon significant numbers also started arriving from France (the Huguenots), Scotland, Ireland, Germany, Wales, the Netherlands and Sweden. Jews came from Spain, fleeing the Catholic Inquisition there. Throughout the colonial period, South Carolina had one of the most diverse white populations of any colony.[43]

# The Earliest Settlers on Edisto Island

Land along both sides of the lower Ashley River soon was all given out, and surveyors began laying out parcels for new settlers on James Island, Johns Island and farther inland.

Lord Ashley, one of the most powerful proprietors, still at home in England, was entitled to a twelve-thousand-acre barony but was displeased with the location chosen for him. The colony's surveyors had laid it out on the south bank of the Ashley River, opposite the future town of Dorchester, hence many miles upriver from Charles Towne. In 1674 Lord Ashley instructed his agent at Charles Towne, Maurice Matthews, to obtain for him a comparable barony on Edisto Island (then called Locke Island). He ordered another official, Henry Woodward, to negotiate with the Edisto Indians and purchase the entire island. "You are to treate with the Indians of Edisto for the Island and buy it of them and make a Friendship with them." And he sent out a third person from England, Andrew Percivall, to manage his new plantation and also to lay out a town on "Locke Island" as part of the Ashley Barony.[44] (John Locke, for whom Edisto Island was briefly named, was the confidential secretary of Lord Ashley, and coauthor of the "Fundamental Constitutions" of the Carolina Colony. He later became one of the seminal thinkers of the seventeenth century on civil and religious liberty and the ultimate sovereignty of the people.)

But the leaders of the colony thought it unwise to settle a place as remote as Edisto Island at that early date, and when he arrived, Percivall apparently agreed with them. So they went ahead with the original plan for Ashley Barony on the upper Ashley River, and postponed any plans for Edisto Island. Woodward and Percivall did negotiate a treaty with Indian tribes in 1675, but it was not for Edisto Island. Instead, it cleared the way for Ashley Barony on the mainland by purchasing "great & lesser Cassoe lying on the River of Kyewah [the Indians' name for the Ashley River] and the River of Stono & the freshes of the River of Edistoh"—that is, the entire Lowcountry mainland along the Stono River from the Ashley River to the Edisto River.[45]

So the Edisto Indians sat out the first decade of the Carolina Colony, undisturbed on their island except perhaps for occasional English visitors, who must have liked what they saw and wanted some of it. Then, in early 1683, the Edisto and other Lowcountry tribes sold Edisto Island and the other sea islands to the English for £100, and the Edisto soon moved off the island and resettled at or near their ancestral home at Port Royal.[46]

On October 26, 1683, Paul Grimball, a recently arrived merchant from England, obtained a grant of 1,290 acres at Point of Pines on the North Edisto. From this large tract he soon carved out a small farm and built a home for himself, his wife and children. They were the first documented white settlers on Edisto Island.[47]

Grimball built a small but substantial house facing the wide North Edisto. Its walls, at least for the ground floor, were of tabby, a solid masonry made from oyster shells. A portion of those walls still stands today as the oldest European relic still identifiable on Edisto Island.[48] Grimball planted seventy acres of Indian corn (a large amount for those early days), and also peas, onions and tobacco. From a breeding stock of swine probably imported from Barbados, he soon had a herd of one hundred pigs. At first, he probably had European indentured servants to work the farm.[49]

Grimball also must have rented or built a dwelling in Charles Towne, for he had official duties there part of each year (see below). The Edisto plantation was forty miles from Charles Towne by the outside passage, which could be covered in four to six hours

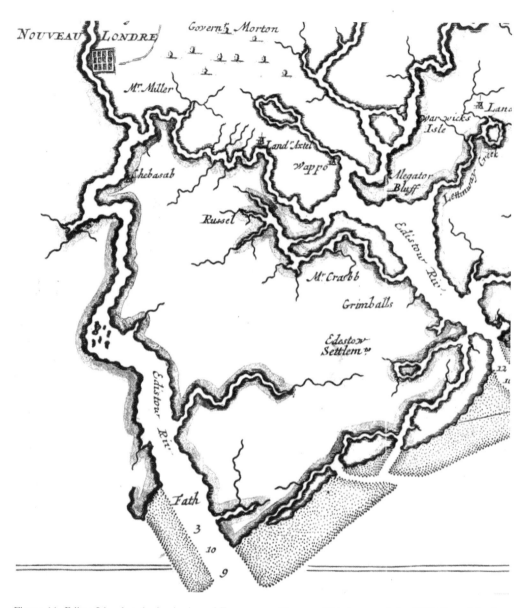

Figure 11. Edisto Island at the beginning of European settlement. This is part of the 1696 Pierre Mortier map of Carolina. All "Edistow Settlements" were on the north side of the island, closer to Charleston. *Courtesy of EIHPS.*

by a small, fast sailboat in good weather with favorable winds. By 1683 there were also already settlers on Johns Island and Wadmalaw, so Edisto may not have seemed as isolated as it had eight years earlier. Still, for a few years, it was the southernmost outpost of the Carolina colony.[50]

Joseph Morton, governor of the colony from 1682 to 1684, and again briefly a few years later, had a close association with Edisto Island. His first home was "at Edisto"—

that is, either on Edisto Island or very close by on Wadmalaw Island.[51] New settlers, including Crabb and Russell, were on Edisto Island by 1696 (Figure 11). Joseph Russell received a 570-acre grant on Little Edisto in 1710, but he may have settled informally on Little Edisto before 1696 and formalized his grant in 1710.[52] The largest creek on the north side of Edisto Island is named for him.

Edisto Island soon ceased to be the southernmost English outpost on the Atlantic Coast. A group of Scots arrived in Charles Towne in October 1684 with instructions from the Proprietors in London to give them not only a huge quantity of land but also self-government in a separate county. Their leaders were Baron Cardross and the Reverend William Dunlop. Port Royal County, south of Colleton County, was created for them, and they settled near present-day Beaufort. But their numbers were reduced by disease and defection at Charles Towne, and only fifty-one Scots actually took up residence at Stuart Town in November 1684.[53]

The Scots were not content quietly to build themselves a prosperous little colony at Port Royal. Their leaders were a proud and contentious group, unwilling to coordinate policy with the more experienced English at Charles Towne. And they had grandiose ideas that did not take into account the larger realities on the southeast Atlantic Coast. They told the local Indians they wanted to establish a trade route to Mexico, and that they planned to occupy an abandoned Spanish mission in the Georgia sea islands.

Spanish intelligence at St. Augustine soon heard all about these plans, and their governor reacted predictably. He dispatched a punitive expeditionary force up the coast in the summer of 1686. Spanish warships sailed into Port Royal Sound, landed soldiers, killed the livestock and burned Stuart Town to the ground. The Scottish settlers saw the Spanish coming and hid in the woods, so none were hurt. But they retreated north and never rebuilt Stuart Town. A number of these Scots later ended up on Edisto Island.[54]

The Spanish were not finished. A few days later they sailed into the North Edisto River and spread devastation there. Lord Cardross had ridden overland and alerted Governor Morton, but the council had not had time to send a defensive force to Edisto, and the Spanish struck quickly. They burned Paul Grimball's and Joseph Morton's and several other houses in the vicinity of the North Edisto. A brother-in-law of Governor Morton was killed, and thirteen of his African slaves were carried off. Grimball apparently hid his family safely on the island.[55]

Still, the Spanish were not finished. They prepared to sail north, intending to sack Charles Towne and drive the English permanently out of "their" territory. But a hurricane arose and battered the Spanish fleet at the mouth of the North Edisto. One of their ships went down and with it, the expedition's commander. The remnant returned to St. Augustine.

Paul Grimball soon returned to Edisto Island, rebuilt and continued to develop his plantation at Point of Pines. The Carolina colony devised an early warning system against the Spanish, with the help of friendly Indians, and the Spanish never successfully attacked as far north as Edisto again.[56]

# Paul Grimball, the Man and the Politician[57]

Paul Grimball was involved in the turbulent politics of Charles Towne from the time he arrived in the colony in 1682. Governor Morton appears to have been his sponsor and mentor. That same year, Morton appointed Grimball an assistant justice of the Berkeley County Court. In 1684, Grimball became a Proprietor's deputy on the Grand Council of the colony. In 1688 the Proprietors appointed him secretary of the province. As such, he was responsible for most of the written records, from court actions to land grants, deeds and wills.[58]

Grimball worked conscientiously to improve record keeping, archiving and reporting to the Proprietors in London. The job provided a steady income from documentary fees, and from that money Grimball paid a salary to a series of deputy secretaries, who did much of the work under his supervision. In 1692 the Proprietors in London credited Grimball, after prodding his predecessors for eighteen years, with being the first secretary of the colony who bothered to send to London sufficient copies of key documents to enable them to fulfill their own responsibility to report to the king on the management of the colony. They considered Grimball's position "the Officer of the greatest trust in the Governmt next to the Governor."

As a council member and secretary, Grimball actively supported Morton's successor, Governor James Colleton, even when Colleton took the extreme step of declaring martial law to stop the enslavement of Indians and illegal trade with pirates. The Goose Creek faction (who opposed the Proprietors) overthrew Governor Colleton in a coup d'état and replaced him with Seth Sothell in 1690. But Secretary Grimball, loyal to Colleton, refused to deliver the official records and great seal of the colony to the new governor, who had him put in prison. In February 1691, while Grimball was still in prison in Charles Towne, a constable with an armed guard landed at Point of Pines in the night and searched Grimball's house in the presence of his terrified wife and children. They also searched the nearby home of Grimball's son-in-law, John Hamilton.

In due course the alarmed Proprietors in London sent out a new governor, Philip Ludwell. He arrived in Charles Towne in April 1692, armed with documents to replace the impostor, Sothell, and his appointees. Grimball was released from prison and restored as secretary. He filled the position until his death in 1696.[59] He served under five different colonial governors and survived with his reputation for personal probity intact.

Paul Grimball apparently loved his plantation on Edisto Island and spent as much time there as his official duties permitted. His family mostly stayed on Edisto even when he was in town. In 1692, he wrote to the Proprietors that the new governor, Ludwell, expected him to spend an unreasonable amount of time in town. The Proprietors reminded the governor that the deputy secretary, who lived in town, could do most of the secretary's work; that Grimball was highly valued for his years of diligent service and loyalty to the Proprietors; that he was now getting old; and that the governor should ease up on him. (Apparently he did.)

A glimpse of Paul Grimball's personality is preserved in a 1690 letter written by John Stewart, a Scottish friend in Charles Towne who knew him well. As summarized by a recent scholar, Stewart thought Grimball "was hysterically funny in company, honest, 'hot and martiall,' inclined to 'the Love of a penny,' and 'of good sense to be so old.'"[60]

Paul Grimball became quite wealthy by the standards of the early Carolina colony. He got his start and qualified for a large land grant on Edisto Island by "head rights" for several adult male European indentured servants he brought over. Later, he bought several African or Afro-Caribbean slaves. When in 1689 he listed his material losses from the Spanish attack on Edisto Island three years earlier, they totaled more than £1,100. That wealth was in addition to the value of his land, indentured servants and slaves, and he also owned properties elsewhere. On Edisto, he raised crops and livestock for slaughter, as well as horses for sale.

Paul Grimball and his wife Mary had five children, and their genes were in many subsequent generations of Edistonians, some of them prominent. Daughter Mary soon married John Hamilton of Edisto Island, who was a deputy secretary of the province, and one of their descendants was Paul Hamilton, future governor of South Carolina and U.S. secretary of the navy under President James Madison (1809–17).

Paul and Mary Grimball's second daughter, Ann, married in succession two early Edisto Island landowners, Christopher Linkley and Charles Odingsell, the latter another former deputy secretary of the province under her father. Paul and Mary's third daughter, Providence, married twice but had no children; her first husband was an early Edisto Island planter, Lawrence Dennis. The Grimballs' son John was a hat maker in Charles Towne. He was married with two sons, but his family did not live in Carolina; he may have married before he left England, and left his sons there.

Paul and Mary Grimball's son Thomas, apparently their youngest child, peopled the colony with descendants named Grimball. He married Elizabeth, daughter of early Edisto landowner William Adams. They lived on Edisto Island, having inherited Paul Grimball's Point of Pines Plantation, now 1,600 acres. They had four sons: Paul, Thomas, Joshua and Isaac Grimball. Their progeny married into many families prominent on Edisto in the 1700s, among them Baynard, Calder, Clark, Eaton, Jenkins, Maxwell, Mikell, Rippon and Sealy.[61]

## The Second Wave of Settlers on Edisto Island

In the late 1690s and early 1700s the colony issued a steady stream of land grants on Edisto Island, and it began to fill up. Thirty-two surnames are on a 1715 map of Edisto (Figure 12), and another fourteen names are just across the South Edisto River on Fenwick Island, which was traditionally managed from Edisto. Some of those names soon disappeared from Edisto without a trace, including Williams, MacPherson, Crabb, Huzar, Hanna, Bee, Hendrik, James, Fox and Downs. Other names clearly match early documents, but did not remain long on the island. Cheverall (Sacheverell), Bowers, Hamilton, Dennis, Abbott, Sealy, Palmeter (Palmenter), Russell, Whippy, Peters and Wats are in that category. A few of the 1715 names took root and are found on Edisto Island down through the centuries: Fripp, Bailey, Whitmarsh, Grimball, Mitchell, Wilkinson and Clark.

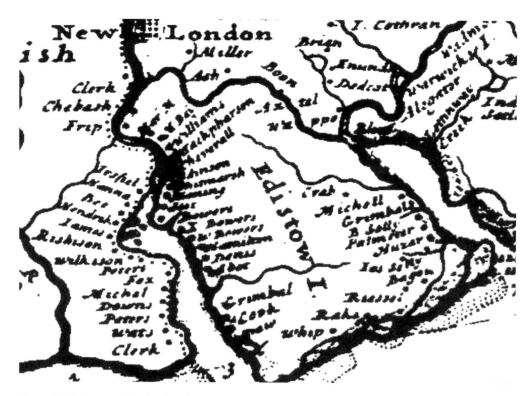

Figure 12. Edisto and Fenwick (left) Islands in 1715. Detail of map by Herman Moll names forty-five white settlers; locations are not precise. New London was an early name for Wiltown. Names are transcribed in *Documents on Edisto Island History.*

## The Hamilton Family on Edisto

John Hamilton was one of the Scots at short-lived Stuart Town in the 1680s who stayed on to make a new life for himself among the English at Charles Towne. He soon married Mary, daughter of Paul Grimball, and built a house on the island "nearby." John Hamilton's house was searched for records by Governor Sothell's men in 1691 on the same day they searched the Grimball house at Point of Pines. In 1693, Grimball made son-in-law Hamilton his deputy secretary of the province.[62] This was a salaried job that probably required Hamilton to spend most of his time at a home in Charles Towne. He resigned the deputy-secretaryship in 1695 when he was elected to the general assembly, in which he served several terms.[63]

John Hamilton and Mary (Grimball) Hamilton had three children. Their daughter Mary married twice and had children. Their son Paul Hamilton I married Martha, daughter of Edisto settler William Bower. They had three sons and two daughters: Paul, John, Archibald (father of the future governor), Martha and Dorcas. Martha Hamilton married one of the early Presbyterian ministers on Edisto, the Reverend John McLeod (pastor, 1741–54), and they had children. The third child of John and Mary Hamilton was Ann, who married three times and also had children and grandchildren. Many of these descendants probably stayed on Edisto Island, but the male line with the Hamilton name was gone from the island by the end of the 1700s.

Paul Hamilton, son of John and Mary, grandson of Paul and Mary Grimball, was "a man of great method and regularity full of reflection and provident." He was also very rich (see below), and has long been credited with building Brick House ("America's first manor house") on Edisto Island about 1725.[64] It was a large, elegant house of brick, which was unusual in its day, even in Charles Towne. The bricks were imported and the quoins were stucco. Paul and Martha Hamilton apparently lived at Brick House, the grandest house on Edisto in its day, until his death about 1738.[65] The house burned in 1929, but the walls still stand.

Who built Brick House, however, is not really known. A family memoir written many years later by Governor Paul Hamilton, nephew of Paul Hamilton I, seems to state that his uncle built this house.[66] But a recent analysis of this and other old documents by William Albergotti offers another intriguing possibility. He notes that most historians

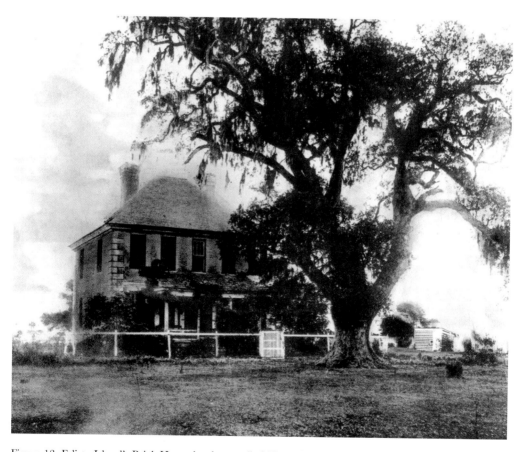

Figure 13. Edisto Island's Brick House has been called "America's first manor house." The bricks were imported; the quoins are stucco. Built about 1725 or earlier, it was Edisto's oldest house until it burned in 1929. *Photo courtesy of EIHPS.*

have assumed that Paul Grimball (grandfather of Paul Hamilton I) rebuilt his home at Point of Pines after the 1686 Spanish raid, possibly on the original tabby foundation. But Albergotti suggests that Grimball's second home may not have been at Point of Pines at all. Loath to rebuild on the same exposed site the Spanish had burned, he may have built Brick House on Russell Creek about 1690 and lived there until his death in 1696. Clearly, Spanish raids were still a concern in 1690, and this is a location that seagoing vessels could not reach. If so, that would make Brick House about thirty-five years older than most historians have assumed.[67]

## Edisto's Planter Class in the 1700s

A 1732 tax report for Edisto Island lists fifty-seven men and one woman who owned land, slaves or both on Edisto Island.[68] By far the richest man on Edisto Island in 1732 was Paul Hamilton, the son of John Hamilton and grandson of Paul Grimball. Hamilton owned 2,300 acres on Edisto and another 3,000 on nearby islands and the mainland. His wealth just in land was assessed at more than £3,000, colonial currency. He also owned thirty-four African slaves, more than any other man on the island.

Ten other men owned very large plantations of 1,000 acres or more on Edisto and nearby islands. They were William Bower, Ralph Bailey, William Edings, John Frampton, Paul Grimball (grandson of the first Paul Grimball), George Norton, Charles Odingsells, Joseph Russell, Joseph Sealy and John Stewart. Another twenty men—Archibald Calder, James Clark, Ichabod Fry, Thomas Grimball, Isaac Grimball, John Hamilton, James Lardant, James Meggett, John Meggett, William Mellichamp, Ephraim Mikell, Thomas Rake, Edward Rippon, John Sams, Joseph Sealy Jr., Richard Stevens, Joseph Watson, Robert Whippy, William Whippy and Ichabod Winborn—each owned between 290 and 870 acres, enough land to earn a comfortable living.

Except for the Grimball and Hamilton families, only sketchy information is available about most of these early settlers, but three deserve special mention: Archibald Calder, Thomas Rake and Joseph Fickling.

Archibald Calder was listed in 1732 as owning only 350 acres on Edisto Island, but clearly he managed well and prospered, for by 1767 he had bought or inherited more than 1,400 acres on Little Edisto, Bailey Island and the northwest corner of Edisto Island.[69] It is not clear on which of these properties he lived, but he took a special interest in water transportation from the South Edisto to the North Edisto River. He was appointed one of the commissioners in 1741 to clear and dig the canal between Edisto and Jehossee Island that came to be known as Watt's Cut.[70] It was a narrow and shallow waterway for almost two hundred years, but must have been a very useful shortcut for plantation work boats and passenger "barges" (large rowboats powered by slaves), which provided basic transportation around the island and to the mainland, until the age of steam in the 1800s.

The Rake family of early Edisto Island exemplifies the upward mobility available in America to European emigrants willing to work hard and take risks in a new land. A youthful Thomas Rake sailed from Bristol, England, to Virginia in 1676, apprenticed (indentured) for five years to one Osmond Crabb.[71] Twenty years later Rake had a family, had re-emigrated from Virginia to Carolina and was raising livestock on Edisto Island.[72] In 1697, Rake obtained warrants for his own land on Edisto totaling some three hundred acres, built a house and continued farming. We do not know the name of Rake's wife, but the couple had at least three daughters and one son, Thomas Jr. The Rakes apparently were active in the politics of the Carolina colony, for when Arthur Middleton spearheaded an anti-Proprietors petition to the Crown of England in 1717, both Rakes, father and son, were among the signers.[73]

Thomas Rake Jr. bought more land and apparently diversified his father's livestock farm by planting rice on a commercial scale. In 1732 he owned 670 acres and nineteen slaves, and was a moderately wealthy man. The Rake plantation, later known as Red Top, was in the northwest corner of the island abutting Russell Creek. When he died in 1762, Thomas Rake Jr. owned slaves valued at £4,780; thirteen tons of market-ready rice worth at least £350; and £1,000 in cash reserves. His livestock, tools and household furnishings pushed the value of his movable property over £7,500—and that did not include his house or seven-hundred-acre plantation.[74]

We know Thomas Rake Jr.'s wife only as Mary. They had no male heir, but a daughter married into the Baynard family and had children. Meanwhile, the sisters of Thomas Rake Jr. had married into three other Edisto families: Calder, Fry and Fickling (see below). It is no stretch to assume that the memory and the influence of the Rake family continued for many generations after the surname itself disappeared from Edisto Island.

All the Edisto plantations taxed in 1732, taken together, contained 21,614 acres of land. The total assessed value of plantations owned by Edistonians, including those located elsewhere, was about £20,000. Assessed values varied, but the average was less than ten shillings per acre. The land tax rate was miniscule (0.21 percent), so all the 21,614 acres in Edisto plantations brought in only about £26 that year in land tax. Clearly, land tax was not a major source of revenue for the colonial government.[75] By contrast, the tax on slaves (below) was substantial. It is somewhat surprising how many Edisto taxpayers owned little or no land in 1732. William Conyers, Matthew Crees (Crews?), John Floyd, William Nash, Joseph Scott, John Sealy and William Spoade each owned 200 acres or less. John Andrew, William Baynard, Paul Cole, James Ellis, Thomas Hayn, John Jenkins Jr., William Jenkins, Lawrence Mellichamp, Daniel Mitchell, James Mitchell, John Nash, Benjamin Sealy, William Sealy, Samuel Stevens and John Wells each paid taxes on one to six slaves but owned no land at all. A few of those taxpayers probably were young sons of large landowners who had not yet come into an inheritance. But most of them probably were salaried overseers, and a few may have been artisans: blacksmiths, harness makers, masons or carpenters. William Tilley is listed on the return as the owner of "a store in the country."

In 1732, Edisto planters owned a total of 546 slaves who worked on their owners' Edisto plantations and their operations elsewhere. The tax was a flat one pound per slave each year, so the slaves owned by Edisto planters brought the government thirteen times more revenue in 1732 than their 34,000 acres of land.[76]

In 1719, after years of wrangling between locally elected assemblymen and appointed governors, South Carolina's colonial leaders overthrew the Proprietary government and requested direct rule by the king and his ministers. For several years after 1719 the colonists virtually ruled themselves, while they worked out the new relationship between Charles Towne and London, which lasted until 1776. Self-rule has very deep historic roots in South Carolina.[77]

The new government and politics in South Carolina after 1719 also had an effect on land ownership records. All landowners were asked to re-register their landholdings. To do so, they had to write out in narrative form, and deposit at the auditor's office, all the facts they could assemble about each plantation and tract: its size and location, its boundaries and its history of ownership, insofar as known, from the original grant through each inheritance and sale to the present. The same filing was encouraged for each future transaction.

Today, these "memorials" provide descendants and historians a very valuable window into the early chains of ownership of specific land parcels and the broad patterns of ownership. Much of the information in Chapter 7 on ownership of specific plantations during the colonial period comes from these memorials. And all the land memorials that can be identified as clearly pertaining to Edisto Island, from 1722 to1773, are summarized in *Documents on Edisto Island History*.

The Ficklings were another early Edisto family that started with almost nothing but rose to prominence within two generations. Jeremiah Fickling (1705?–1764?) probably was born in Bermuda, and settled on Edisto Island about 1730. His parents had immigrated to America from Norfolk County, England. Jeremiah and his wife, Mary Elizabeth Allen of Colleton County, had six sons. Since Jeremiah never registered any land of his own, he may have hired himself out as an overseer. His fourth son, Joseph Fickling (1735–1799), however, established himself as a landowner. In 1764 he bought 200 acres (possibly on Watch Island, now Botany Bay Island) from John Frampton, and in 1768, 227 acres more from James and Elizabeth Clark. Joseph's first wife, Mary Barbara Calder, was the mother of his four sons and a daughter. At age fifty-three, widowed, Joseph married a widow, Mary Mikell Evans, the daughter of John Mikell of Edisto Island. With 400 acres, four sons and hard work, Joseph Fickling was a moderately wealthy man, and he bequeathed fifteen slaves to each of his sons. In addition, at midlife he apparently was very political and very popular among his peers, for in 1775 Joseph Fickling was elected captain of the first Edisto Island company of the Colleton County regiment for the War of Independence. The next year, two of his sons enlisted as privates in the second Edisto Island company and another son, Joseph Jr., was elected second lieutenant (see Figure 15). Though the family included many males, the Fickling surname disappeared from the ranks of Edisto Island planters well before the Civil War.[78]

By the middle 1700s, Edisto Island was largely "granted out," and probably pretty solidly settled. Most planters had sold off the oak and other usable timber while clearing their plantations, and were raising cattle, corn and other food crops. Some were experimenting with rice and indigo as cash crops (Chapter 4).

The typical white family residence on Edisto Island in the 1700s was a small, simple frame house of one story. Few of these houses survived to the Civil War, much less to the

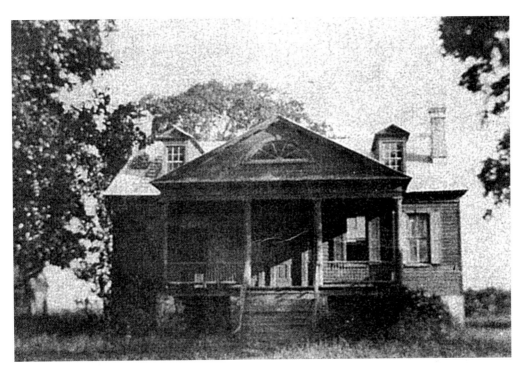

Figure 14. Old House, probably built between 1735 and 1760, is Edisto's oldest house still in use. The columned porch, twin dormers and fanlighted entrance are Neoclassical ornaments added in the nineteenth century. *Photo courtesy of EIHPS.*

present. Most of them were torn down and replaced in the early 1800s with the much larger, two-story sea island–style frame houses associated today with Edisto's "Golden Age." Only one house, originally called Four Chimneys but today called Old House, still stands on Edisto Island from the pre-Revolutionary period (Figure 14). It should be visualized without its columned porch and other Greek Revival elements added in the 1800s to appreciate the boxy simplicity of most Edisto houses in the colonial period.[79] The largest exception to the generalization about simple frame houses in the 1700s is, of course, Brick House. It must have been the envy of every planter on the island until larger houses began to be built in the 1790s.

## Turmoil in the 1700s: Human Conflicts and Natural Disasters

Paul Grimball, the Hamiltons and others resettled on Edisto Island after the Spanish raid of 1686, and by 1690 life probably had returned to normal. The island's white population was growing steadily and a sense of community was probably forming. But the next major shock came from hostile Indians, since the frontier was only fifteen miles west of Edisto, at the Combahee River.

Trade between the settlers and the Indians was a lucrative business, and anyone could try it. Traders purchased deerskins from many Indian tribes, far into the interior, and shipped them to Europe at a handsome profit. At the same time they retailed whiskey, iron tools, cloth and decorative items to the Indians at inflated prices. The colonial government tried unsuccessfully from 1680 until 1715 to regulate this trade. But every attempt to legislate controls, licensing and government supervision of the traders was defeated or vetoed for thirty-five years because governors and other high officials personally benefited from the unregulated trade. By 1715 many Indians were permanently in debt to the traders, some of whom applied pressure by physical abuse. Indians also were still being kidnapped into slavery.[80]

All the tribes on the frontier were angry, but the Yemassee were the first to erupt into violence. Muskhogean related to the Edisto and the Yemassee occupied the mainland between the Combahee and Savannah Rivers. Besides the trading abuses, they resented the settlers who were moving into their territory without a treaty. In a surprise attack on several plantations near Port Royal in April 1715, the Yemassee killed about one hundred men, women and children. Then, with their Indian allies, they systematically hunted down and killed all the traders they could find. The colonial government raised a militia to defend a perimeter near Charles Towne. Settlers abandoned their homes in outlying areas and flooded into town. Edisto Island probably emptied for several weeks, as every able-bodied white settler, and perhaps some African slaves, joined the defense force.

In June 1715 the militia defeated part of the Yemassee at Port Royal and Salkehatchie. Then the powerful Cherokee were persuaded to help the English, and they turned the tide. But other tribes, especially the Catawba and Creek, continued to raid settlements all over South Carolina until 1718. In all, four hundred settlers were killed. Property losses were estimated at the equivalent of $22 million in today's dollars, and defense costs were another $10 million. The Carolina colony felt insecure for years, and its economy took a long time to recover.

As late as the 1740s and 1750s, friendly "settlement" Indians in the Lowcountry, including the Edisto, were still being harassed and sometimes killed by hostile Indians, mostly Creek, who were incited by French authorities then controlling the Mississippi Valley. However, Georgia was being settled as a separate English colony starting in the 1730s, and soon constituted a buffer between South Carolina and the hostile Indians to the south and west. In one last sputter of violent resistance, two Indians attacked a house on Edisto Island in 1753 and murdered a settler and her two children. The newspaper that reported the tragedy did not identify the Indians by tribe, nor the names of the victims.[81]

By 1720, African Americans were 64 percent of the Carolina population, and in 1740, 66 percent. White slave owners and other settlers worried constantly about a slave rebellion, and there were plenty of precedents in the British West Indies. Rumors circulated that the Spanish in Florida were inciting slaves to revolt. Circumstantial evidence was strong: enslaved people clearly knew that freedom lay only two hundred miles south, and a few runaways made it to St. Augustine.[82]

Close to Edisto, planning for the Stono Rebellion was a well-kept secret among about twenty slaves in St. Paul's Parish along the Stono River. The revolt happened on September 9, 1739. It was a Sunday morning, the slaves' day off, when many owners and other settlers were in church. The escaping slaves killed two storekeepers at Stono Bridge, stole guns and ammunition and headed south along the main road toward Florida, picking up other escapees, killing whites and burning and destroying as they went. They were discovered in late afternoon. A militia of owners was quickly raised and by evening had fought and won a pitched battle with the African Americans who were fighting to escape slavery. Part of the militia was called out of the Presbyterian church at Willtown, near Edisto Island, and the battle took place on a plantation near Parkers Ferry on the Edisto River.

The owners' retribution was swift and overwhelming. Out of perhaps one hundred enslaved Africans who escaped, fourteen died in the initial battle; several others were caught trying to run home and were summarily executed that Sunday night. But a large number escaped initial recapture. "Settlement" Indians helped track the escaped slaves, and during the following week at least forty more were caught and killed, including a group of thirty who were tracked down on September 15. A leader of the revolt who hid in the swamps was hunted for three years before he was caught, tried and hanged. Accounts vary on how many owners and other white settlers died in the Stono Rebellion; the highest estimate is twenty-three.[83]

Apparently none of the Stono rebels was from Edisto Island, but it all happened very close to those planters' homes. Moreover, the black-to-white population ratio was even more lopsided on Edisto than the average for South Carolina as a whole, quoted above. The Edisto owners' fears were proven real and justified. The colony's commons house passed new laws the next year that addressed some of the obvious security loopholes, and sought to ensure both humane treatment for enslaved people and a closer watch over their activities. Eventually, the owners' fears of a slave revolt gradually subsided, but always remained in the backs of their minds.[84]

Other disasters in the 1700s came from nature. The hurricane of September 15, 1752, became legendary in the South Carolina Lowcountry. Charles Town was hardest hit: the eye of the storm crossed the coast just west of the town on a rising tide, and the surge was ten feet above high tide. Large ships landed in the streets, wharves were demolished and half the year's rice crop was ruined. There was also heavy damage forty miles to the north and south, which included Edisto Island. Trees were downed, roads and bridges washed out and farm buildings collapsed. The cleanup must have taken months, and the crop losses were staggering. This devastating hurricane followed a severe drought and precipitated a serious monetary crisis in the colony. Thus it had both economic and political repercussions, further weakening the already frayed relations between the elected commons and the appointed royal governor, James Glen.[85]

Another hurricane struck only four years later, in 1756. A six-foot tidal surge ravaged the coast from St. Simons Island, Georgia, all the way to Charles Town.[86]

Twenty years later, there was another war.

# Edisto Island in the Revolutionary War[87]

In the spring of 1776 South Carolinians decisively repulsed a powerful British fleet and saved Charles Town in the Battle of Sullivan's Island. In the fall of 1778 General Sir Henry Clinton, in overall command of British forces, sent an army by sea from New York to Savannah, while another army marched overland from Florida into Georgia. They easily captured Savannah and garrisoned much of the interior of Georgia. For South Carolinians, the enemy was now on their borders again.

In the spring of 1779, British General Augustine Prevost crossed the Savannah River and marched toward Charles Town with about three thousand men. American General William Moultrie, the hero of the Battle of Sullivan's Island, fell back to Charles Town's inner defenses with a similar sized army, while his superior, General Benjamin Lincoln, hurried from Augusta to attack Prevost from the rear. The British and Americans fought on June 20 at Stono Ferry. The British could not break out of their box on Johns Island, so on June 23 they started hopscotching back to Beaufort across Johns, Wadmalaw, Edisto, St. Helena, Ladies and Port Royal Islands. Charles Town was saved again, but the sea islands were wide open and mostly undefended. Most white families apparently took refuge on the mainland, inside the Patriot lines.

For the sea islands, including Edisto, this was the ugliest chapter of the war. A nineteenth-century historian wrote that "the British committed the most cruel depredations…Houses were stripped of plate, jewelry, clothing, money and everything of value that could be carried away. Livestock was wantonly slaughtered, and in a few cases females were violated by the brutal soldiery." Thousands of slaves

> *who had been promised freedom, repaired to the British camp, and informed the soldiers where their master's property was concealed…Three thousand negroes were carried out of the state, many of whom were shipped to the West Indies and sold. Hundreds died of camp fever upon Otter Island [near Edisto Beach], and for years afterward their bleaching bones strewed the ground thereon. The whole loss was more than four thousand.[88]*

South Carolina historian Walter Edgar adds that "a number of homes were burned, and so was Sheldon Church," near Beaufort. "The conduct of Prevost's troops…and the wanton destruction of property provided a bitter foretaste of the civil war that would soon engulf South Carolina." Prevost's troops occupied Beaufort from May to September 1779 and then pulled back to defend Savannah.[89]

In October a fleet arrived off Georgia from France, allied to America, but a joint attack on Savannah by an American army and the French fleet failed to dislodge the British. In December the British put together a gigantic invasion force in New York Harbor to attack Charles Town again. Sir Henry Clinton sailed south with one hundred ships and more than eight thousand men, but the fleet, battered by unrelenting winter storms, took five weeks to rendezvous off Georgia and another week to effect a landing in the sea islands south of Charles Town. On February 11, 1780, Clinton's fleet sailed into the North Edisto River. Once again, Edisto Island was completely unprotected from an enemy invasion.

Clinton landed his troops on the south end of Simmons Island (now called Seabrook Island), and started them marching north across Johns Island toward Charles Town. By February 24 parts of the invasion force had crossed the Stono River and were on James Island, facing Charles Town. Meanwhile, General Lincoln had had weeks to perfect his defenses in Charles Town and to convince General Washington to dispatch reinforcements overland from New York. With the North Edisto full of British ships and all American forces pulled back to Charles Town, the Edisto plantations were again at the mercy of British foragers, but some Edisto planters apparently remained on the island to try to prevent looting. General Clinton's troops interpreted his ambiguous orders as allowing the removal of any militarily useful animals and provisions from abandoned farms, on the assumption that only Rebels would run away. Both army and navy units plundered and destroyed on Edisto, Wadmalaw and Johns Islands. They particularly needed horses to mount their cavalry and pull their cannon. A British navy captain, Peter Russell, recorded a complaint from some Edisto civilians that British sailors had killed their cattle and hogs and left them to rot. However, there are no reports that any civilians were personally harmed.[90]

When the British attack fleet succeeded in crossing the bar and entering Charles Town harbor on March 20, 1780, Charles Town's fate was sealed. The British army had already surrounded the city on the landward side. Now the army and navy could work together and pound the city into submission. General Lincoln fought hard and held out for seven more weeks, before he surrendered the city and his army on May 12. Charles Town remained under British control until the British surrender at Yorktown, Virginia, in October 1781.[91]

There are no reports of any skirmishes or atrocities on Edisto or nearby islands during these final seventeen months of the war. Some Edistonians probably returned home, particularly if they had men in the household who were not off in one army or the other, for like most communities in South Carolina, white Edistonians were divided in their loyalties.

A Colleton County Patriot regiment was raised in August 1775 by Joseph Glover of Round O (near St. George), who became its colonel. Edisto, Wadmalaw and Johns Islands each contributed a company, as did ten other communities from Beach Hill (near Dorchester) to the Salkehatchie River. The Edisto Island company was commanded by Captain Joseph Fickling; his lieutenants were John Seabrook and James Clark. Theirs was one of the largest companies in the entire regiment, at least at the beginning of the war, with two sergeants and ninety-five privates. Unfortunately, no roster of the enlisted men has come to light.[92]

Captain Joseph Fickling (1735–1799) was a wealthy planter on Edisto Island. His three sons served in a different Edisto Island company of the same regiment that was raised in 1776. That company was commanded by Captain Joseph Jenkins. Joseph Fickling Jr. was his second lieutenant and Jeremiah and John Fickling were privates.[93] The roster has fifty-two names, including officers. This company's roster (Figure 15) is transcribed in *Documents on Edisto Island History*.

No records have been found of the actual service of these Edisto Island companies. It is a reasonable assumption, however, that they saw active duty during at least part of

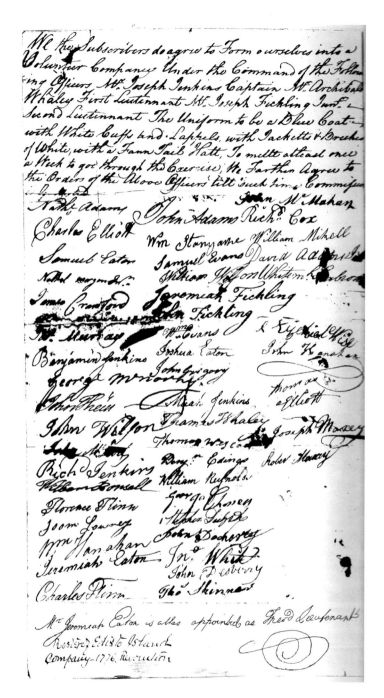

Figure 15. Roster and regulations of the 1776 Edisto Island company, Colleton County Regiment of Foot. The complete text is transcribed in *Documents on Edisto Island History.* Courtesy of Clara C. Mackenzie.

the war, most likely patrolling in the Lowcountry and in the defense of Charles Town in both the 1779 and 1780 campaigns.[94]

At least one Edisto family has an explicit tradition that its ancestor was killed on Edisto Island while serving in the Revolution. James Murray (1740–1779), whose name appears on the 1776 Edisto company roster, is buried in the Jenkins family cemetery on Edisto Island. He had arrived on the island just a few years earlier and married Abigail Jenkins. A direct descendant wrote in a family history notebook a century later that "he [was] killed by the explosion of a cannon while defending the Island from the enemy (British) leaving one child—Joseph James Murray." No contemporary document has been found to substantiate this oral tradition, but it is quite plausible and is consistent with the 1779 date of death on his gravestone. The one son, Joseph James Murray, founded a far-flung Murray family, some of whom still live on Edisto Island today.[95]

At least three Edisto Island planters appear to have suffered after the war for known Loyalist sympathies. They were William Meggett, Isaac Rippon and Joseph Seabrook. Each of them submitted a petition to the state legislature in 1783 explaining "his conduct during the late war" and asking "to be relieved of the amercement levied upon him." An amercement was a financial penalty imposed by the legislature.[96] It is not clear whether their petitions were granted, but all apparently remained on Edisto Island. There may well have been other Loyalists from Edisto who did not return to the island after the war, but if so, no records have been found.

## CHAPTER 3

# EDISTO'S AFRICANS

This chapter focuses on what is known of the ethnic heritages of African Americans on Edisto, and the slaving transactions that brought them to the island. Chapter 5 describes the conditions under which slaves actually lived, worked and died on Edisto Island, especially during the "Golden Age" of plantation prosperity from 1790 to 1861.

South Carolina Indians were also enslaved from time to time between 1670 and 1720 by unscrupulous settlers (Chapter 1). But it was strictly against the laws of the colony, which preferred friendly relations and lucrative trade with the Indians. No record has been found that any of the Edisto Indians were enslaved, though some of them probably were still living on the island when white settlers started clearing land and building houses.[97]

## What Does "Slave" Mean?

There is no one term that accurately summarizes all aspects of an enslaved person. Slaves were African men, women or children (or the descendants of Africans) who had been removed by force from the only community they knew, herded with strangers into coastal prisons, sold to a foreign businessman and transported to America in sailing ships under conditions that ranged from miserable to unspeakable. An African who survived the "middle passage" was then sold to another stranger, taken to a plantation in a strange new country, given minimal housing and strange food, forced to work hard every day alongside strangers, expected to learn a new language in order to survive and prevented from ever leaving that place unless sold to start over in another strange place.

In time, these captured Africans became functioning members of a community of workers. While enslaved, they developed talents; formed friendships and rivalries; played by the rules, broke the rules or made the rules; established families; and reared children. As slaves, Africans and their descendents were also spiritual people with religious beliefs, often expressed in private rituals or public worship. These captured Africans and their descendants eventually aged, died and were buried in this new land, often in unmarked graves, separated forever from the spirits of their ancestors in Africa.

So the word "slave" falls far short of expressing this existence, because it evokes mainly the one-sided economic relationship between worker and owner: slaves were property. For lack of a better single-word term, however, this author sometimes refers to Edisto's Africans and African Americans as slaves before 1862. It is an imperfect and uncomfortable shorthand.

Paul Grimball, the first documented white settler on Edisto Island (Chapter 2), probably cleared his land and built his first house at Point of Pines in 1683 mainly with the labor of white indentured servants that he brought with him.[98]

But to build and operate a substantial farm on the frontier (which is what Edisto Island was in its first years) required lots of labor, and early landowners like Paul Grimball probably started right away to explore how they could purchase at least a few slaves of African descent. Sugar planters in Barbados and other British islands in the Caribbean had been using African slaves for more than fifty years and had gotten very rich. Grimball undoubtedly had friends in Charleston who had emigrated directly from the islands and had brought Afro-Caribbean slaves with them between 1670 and 1683.

Grimball wasn't thinking of large numbers of slaves. In those early years, a handful was an adequate number for the required work; a dozen was a lot. The large plantations with even fifty slaves on Edisto Island were not yet a reality. But Grimball soon made his purchases, and the first people of African descent probably arrived on Edisto Island in 1684 or 1685 as slaves.[99]

## Slave Trading in Charleston, 1670–1807

When Paul Grimball and other settlers began buying slaves for their Edisto farms in the 1680s, Charles Towne had no organized public market for buying and selling slaves; this apparently did not evolve until 1695 or later.[100] Virtually all the African-descent slaves in South Carolina in the first thirty years of European settlement came from Barbados. Prospective buyers wrote to a friend or merchant in Barbados (or went there in person on one of the regular commercial ships out of Charleston), and negotiated a private sale of five or ten slaves.

Slaving ships sailed regularly from Africa to Barbados, Jamaica and other Caribbean ports in the 1600s, but virtually none came to Charles Towne before 1700; from the perspective of the slave traders, there simply was not enough demand to justify a shipload of people. Small batches of African captives turned up quietly for sale at reduced prices by pirates from time to time in these early years; some slaves brought to South Carolina this way already had Spanish names.[101] In Barbados, a Carolina settler could purchase African captives directly from the slave ship that brought them, or, for a higher price, people that had already worked on a plantation and were considered "seasoned slaves."[102] But the number of slaves remained quite small, and whites continued to outnumber blacks in Carolina until about 1708. The main reason for the increased numbers of slaves brought to Carolina after 1700 was that labor was the colony's scarcest resource.[103]

The perceived strength and stamina, compared to both whites and Indians, of the Africans who survived the middle passage and the brutality of being enslaved was another important rationalization that led planters to prefer purchasing African-descent slaves. This trend led to the rapid transition to an African American slave economy in South Carolina after 1700.[104] Charles Town soon became one of the highest volume and most diversified centers for African slave importation in North America.

Without astronomical numbers of enslaved workers (compared to a few white owners), the Carolina Lowcountry, and Edisto Island in particular, never could have achieved its spectacular starburst of affluence (for the plantation owners) that white descendants call the "Golden Age" (Chapters 6 and 7). To understand this contribution of labor, it is helpful to examine briefly just how many Africans eventually were imported into South Carolina as slaves.

A leading scholar on the Atlantic African slave trade, Philip Curtin of the University of Wisconsin, places South Carolina's slave population in a global context.[105] Curtin estimates that 345,000 African and Afro-Caribbean slaves were imported into the thirteen original American states from the 1600s to 1807, the last year the trade was legal. He adds another 28,000 people sold into slavery in the Louisiana Territory before it became part of the United States in 1803, and perhaps 54,000 who were smuggled in on the Southeast and Gulf Coasts between 1808 and 1861 (after the slave trade became illegal), and arrives at an estimated total of 427,000 people imported into slavery in the United States.

Those 427,000 Africans brought into the United States were less than 5 percent of the people taken by force from Africa to all of the Americas during that period. Curtin calculates that total at about 9.4 million (and this number does not include those who died while being transported to the Americas). He believes that 42 percent of them went to Caribbean islands and 49 percent went to South America. Brazil alone received 38 percent, or 3.6 million slaves—eight times as many as the United States.[106] Of course, all of these figures are informed estimates, based on old and incomplete shipping records that have been statistically adjusted in various ways. Curtin warns they may be off by 20 percent or more, but they are among the best estimates available.

Probably about 150,000 of Curtin's North America total of 345,000 African slaves entered through South Carolina during the entire period of legal importation.[107]

Another scholar has calculated African slave imports to North America for each decade of the 1700s, at least roughly, using historical data from the colonial period compiled by the U.S. Census Bureau. The figures in Table 1 provide an approximate sense of the rise and fall of the slave trade through Atlantic ports, including Charles Town, during the eighteenth century.[108] Both the American Congress and the British Parliament had been expected to make the trade illegal after 1807, and both did so. [109]

*Table 1.*
*Slave Imports into Southern North American Mainland, 1701–1775*

| | |
|---|---|
| 1701–1710 | 9,000 |
| 1711–1720 | 10,800 |
| 1721–1730 | 9,900 |
| 1731–1740 | 40,500 |
| 1741–1750 | 58,500 |
| 1751–1760 | 41,900 |
| 1761–1770 | 69,500 |
| 1771–1775 | 15,000 |
| Total | 255,100 |

Source: Curtin, *Atlantic Slave Trade*, 1969.

# Ethnic Origins of the Africans Brought to Carolina

Data are also available on the proportions of captive people shipped to South Carolina from eight different parts of Africa. This information covers a shorter period, from 1733 to 1807, so the figures are not directly comparable to the total captive trade figures set out above. But Table 2 does indicate the broad proportions of different African peoples who were enslaved on South Carolina plantations.[110]

The ethnic origins of African slaves in South Carolina differed significantly from those captured and shipped by British traders to the Americas as a whole. The differences appear to stem almost entirely from the preferences (or prejudices) of the South Carolina planters, and their willingness to pay premium prices for their preferred captives.

South Carolina planters, in particular, strongly preferred people from the Senegambia region of West Africa. Many of them were Bambara and Malinke people from the interior of the continent. South Carolina rice planters, as will be seen below, wanted Gambians who understood rice cultivation in Africa to work their plantations. Almost 20 percent of the captives who landed in South Carolina were from this region, compared to only 5.5 percent shipped out of Africa in British slaving vessels. South Carolina planters also bought large numbers of Africans from the Windward Coast and the Gold Coast.

*Table 2.*
*Slaves Imported into South Carolina,*
*1733–1807, by Origin*
*Percent of slaves with identifiable origin*

| | |
|---|---|
| Senegambia | 19.5 |
| Sierra Leone | 6.8 |
| Windward Coast | 16.3 |
| Gold Coast | 13.3 |
| Bight of Benin | 1.6 |
| Bight of Biafra | 2.1 |
| Angola | 39.6 |
| Mozambique/Madagascar (East Africa) | 0.7 |
| Total | 100.0 |

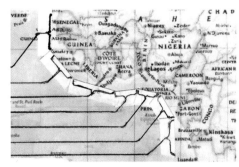

**Modern West Africa**

Windward Coast: Cape Mount to Assini, including present-day Ivory Coast and Liberia.

Gold Coast: Assini to the Volta River, including most of today's Ghana.

Bight of Benin: Volta River to Benin River; today's Togo, Benin and western Nigeria.

Bight of Biafra: Benin River to Cape Lopez: today's eastern Nigeria, Cameroon and part of Gabon.

Source: Curtin, *Atlantic Slave Trade*, 1969.

A disproportionate number of African slaves in South Carolina also were from Angola: almost 40 percent, twice the all-time British slavers' average of 18.2 percent. "Angola" was a common name for a large region of the central African coast near the Congo River, and included the Kongo and several related peoples. The Angola captives apparently were accepted in large numbers by South Carolina planters, despite their reputation as a rebellious people, because near the end of the slaving period few captives were available except Angolans and Ibos. The renowned Gullah culture of the Carolina sea islands (see Chapter 5) apparently took its name from Angola, the origin of so many of these people.[111]

Above all, the South Carolina planters rejected captives from the Bight of Biafra. From this region came the Ibo people and a related group called Igbo. They made up the largest single part (30 percent) of all captives shipped on British vessels from 1690 to 1807, but they were only 2 percent of the captives brought into South Carolina. This strong planter prejudice against Ibo people as slaves appears to have reflected a view that they were both fierce fighters and prone to suicide when enslaved. By contrast, huge numbers of Ibo captives were routed to Virginia (37.7 percent of all Virginia slaves).

To summarize, then, the ethnic origins of Africans who became slaves in South Carolina were heavily skewed toward the Kongo and other peoples of central Africa, followed by large numbers from Senegambia, the Windward Coast (Ivory Coast and Liberia) and the Gold Coast (Ghana). In the absence of more precise data, we can only assume that Edisto's original mix of African ethnic groups was similar to that of South Carolina as a whole.

## African Slaves on Rice Plantations: A Unique Case

Edisto Island proper never became an important rice producer (see Chapter 4), but there was a time in the 1700s when many planters experimented with it, and small-scale production seems to have continued into the late nineteenth and early twentieth centuries. Jehossee Island, however, did become a major rice producing plantation, and since Jehossee has historically been considered part of Edisto, African slaves on rice plantations are an integral part of Edisto's history.

The connection between South Carolina and Gambia through slavery received a lot of attention from scholars in the late twentieth century, so we know a lot about it. We know, for example, that people from the Gambia River on the west coast of Africa were highly valued for their knowledge of rice cultivation and processing. Some historians believe these Africans taught the white planters how to grow rice.[112] Another historian sees adaptive behavior and experimentation among both African Americans and whites. He notes that rice was grown at Jamestown, Virginia, long before South Carolina was even settled, and reminds us that successful, large-scale rice culture in South Carolina evolved over many years of trial and error. Nevertheless, he also concludes that "the African influence on the development of rice cultivation in Carolina [was] a decisive one."[113]

"Senegambia" as a source of captives who became slaves in Carolina included much more than the Gambia River delta. A thousand miles inland from the coast, along the Niger River near Timbuktu, rice had been grown perhaps as early as 3,500 years ago. There, the annual rains flooded millions of hectares, creating a vast inland delta, and the people had learned to plant different varieties of rice under different conditions of water depth, drainage, growing season, etc. Inland rice growing peoples of the Niger River and its tributaries (today's Republic of Mali) included groups called Bambara, Marka, Fula, Malinke, Songhai and Mande.[114] All of them probably contributed to the pool of captives herded to the coast and sold into slavery at the Gambia River or at slave "factories" farther south and west.

And that is not all. Rice growing expertise stretched along the Guinea Coast of Africa "from as far north as Cape Verde in Senegal, and to the south and eastward as far as the Bandama River on the Ivory Coast." Though not as renowned as the Gambians, these peoples knew how to raise upland (dry land) rice, floating rice and swamp rice, depending on the terrain and rainfall available. These rice growing peoples of the coastal rainforest and mangrove swamps included the Baga, Mende, Temne, Kisi and Joola.[115] They, too, undoubtedly were among the enslaved, for they lived in the slave-exporting regions called Sierra Leone and Windward Coast (Table 2), which together supplied over a fifth of the people who became slaves in South Carolina. Some of these people almost certainly ended up on Edisto Island.

## Slave Population on Edisto in the 1700s

The population of slaves in South Carolina grew by more than a third between 1703 and 1708, while the white population grew by only 7 percent. But the whole colony still had less than ten thousand souls, including enslaved Indians.[116]

Edisto Island's population was still minuscule in 1708, but precise figures are not available. Given that it still was an outlying settlement, there probably were only a few dozen white settlers and their families, and a similar number of African slaves.

*Table 3.*
*South Carolina's Population*

|  | 1703 | 1708 |
|---|---|---|
| Whites | 3,800 | 4,080 |
| Negro Slaves | 3,000 | 4,100 |
| Indian Slaves | 350 | 1,400 |
| Total | 7,150 | 9,580 |

Source: Wood, *Black Majority*, 1974.

The next available documented figures are for 1720, and they provide a breakdown by the colony's eleven parishes. St. Paul's was the parish that included Edisto Island (Table 4).[117] The three islands in St. Paul's closer to Charles Town than Edisto—Wadmalaw, Johns and James—probably had most of the parish's population. Edisto was still relatively less developed, so the first three islands also would have had higher ratios of slaves than Edisto. (The two parishes farther south—St. Bartholomew's and St. Helena's—still had majority white populations.) Thus, in 1720 Edisto Island probably had about 15 percent of the parish's population, perhaps 150 whites and 200 African slaves.

*Table 4.*
*Population, St. Paul's Parish,*
*South Carolina, 1720*

|  | Free | Slave | Total | Slave % |
|---|---|---|---|---|
| St. Paul's | 1,005 | 1,634 | 2,639 | 62 |
| South Carolina | 6,262 | 11,828 | 18,090 | 65 |

Source: Wood, *Black Majority*, 1974.

Between 1720 and 1732 Edisto Island experienced a rapid growth in population, especially of its African slaves. The next figures are from tax records, and provide details specific to Edisto Island (Table 5).[118] They are shown in greater detail in *Documents on Edisto Island History*.

*Table 5.*
*Edisto Island Population, 1732*

|       |      |
|-------|------|
| Free  | 195  |
| Slave | 546  |
| Total | 741  |

Source: SCDAH, "1732 Tax List."

No other statistics are available until the end of the eighteenth century, but clearly the African slave population of Edisto continued to grow steadily while the white planter population leveled off. By the 1730s, virtually all the tracts that were going to be occupied by landowners and their families were already occupied, but landowners continued to buy slaves so they could expand production. Productivity of agriculture on Edisto Island apparently was increasing steadily, both as a cause and as a result of the growing slave population.

The federal census of 1800 on Edisto shows 206 free persons of all ages and 1,823 slaves of all ages. Thus, between 1732 and 1800 Edisto's population went from 74 percent to 90 percent people of African descent.[119] The proportion would hover near that figure for the next 150 years.

The 1800 census also records that exactly one free person of color was living on Edisto Island. His name was Robert Mason.[120] He had no family living with him, and no other information about him has turned up. Very likely he was a skilled craftsman, able to support himself in a way that was valued by the planter community, or he probably would not have been there.

# The Illegal Trade in African Captives after 1807

Beginning January 1, 1808, slave trading ships were subject to confiscation and their officers were subject to prosecution, if caught either by the Royal Navy patrolling the coasts of Africa or by the Revenue Cutter Service patrolling the U.S. coasts. However, the American laws were "very badly enforced"; the desire to purchase African captives remained strong; potential profits to slave traders remained high; and ship owners and captains continued to take the risks.

Professor Curtin, cited above for the magnitude of the slave trade before 1808, believes some fifty-four thousand additional Africans or slaves of African descent were smuggled into the United States through the coast from Maryland to Texas between 1808 and 1861.[121] He provides no breakdown, but it seems likely that perhaps fifteen to twenty thousand of those were landed in South Carolina. There is no way of knowing how many of those ended up on Edisto Island: perhaps a few hundred, perhaps a thousand. A mitigating factor was that other sources of labor were available. Slaves born in the United States could still be purchased legally in Charleston right up to 1861, and Edisto planters, among others, could afford the higher prices for slaves from Virginia and other places with a surplus of labor.

## An Edisto Family from "Angola"

Very few Edisto Island African American families are able to trace their ancestry back to a specific African captive individual or even an ethnic group in Africa. It is difficult enough for African Americans today to connect their families to any ancestor before 1870 (the first federal census to list all people of African descent by full names), unless that ancestor was free before the Civil War. Most people who lived as slaves had no surnames, and their given names were seldom recorded in any public records. Even the few genealogists fortunate enough to find an enslaved ancestor's name in a plantation journal or a white owner's will rarely are able to trace that person's lineage back several more generations to a person born in Africa—much less to a specific place in Africa. This extreme difficulty partly accounts for the resounding popular success of Alex Haley's book, *Roots*, which showed the American public in 1976 that it *could* be done. The same continuing difficulties make just as remarkable the story of one Edisto family that knows exactly who their original African ancestors were.

Those captured ancestors arrived about 1820, more than a decade after the importation of new African captives had become illegal. The story of their enslavement was told in great detail in the 1970s by Sam Gadsden, then in his nineties and since deceased. He was a great-grandson of the head of the African family that was captured, and Mr. Gadsden had heard it from his great-aunt, who had actually been born in Africa, and had had her childhood memories reinforced and amplified by her father and other relatives during her adult lifetime. The Gadsden family's oral tradition, repeated verbatim over many generations in the tradition of an African *griot*, has been judged by experts to have a high degree of reliability. This is a summary of the story as told to and published by Nick Lindsay:[122]

Two sons of an African prince were named Kwibo Tom and Wallie (Woli?). They had an established trading relationship with a Dutch ship captain in the early 1800s. These brothers knew how to obtain elephant ivory, gold and diamonds from the interior of their part of Africa, and they traded these to the Dutch captain for printed cloth and clothing and decorative goods, which they used in trade with other Africans. After many years of this kind of trading, Kwibo Tom and Wallie made a different deal with the Dutch captain, with the approval of their father, the prince. They would accompany the captain across the ocean with their own cargo of ivory and other African goods to trade for a shipload of clothing and other small manufactured goods Africans valued, and then return home. They would pay the Dutch captain with part of their ivory and gold, and he promised to return them safely to their father. They boarded his ship with their wives and children and sailed away to get rich by trading on their own account. But the Dutch captain betrayed the trust of the prince, sold his passengers into slavery in South Carolina and kept their valuable cargo for himself. He turned out to be a pirate.

The Dutch captain knew the trade in African captives was no longer legal in the United States, so he did not sail into Charleston. Instead, he sailed into Bohicket Creek and sold both families to a Mr. Clark on Wadmalaw Island. Clark then distributed members of the two large families among his various plantations, including several on Edisto Island.

Kwibo Tom and Wallie were allowed to visit freely from one plantation to another, and were encouraged by Clark to father as many children by as many wives as they liked. Kwibo Tom's African wife and children were transferred to Clark's daughter, Lydia, as a wedding portion when she married William Meggett Murray in 1825, and they all went to live on his plantation, Jack Daw Hall, at Frampton's Inlet. Wallie's wife and children were sent to another plantation called Clark's on Edisto Island. Murray later transferred two of Kwibo Tom's daughters to be slaves on the Presbyterian Parsonage farm, and they eventually married two Gadsden brothers. Those two women were sisters of Sam Gadsden's grandmother, Rebecca.

And where in Africa were these families kidnapped from? Though Sam Gadsden told this part of the story in two very different versions, the version now accepted by a leading African American expert on African history and the slave trade is that they were from central Africa near the Congo River, the region broadly called Angola by the slave traders. Specifically, they were of the Vili people of Loango Bay, now in the Congo Republic. And some of their descendants, now numbering in the hundreds, still live on Edisto Island, and know very well who their ancestors were and where they came from.[123]

## CHAPTER 4

# EDISTO'S EARLY ECONOMY

Like all of the South Carolina Lowcountry, there were several distinct economic periods on Edisto Island during the first century after European settlement, each with a different mix of agricultural products. More than a hundred years passed, from 1683 to about 1790, before Edisto planters, like planters on all the other sea islands, hit upon the crop that would bring fabulous wealth to them and their families. During those first one hundred years many plantations were bought and sold several times, as some planters gave up and moved elsewhere, while others probably wondered if they could ever achieve economic security on the relatively isolated island.

The productivity of the soil was never the issue. The issues involved technology and labor. Both the planters and their African slaves had to learn, by sharing information and by trial and error, how to use the resources available—the soil, the flat terrain, the forests, the rainfall, the tidal rivers, the hot, humid weather—how to grow and process products that were marketable in that corner of the world at prices that would supply their needs and leave something over for the planters to reinvest in more land and to purchase more slaves. This last part—more slaves—was crucial from the planters' point of view, for the scarcest resource of all during their first half-century on Edisto was labor. There simply were not enough white indentured servants and African slaves combined to work the abundant, cheap land to provide for more than basic subsistence, and the planters had visions of a more prosperous lifestyle.

## Lumber, Corn and Cattle

The first few landowners on Edisto Island cleared their land a little at a time and concentrated first on growing Indian corn and vegetables and raising cattle and hogs to feed their families and their (mostly indentured white) servants. Some parts of the island were grassland or savannah when the settlers arrived, and thus did not have to be cleared.[124] Early grantees like Paul Grimball and John Hamilton would have considered themselves fortunate if any of their grants included some savannah, because that land could be plowed and planted immediately.

Wood from land clearing had several uses. Pine from the pine barrens and cypress from the freshwater swamps of Edisto Island were sawed into lumber, which was used both for local building and for sale in Charles Towne and in Barbados, where lumber was scarce. Edisto probably did not have enough pine to support a naval stores industry, as did much of the interior of Carolina, but it had lots of live oak, which was highly valued by shipbuilders. Charles Towne had its own shipyards from the earliest days, and built small trading vessels for sale to offshore shippers as well as for the Carolina colony's own use. Local shipbuilders were said to "prefer [live oak] even to the best oak that can be met with in the yards of England."[125] Edisto oak probably also went to Charles Towne to be turned into barrel staves and casks for export to the Caribbean, where huge quantities of sugar were packed in barrels annually for the European market.

Maize, or Indian corn, was being grown in gardens by the Edisto Indians long before the English arrived (Chapter 1), and the settlers adopted it immediately as a major food staple, though some also grew wheat. There was a ready market for surplus corn in Charles Towne and, through Charles Towne, to the Caribbean. Intensively cultivated sugar islands like Barbados were net importers of food by the time Carolina was ready to export. Little corn was used for animal feed; most of it was ground into meal for human consumption. By the mid-1700s, when rice was already Charles Towne's dominant export, lumber products and corn still accounted for about 2 percent each of Charles Towne's export income. Some of each undoubtedly came from Edisto.[126]

Some of the easiest products to raise successfully on Edisto Island were cattle and hogs. At first, livestock was imported from Virginia, New England and Bermuda, and most of it was slaughtered immediately to feed the hungry settlers in Charles Towne. By 1674, however, Carolina had its own herds, and early settlers were selling live animals to new arrivals to get their own herds started. By the 1690s much of the colony's hinterland, including Edisto, had become a free range for proliferating cattle, and the price of beef in Charles Towne was down to a very reasonable rate.[127] On Edisto, the numerous small constituent islands and peninsulas extending into the marshes (see Figure 2) provided natural boundaries for the cattle herds of some landowners.[128]

There were several reasons for free-ranging the cattle. Land was cheap but labor was scarce and, in the early years, farmers could not spare the labor time to build fences and barns. The winters were mild, so cattle could forage for themselves in the woods and marshes year-round, and they multiplied rapidly. Typically, landowners would assign one of their slaves to build a small cow pen and a hut for himself on a remote part of the farm and to live there to guard the cattle. Cows with calves were kept in the pen to protect them from predators, but the rest of the herd roamed free.[129] Cattle brands were registered in Charles Towne to distinguish ownership when herds mingled in the woods. Unbranded cattle would have been free for the taking.[130] The colony's cattle were mostly black in color, but were not as large as the European stock they developed from.[131]

Edisto's hogs were also small and were "rusty redish" in color. They were more often penned up than cattle, but inevitably many of them escaped and roamed the island as feral swine. These wild pigs were hunted for their meat, which was said to have excellent flavor, because part of their diet was "peaches and other delicates." But hogs intended for bacon were penned and fed corn, to harden the fat.[132]

Edisto Island's excess cattle and hogs went to the Charles Towne market from the earliest days, and produced some cash income for settlers, many of whom reinvested the capital immediately in more slaves. In town, some of the animals were slaughtered for local consumption. The rest were exported to the Caribbean as salt beef and pork in barrels. Local tanneries turned the cowhides into leather for both local and export markets. Like lumber and corn, these livestock products were an important part of the opening phase of Edisto's agriculture. But by the mid-1700s meat and leather, combined, had slipped to only about 5 percent of Carolina's exports.[133]

# Rice

Experiments with rice cultivation in the Carolina colony began about 1695 and continued for a very long time. Some of the trial and error took place on Edisto Island. Both dry and submerged cultivation were tried, and both swamp and artificial pond irrigation were used successfully, but on a limited scale. The seed that would produce "Carolina gold" rice probably came from Madagascar. By 1708, rice was South Carolina's single most important export, and by 1748 it accounted for more than all other exports combined. The success of rice soared to an even greater proportion after the Revolutionary War, when planters learned to harness the tides to flood and drain their rice fields with fresh water, in the system that came to be known as tidal freshwater irrigation.[134]

Rice was an important money crop on Edisto Island in the 1700s even though, except on Jehossee, it could only be grown on a small scale. On dozens of plantations across the island there is evidence that rice was farmed on reclaimed marshes adjoining tidal creeks. Thomas Rake, among others, appears to have earned substantial income from rice in the 1760s (Chapter 2). After the advent of sea-island cotton, many Edisto planters apparently continued to plant rice, but typically on a small scale and mainly for local consumption. Throughout the 1800s rice was a welcome variation in the corn-heavy plantation diet.[135]

Part of the surviving evidence of Edisto's small-scale rice cultivation is the straight lines on maps in the 1850s, representing dikes across the narrow marshes near the upper ends of tidal creeks. One example is shown in the map of Shell House Plantation. Other examples can be found in the maps in Chapter 7. Additional evidence has turned up in notations on plantation plats, planters' journals and other documents.

To grow even a small amount of rice in a reclaimed marsh, farmers had to have a source of fresh water on demand, at a slightly higher elevation than the rice field. Typically, they used a nearby swamp that drained into the marsh. If there was no swamp, any depression in the land could be converted into a rainwater impoundment or rice pond. A low dike across the mouth of the swamp or drainage ditch would hold back the accumulated fresh water until the proper time to flood the field. Flushing a newly diked marsh several times with fresh water would leach enough of the salt out of the

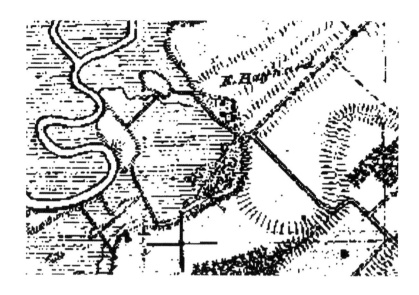

Figure 16. Rice fields at Shell House Plantation, from 1852 U.S. Coast Survey map. The three straight lines connecting small marsh islands with the shoreline are earthen dikes, probably enclosing a rice field. Peninsula at bottom center is today's Marsh Point.

mud to grow rice. After that, the field usually was flooded soon after planting, to prevent the growth of weeds while the rice grew tall, flowered and formed seed. When the fresh water was no longer wanted on the field, a gate or trunk in the outer dike was opened to empty it into the creek at low tide. Building the dikes and trunks, digging the ditches and creating these rice fields was very labor intensive, so it usually was done on a small scale, but after the initial investment, rice production could be kept going year after year with relatively few workers, and some of the seasonal tasks were less onerous than those required for growing and processing indigo or cotton.

Jehossee Plantation was the exception to the rule of small-scale rice farming on Edisto Island. Jehossee was huge, at least when it was fully developed in the mid-1800s (Chapter 7). What Jehossee had that no other part of Edisto had was its fortunate location on Pon Pon (the South Edisto River), just above where the fresh water met the salt. An inexhaustible supply of fresh water from upstate flowed past Jehossee. Around 1790 planters from Georgetown, South Carolina, to Georgia began to harness this rich treasure to grow rice on vast fields reclaimed from marsh lands along the Waccamaw, Pee Dee, Black, Sampit, Santee, Cooper, Edisto, Ashepoo, Combahee, Coosawhatchie, Savannah and Altamaha Rivers. Both sides of Pon Pon were devoted to large-scale rice planting in the 1800s, but the plantations on the west side of the river lay in St. Bartholomew's Parish, and thus are not part of Edisto's history.

Each high tide in the South Edisto River caused not only the salt water to rise several miles inland but the fresh water behind it to rise as well, until the tide went out. Thus Jehossee experienced a twice-daily rise and fall of *fresh* water along its margins. Once a part of the marsh had been enclosed with dikes, and water control gates or trunks were installed in the dikes, it was a simple matter (in principle) to flood the fields with fresh water simply by opening the trunks on the upriver end during successive high tides and closing them during low tides, until the fields were covered to the desired depth. Later, the fields were drained by opening gates in the dikes on the downriver end at low tide. As more and more sections of marsh were enclosed, internal dikes then were built to divide the fields into sections so they could be flooded or drained a few at a time, allowing a smaller labor force to work them in rotation. Internal networks of feeder canals and drainage ditches completed the infrastructure. The several hundred acres of natural high land at Jehossee were used for housing, roads, mills and fields to grow corn and other provision crops for the workers. A large section of high land was kept in forest to provide all the plantations' needs for lumber and firewood.

Wetland rice growing and processing on Edisto went through the same stages each year, whether on a small scale or a large scale. The fields were drained and plowed in March, usually by mules or oxen. The ground was further worked with hoes in April, leveling it and preparing trenches. Workers dropped the seeds into the trenches by hand and covered them with a foot. When the rice plants sprouted, the field was flooded again and then periodically drained and flooded to impede the growth of weeds. Some hoeing and weeding had to be done during the summer, but not nearly so much as with dry land rice or cotton. When the grain appeared on the stalks, it was the task of slave children to go into the fields each day to chase off the birds, especially bobolinks, that tried to eat the grain. In September the fields were drained and harvested. Workers used a hand tool called a rice hook to cut off the stalks near the ground, and carried them in bundles or by the cartload to the threshing floor.[136]

Processing the rice was very labor intensive and exacting work. Care had to be taken in all the stages not to damage the grains or contaminate the rice with dirt and trash. Either would greatly reduce its market value. Every step of this kind of rice processing had been practiced in parts of West Africa for many generations, so Africans from those regions were highly sought after as slaves by Carolina rice growers (Chapter 3).[137]

Threshers separated the rice grains from the stalks by spreading them out on a dry, hard surface and flailing them with a leather strap attached to a stick. Then the loose piles of grain were scooped into flat coil baskets for winnowing, that is, repeatedly tossing the rice in the air and catching it in the basket so the breeze could carry off the chaff. Next, a large scoop of grain was placed into a hollowed log (mortar) and pounded repeatedly with a wooden pestle to remove the husks from the edible grain. Grains and husks were then separated by a final winnowing, and the rice was packed into wooden casks for storage or shipment to market.[138]

During the 1700s South Carolina became the most prosperous of all the English colonies in America, largely due to its rice production. The Caribbean and European market for rice was strong, and wholesale prices in Charles Town were high. So Edisto's landowners with rice to sell had a ready source of new capital.[139] In the colony as a whole, annual rice exports climbed steadily throughout the eighteenth century, from 270,000 pounds in 1700 to 6.2 million pounds in 1720, to 30 million pounds in 1730 and to 66 million pounds in 1770. Carolina Gold was a great success story even before the technological innovation of tidal freshwater irrigation around 1790, and Edisto Island undoubtedly shared in that success.[140]

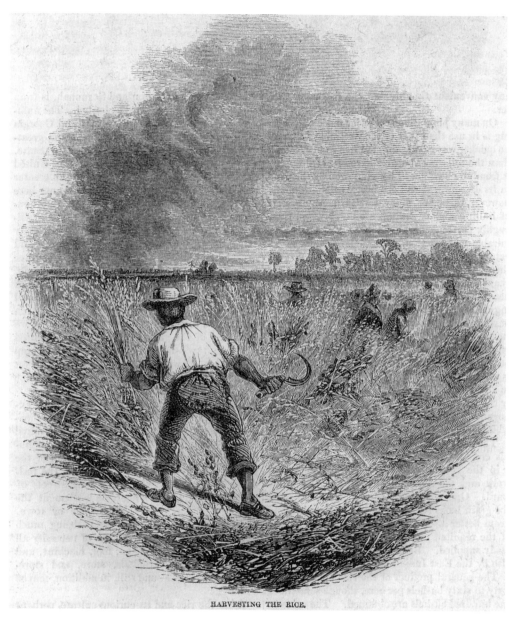

Figure 17. Harvesting rice with a rice hook on a South Carolina plantation. Engraving from *Harper's New Monthly Magazine*, 1859. *Courtesy of South Caroliniana Library, University of South Carolina, Columbia.*

# Indigo

While small-scale rice production brought reliable income to some Edisto planters during the 1700s, they continued to search for and experiment with other crops that would grow well and produce income from their underused high land, as did settlers elsewhere in the Lowcountry. Indigo filled that bill, for a short time.

Indigo, a dark blue textile dye, was known in the Caribbean, Virginia and Carolina from the 1600s, but it was first successfully planted, processed and marketed by Eliza Lucas Pinckney, a young woman in St. Andrew's Parish near Charles Town, in the early 1740s. She and her husband, Charles Pinckney, made the seed available to many other Lowcountry planters in 1744, and indigo soon was being produced in large quantities for the English market. From 1748 to 1775 the British Parliament actually paid a bounty for American indigo, effectively increasing the import price by about 20 percent. Unfortunately for the American colonies, however, Britain closed the door to indigo from North America with the onset of the Revolutionary War, and France had sources it preferred from its own colonies, so South Carolina was abruptly left without a ready market. Production dropped in the 1780s as Charles Town's wholesalers searched for new markets. Then it stopped completely, less than forty years after it had started.[141]

In the mid-1740s, Edisto Island planters were among the first to jump on the indigo bandwagon, and they apparently were heavy producers during its brief heyday. Several older Edisto residents today can still point to depressions in the ground that were once "indigo pits," according to family traditions passed from generation to generation for two hundred years.[142]

Indigo plantations were not extensive, for the processing was unpleasant and very labor intensive. Fifty or sixty acres would produce all the indigo that a few workers could handle, and a few workers is all that most Edisto planters had in the mid-1700s. Conveniently, indigo not only grew on high ground not needed for rice, but was also harvested and processed before the rice, so both crops could be grown on the same plantations with limited manpower. Some planters also apparently tried to rotate the indigo crop to new land each year.[143]

The variety of indigo grown in the Carolina Lowcountry was brought from the West Indies, where it was also grown successfully. It was planted in rows in well-plowed fields after all danger of frost, and harvested in the summer when the plants, two to three feet tall, began to bud, and before any of the leaves turned brown. The entire plant was cut off with a knife or sickle near the ground and laid gently on a cloth to avoid bruising and to keep it clean. Then the plants were carried immediately to the first vat, eighteen or twenty cloth bundles at a time—the fresher the plants when started through the processing, the better the quality of indigo produced.[144]

Processing indigo required three large vats connected by pipes, built to allow gravity flow of liquid from first to second, and from second to third. Some growers built square vats of wood on stilts, but others built more permanent brick-lined vats on sloping ground. Whole plants were laid in the first vat, covered with fresh water and allowed to "digest" all day. When fermentation reached just the right stage, usually after about twelve hours, the valve was opened at the bottom of the vat and the liquid drawn off into the second vat. The macerated stems and leaves in the first vat were then removed and discarded—some planters used them for fertilizer—and another batch could be started.

In the second vat the liquid was stirred and beaten with wooden paddles attached to a wheel that was usually hand cranked, which caused the indigo salts to begin to coagulate.

The master indigo maker would dip out samples, often in a silver cup, and watch for just the right rate of precipitation of the solids to stop the beating. (Some Lowcountry producers added limewater at this stage to speed up the process, a shortcut that caused French indigo buyers to scorn all Carolina indigo.[145]) After all the solids had settled to the bottom, the excess water was drained off and discarded. Then the sludge (called "feces") was allowed to drain into the third and final vat. There it was allowed to settle and separate some more. Then the workers scooped the wet indigo sludge into cloth bags and hung them up to drip until dry. Finally the stiff paste was packed into flat boxes to cure into hard, dry cakes in a shady place because sunlight would damage the indigo.[146] The dry cake was then packed in casks of several hundred pounds each for shipment.

In 1748, only four years after production started in South Carolina, 117,000 pounds of indigo earned 10 percent of the colony's export income. In the final year before the Revolutionary War, South Carolina exported 1.1 million pounds of indigo.[147] Some historians believe Edisto planters did particularly well on indigo. They processed it with care and earned a reputation that associated the Edisto name with high-quality dye. Owners of several well-known plantations on Edisto Island appear to have gotten their early starts on profits from indigo. Among them were Old House, Brookland and Brick House.[148]

# The Advent of Sea-island Cotton

Even before the market for South Carolina indigo collapsed in 1776, planters on Edisto and nearby sea islands were continually inquiring and experimenting with other cash crops. Cotton seemed a tantalizing possibility. Good quality, long-staple cotton (but not sea-island cotton) had been grown on a small scale for plantation use on Skidaway Island, Georgia, as early as 1767. Similar local plantings are documented by the Burden family of Johns Island, South Carolina (between Edisto and Charleston), by 1788, and possibly ten years earlier. But in those years even simple cotton gins were unavailable in the sea islands, and the seeds had to be picked out by hand before spinning the lint into yarn—an extremely tedious process that could produce only about one pound of clean cotton per person per day.[149] All of that changed dramatically within a few years. The sea islands embarked on an economic revolution that would make them world famous, and Edisto Island in many ways would be at the center of that revolution.

There is a widespread impression among descendants of sea island planters that Eli Whitney's invention of the cotton gin in 1793 allowed sea-island cotton production to take off. That is not true. Whitney's cotton gin indeed revolutionized production of short-staple or upland cotton, but its saw teeth ruined long-staple cotton, and it was never used in the sea islands.[150] The development of sea-island cotton, and the gradual improvements both in growing it and processing it, are much more complicated stories.

There is also a widespread belief that sea-island cotton was *introduced* into Georgia and South Carolina from the West Indies. It wasn't. Sea-island cotton actually was a previously nonexistent cultivar of long-staple cotton (*Gossypium barbadense*). It was *developed* by a few sea island planters through careful seed selection over several years, starting, to be sure, with some high-quality black seed from the West Indies. The story begins in 1785.[151]

During the Revolutionary War a number of prosperous planters from the sea islands (including a few from Edisto Island; see Chapter 2), as well as large numbers of backcountry South Carolina settlers, remained loyal to the Crown. Not a few of those planters chose to leave or had to leave the country after the war, and some went to the West Indies. Some managed to return later, and most corresponded with relatives and friends who remained on the sea islands. In 1785 three Loyalist planters, who had recently moved from Anguilla to the Bahamas, each sent packets of long-staple cotton seed to a friend or relative on St. Simon's Island, Georgia. The Anguilla variant of *G. barbadense* grew well and made beautiful cotton in the tropical climates of the West Indies, but had not yet been successfully grown on the mainland, because the plants took a very long time to mature, and South Carolina's November frosts always killed the plants before they fruited. In Georgia, the plants grew but did not blossom in 1785. Still, the very mild winter of 1785–86 allowed the plants to survive, put up new stalks and bear fruit (cotton bolls) the second year. The Georgians replanted that seed, and the third-year crop grew from seed to fully developed cotton bolls well before frost. A key change had taken place in the genetic makeup of these plants: they had "adapted" to begin flowering during the long, hot summer days, without waiting for the shorter days of fall. A new cultivar had been developed.[152]

Sea-island cotton seed was passed from planter to planter within a few years. The first commercial crop in South Carolina was grown on Hilton Head Island in 1790; by 1793 it was on all the sea islands. By 1808, sea-island cotton was grown extensively on seven islands in South Carolina. Edisto was in the center, with three islands to the north (Johns, James and Wadmalaw) and three to the south (St. Helena, Ladies and Port Royal). The entire crop was exported; there never was a significant domestic market for sea-island cotton before the Civil War. Exports from South Carolina shot up from approximately 10,000 pounds in 1790 to more than 1 million pounds in 1794 to 8.3 million pounds in 1800.[153] And that was just the beginning.

From the outset, the fine, silky texture of sea-island cotton caught the attention of British, French, Swiss and other European manufacturers of high-quality textiles. They were willing to pay a premium for it over the price of American short-staple cotton, which was booming simultaneously in upland areas across the Southern states. But competition among the sea island planters for this specialized market quickly led to greater emphasis on quality than quantity. And a few planters soon found that amazing gains in quality could be achieved by rigorously selecting the best plants each year from their own crops, and planting the succeeding crop only from that seed. In just a few years, starting in 1804, Kinsey Burden of Johns Island had seed that produced cotton with "a fiber from 1½ to 2½ inches long, strong and fine, and with a lustrous creamy tint." By the middle 1800s, several planters and plantations across the sea islands were household names for extra-fine sea-island cotton. Among the names were William Seabrook of Bleak Hall, the Townsend plantation on Edisto Island.[154]

Growing sea-island cotton and preparing it for market were complex and labor-intensive operations. Both the growing and the processing underwent significant changes over the 130 years it was produced, from 1790 to 1920. Planters and African slaves worked hard to understand the crop, to reduce labor requirements, to increase yields per acre and to enhance and protect the quality of the final product.

# Growing Sea-island Cotton[155]

Edisto's planters knew exactly where they should plant cotton. It needed their best high land fields; the well-drained sandy loam that was never used for rice had been underused by indigo, and now (in the 1790s) was little used for anything except provisions. Thus they started with fields that had already been cleared of oak-hickory forest or maritime forest (see Chapter 1). When the cotton weakened the soil of those fields, they just cleared new fields and planted them in cotton, until they ran out of prime land. By the early 1800s some planters were clearing low, swampy land and ditching it for cotton; if adequately drained, this was good cotton land, but many planters learned the hard way that a lot of rain in a short time can quickly rot a field of otherwise healthy cotton plants, and drainage systems underwent continual improvement until after 1900.

When all other available high land was in cotton, planters learned they could even grow cotton on a pine barren, if they mulched and fertilized it heavily and if they ditched it well to compensate for its high water table. Finally, planters turned to their salt marshes and discovered that indeed cotton would also grow in carefully diked marsh mud from which the salt had been leached by repeated immersion with rain or swamp water. In fact, some of the best cotton was grown on recovered marshland.[156] But the initial labor investment in dikes, canals and trunks was so steep that marsh cotton was mostly a small-scale solution. Very probably, some Edisto marshes diked earlier for rice were converted to cotton planting before the Civil War. None of those fields, however, were returned to cotton after the Civil War.

Planters understood the value of crop rotation and fallowing their fields, and sometimes used these techniques to reinvigorate their soils. But as demand increased for high-quality sea-island cotton, few resisted the temptation to plant every available acre. Instead of rotation, they invested labor time in extensive regimes of fertilizing their fields with animal manures, salt mud, salt marsh plants, crushed oyster shell and other materials available on the plantation. After the Civil War, when planters had to pay wages for labor, they invested heavily in commercial fertilizers, usually with good results.

Cotton fields needed to be protected from wind; aside from the occasional hurricane at harvest time,[157] from which nothing could protect the cotton, young plants were vulnerable to spring and summer windstorms. Most planters left a strip of trees along the margin of each field as a windbreak. Where no mature trees were available, they sometimes planted young ones.

Successful sea-island cotton growing required the following steps, some simple, some complex: seed preparation, land preparation, planting, thinning, cultivating and picking.

Planters stored their own best seed from the gin for the following year's planting, although a few purchased high-quality seed from other reputable planters. Some practiced systematic seed selection on a three-year cycle.[158] Whatever the source, the seed needed to be rubbed through a screen to remove any remaining lint and trash that might interfere with planting and germination.

Preparing the land for planting began with "listing" immediately after picking, or in January at the latest. Organic trash, including the old cotton stalks, weeds and grass, was moved into the alleys between rows and given time to decay. In February, surplus cotton seed, animal manure, salt marsh and pluff mud were added to the compost, and then covered with soil from the old beds to create new ridges on top of the accumulated mulches and manures.

All this heavy work was done by gangs of workers with hoes; Edisto's planters were notorious even among their sea island brethren for their disdain of that ancient labor-saving device, the animal-drawn plow.[159] The cotton ridges were typically five feet apart, with deep valleys between them, connecting to ditches and canals that drained into tidal creeks.

Cotton was planted when soil moisture and air temperature were just right, usually between March 20 and April 15. If a frost came after the plants were up, the entire field had to be replanted. Sunny high fields were planted first, and low wet fields last. Seeds were dropped by hand either continuously in a furrow along the top of each row (called "drilling"), or several in each hole made with a hoe, one to three feet apart (planting in hills).

The cotton plants were thinned repeatedly, simply pulling up and discarding the unwanted ones. The goal was to leave one, two or three of the healthiest, strongest cotton plants in each hill, with adequate growing space between the hills.

The cotton had to be cultivated at least four times before it began to send roots down the sides of the ridges; then it was left alone. Cultivating killed the weeds that competed with the cotton for water and space, pulverized the soil around the plants and mounded the soil into hills around the stalks. All this was done with the short hoe, under the broiling summer sun. For good reason, the field slaves hated this job more than any other job except (on some plantations) digging and hauling the heavy pluff mud to the fields in February. On a few plantations, part of the cultivating was done with a horse-drawn skimmer plow invented by John F. Townsend of Bleak Hall, Edisto Island.[160] Even when the skimmer was used, the job was finished with the hoe, forming the hills around each stalk.

Unlike upland, short-staple cotton, sea-island cotton matured ("fruited") gradually between August and December. Thus, fields had to be picked repeatedly before each cohort of newly opened bolls could be damaged by rain and sun. Typically, that meant picking a field every ten days or so for three or four months. Usually, the labor of slaves of all ages—men, women, boys and girls—was needed for the picking, for speed was of the essence, and even small children could make a contribution. The cotton bolls had to

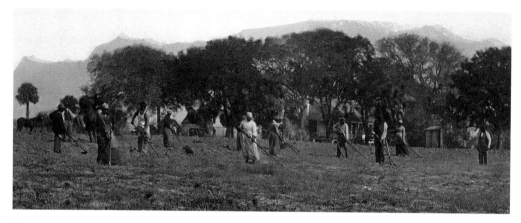

Figure 18. "Listing" a cotton field. Preparation for planting started in midwinter: chopping old stalks, mulching, manuring and shaping new ridges. (Shadow behind trees is a blemish.) *Detail of photo, 1862, by Henry P. Moore, courtesy New Hampshire Historical Society.*

be plucked quickly but neatly from the open husk, leaving behind as much as possible the leaves and other trash. The picker stuffed bolls into a cloth bag and, when it was full, walked to the end of the row and dumped it on his or her cloth sheet, which was weighed at the end of the day. Each worker's weight was recorded and judged against the expectation for a person of that gender, age and strength. An adult was expected to pick seventy or eighty pounds a day; a few could pick one hundred pounds.

## Preparing Sea-island Cotton for Market[161]

On a prosperous, well-furnished sea-island cotton plantation, the cotton house (or houses) had eight separate rooms, one for each of the six stages of preparing the cotton for market, plus two for storing the seed cotton before ginning and the baled cotton ready to ship. The six stages of preparation were drying, sorting, whipping, ginning, moting and packing. It was important to keep the cotton under a roof and out of the sunlight once it was picked, for it needed to be dry for processing, and sun would turn it yellow and brittle. The separate rooms helped protect the cotton from contamination with dirt and byproducts as it became progressively cleaner with each stage of processing.[162]

Picked cotton was first dried to reduce its moisture content to an acceptable level. It was spread on a pine floor with good air circulation to dry for one day if it had been picked in clear weather, two or three if it had gotten wet. The loose cotton was alternately spread and turned until dry. Handling the large heavy sheets of cotton was both arduous and specialized work. The dry cotton was then sorted; any remaining visible trash was picked out, and any damaged or yellowed bolls were removed from what was to be sold. This was a tedious step, but no alternative to hand cleaning and sorting was ever invented. Many overseers required each worker to sort his or her own cotton, as an incentive to pick carefully.

"Whipping" the cotton removed the last small, foreign particles, such as sand or particles of leaf and twig. In the early years this was done by beating it with smooth sticks over a coarse wire screen; after 1830, various mechanical whippers were offered for sale. After whipping, the seed cotton typically was set aside in a clean room for four to six weeks before ginning.

Ginning was the single most important stage of market preparation. It removed the cotton seeds from the lint, without which it would be impossible to spin even clean cotton into thread. Sea-island cotton had a very small, smooth, black seed, which was relatively easy to separate from the fibers, compared to short-staple cotton, which clung tightly to its large, green, hairy seed. Ginning close to the source was extremely advantageous both for quality control and to minimize transportation costs. It took, on average, 1,500 pounds of seed cotton to fill a 300-pound bag with clean, marketable lint. Virtually every plantation on Edisto Island ginned its own cotton while hand-powered gins were in use. Later, when expensive, large-scale gins came into use, most planters had a choice of commercial gins within an hour's cart ride from their plantations.

The earliest gin used in the sea islands was a small, tabletop double-roller machine turned by a hand crank and called a churka gin, a name that came with it from India to the Caribbean in the 1700s. The rollers were of teak. One person cranking and feeding seed cotton into a churka could gin about five pounds of cotton a day. Successively more efficient gins were introduced during the 1800s, some of them quite ingenious. A foot-powered treadle gin was a big step forward; one worker could now gin up to thirty pounds of lint a day. Around 1802 someone found a way for two horses to power a wooden drum or "barrel" as long as a room, from which pulleys drove up to twenty-four small tabletop gins of the type previously powered by a treadle. This system combined the gentle action that sea-island cotton needed with large-scale production. It still required a worker to tend each of the twenty-four gins, but two horsepower delivered six hundred pounds or more of lint per day.[163]

Two major innovations arrived before the Civil War. The McCarthy roller gin was invented in Alabama in 1840 and arrived in South Carolina in 1852, on the plantation of William Seabrook Jr. of Edisto Island (see Chapter 7).[164] The McCarthy gin "revolutionized the ginning of all types of long-staple cotton throughout the world." It featured a single large roller covered with walrus hide, a stationary steel knife that pressed against the back of the ginning roller, another knife that reciprocated back and forth across the fixed knife to break loose the seeds and a grid underneath that allowed the seeds to fall through. Several improvements were made by McCarthy and others between 1840 and 1900, and this gin became the sea island standard after the Civil War. Each gin turned out two hundred pounds of clean lint a day, with only two workers, one to drive the horse and one to tend the gin. Three McCarthy gins could be driven by one horse.[165]

The last major innovation was the steam-driven cotton gin (or room full of gins). Both the long table of small gins and the large McCarthy gins eventually were powered by a steam engine, which was set up in a separate room so the gin room could be kept spotlessly clean. McCarthy gins powered by steam were still in use when Edisto planters gave up to the boll weevil in 1920. Two of these gins remained in the gin house at Sunnyside Plantation on

Edisto Island until 1974, when they were given as museum pieces to the South Carolina Parks Department. In 2003 they were returned to the Lowcountry for restoration and exhibition, one at the Charleston Museum and one at the Edisto Island Museum.

After ginning, sea-island cotton still had two more stages of processing. The next was called "moting." The lint was spread on flat tables while workers, usually women, shook it and gently pulled open any tangles to discover and remove any broken seeds, foreign particles or stained locks of lint. This was the final quality control.

The moted cotton was immediately carried by hand to the bagging room. All sea-island cotton was packed by hand and foot into a standard hemp bag seven and a half feet tall and two and a half feet wide, usually made in Scotland and usually holding three to four hundred pounds. (This small round "bale" made sea-island cotton instantly distinguishable from short-staple cotton, which was packed with a screw press into huge square bales weighing one thousand pounds or more.) The empty bag was attached to an iron hoop in a hole in the floor, and a worker stood in the bag, packing the cotton with his feet as other workers dumped in handfuls of clean lint. As the bag filled, the packer climbed out and used a wooden tamper to pack the cotton to the top. The filled bag was then stitched closed, labeled and stored in a clean room to await shipping to Charleston.

## Sea-island Cotton Exports[166]

Cotton was a very labor-intensive crop, so plantation owners gave much thought to the efficient management of their enslaved workers. The average planter cultivated about six acres of cotton per field hand. To avoid diverting labor from the highly lucrative cotton crop at key stages of production, most planters allocated less land for food crops than needed to support their slave workers, and willingly bought corn, rice and bacon every spring when their own provisions ran out. A common rule of thumb, evidently, was to limit provisions acreage to that "which the hands could attend while working the cotton crop."[167]

The acreage devoted to long-staple cotton on all the sea islands largely stabilized by the 1830s because all available land (or slave labor to do the work) was in use. The cotton plant itself refused to grow and produce reliably anywhere except on the sea islands and a narrow band of mainland adjacent to tidal waters. Apparently this cultivar of *Gossypium barbadense* liked three things about the sea islands: the very long growing season, the salty air and the significantly lower rainfall than the coastal plain only a few miles away.

Thus, total annual exports of sea-island cotton leveled off but held steady at four and a half to five million pounds a year until the Civil War. In the early years, when only Georgia and South Carolina were producing sea-island cotton, South Carolina's share of the export income was about 60 percent. Later, when Florida also produced a substantial amount, South Carolina's portion dropped to 43 percent.

No figures have been found for exports by locality within South Carolina, but from at least 1800 Edisto Island was a recognized leader, both in the quantity and quality of its sea-island cotton.

## CHAPTER 5

# PLANTATION SLAVERY ON EDISTO

L abor on the sea islands from about 1700 to 1861 was provided almost entirely by slaves of African descent and their descendants, and after the Civil War by African American freedmen and women and their descendants. Understanding the economy of slavery is necessary to understanding the society on Edisto both before and after the Civil War.

Edisto's planter aristocracy—men, women and children—simply accepted African slavery as the way things were. Few agonized over slavery as a moral issue. The moral implications of slavery are so obvious to readers in the twenty-first century, both African American and white, that it is difficult to focus on the facts about how this economic and social system functioned. But it is necessary to understand it to address the moral issues with shared knowledge of what actually happened. The moral issues are revisited at the end of this chapter.

Almost without exception, planters and their families also considered most of their slaves lazy, careless with valuable tools, prone to steal and limited in their ability to learn complex tasks. Few whites were able to analyze these "faults" in context, that is, how slavery itself, and resistance to it, could produce certain attitudes and behaviors that could be interpreted this way; they universally assumed that Africans were innately inferior to Europeans as a race. (Slave resistance on Edisto will also be examined at the end of this chapter.) But Lowcountry planters, with inputs from the slaves themselves, did invent the task system of slave labor, which ameliorated some of the most onerous conditions of slave labor and facilitated the highly complex crop production systems outlined in the preceding chapter.

## The Slave Population on Edisto

By 1790 South Carolina had a brand new constitution and a new capital in Columbia.[168] Rice production was booming, making the state the wealthiest (in gross domestic product) of the thirteen in the new republic. Coastal planters whose lands were not suitable for rice were casting about for a new, reliable cash crop. The promising experiments with long-staple cotton on the sea islands of Georgia (Chapter 4) were already being talked about in South Carolina. Edisto Island was on the threshold of a "Golden Age" for its planters.[169]

The first federal census in 1790 showed that Edisto Island had a white population of 223 and a slave population of 1,692. So the island's total population was 88 percent African American.[170]

In 1860, on the brink of the upheaval that would change Edisto Island forever, the census counted 329 whites and 4 free persons of color.[171] So the white population had increased by 48 percent. The slave population, however, had tripled in seventy years; it now stood at 5,082 men, women and children.[172] The population of Edisto Island was now 94 percent African American—surely one of the highest proportions for a large community anywhere in America in 1860.

The majority of slaves on Edisto in 1860 lived in plantation communities of 20 to 50 people. Although William Aiken owned 660 slaves who lived in two villages on his Jehossee Island rice plantation, other Edisto planters owned much fewer slaves. Seventeen cotton planters owned between 100 and 370 slaves each,[173] but these slaves were usually divided among two, three, four or more plantations, so those slaves also lived mostly in communities of 50 persons or fewer.

Sea-island cotton was a very labor-intensive crop, and many proprietors in the early decades of the 1800s had more land than they could plant successfully with the labor of the slaves they owned at that time. So as Edisto's planters got steadily wealthier during the seventy years before the Civil War, they bought more and more slaves. In fact, this wealth affected the national market of slave labor, and many slaves were shipped south from Virginia because they could be sold for higher prices in South Carolina and Georgia. The only large slave market with higher prices than Charleston during this period was New Orleans, from which people were sent to work the plantations of the burgeoning Mississippi Delta and Texas.[174]

## Edisto Plantation Social Structure and Management

The following summary depends heavily on Guion Johnson's systematic study of plantations on nearby St. Helena Island.[175] Fragmentary and anecdotal records from Edisto plantations in the pre–Civil War period show a high degree of similarity. The photos in this section are from Edisto Island, taken during the Civil War. While they are posed compositions, they provide the only known images of some of the people who had been slaves on Edisto.

Small plantations on Edisto Island (three hundred acres or less) usually were directly managed and supervised by the owner in person. Medium-sized plantations (three hundred to six hundred acres) typically had a white overseer who ran day-to-day operations. A few large plantations (over six hundred acres), or a cluster of several adjoining plantations under one owner, almost always had a white manager with considerably more authority than an overseer. A manager was experienced enough and trusted enough to make strategic planting, cultivating and harvesting decisions—decisions crucial to the plantation's overall profitability for the year—while the owner was absent from the island for weeks or even months. Such a manager was considered essential if the plantation owner held political office, enjoyed foreign travel, had a medical or law practice in Charleston or preferred to live elsewhere.

On each working plantation with a resident planter's family, slaves were organized into four social groups, clearly recognized by all members of the plantation community. These groups had all the attributes of class in any society: status, influence, material resources, privilege and some discretion in choosing a husband or wife. The classes were based on work assignments, skills and proximity to power. The four classes of slaves, from the top down, were drivers, craftsmen, house servants and field hands.[176]

Most plantations had one slave driver who was also a slave, though very large places sometimes had two drivers. Plantations jointly managed with others each had resident slaves and a driver who was a member of that community and knew every member of it intimately. The driver would keep the keys to the bulk food storehouses and issue the weekly food rations to each slave. He laid out the daily tasks for each field hand, stayed in the field all day with the workers, passed judgment on the quality of their work and doled out instant punishment or rewards to the workers within guidelines laid down by the overseer or owner. Drivers carried a small whip or club as a symbol of authority, and would use it. The driver provided continuity in plantation operations when white overseers changed, which tended to be frequently. He was the core repository of the plantation slaves' memory of planting, cultivating and harvesting techniques, of how the owner wanted things done.[177]

A ruthless or corrupt driver could make life miserable, not just for a few field hands but for the entire slave community on a plantation. The only recourse for unjust treatment was to try to appeal to the owner or his family in some way. There was no legal redress.

A real incident of driver abuse (with surprising consequences) happened on the Edisto plantation of Major William Murray before the Civil War.[178] The overseer was a white man named Muirhead, but the slaves disliked him and called him Mule Head behind his back. At one point a driver died, and instead of promoting someone from the ranks of the plantation slave community, Murray allowed Muirhead to bring in a stranger from another plantation as driver. The new driver was a smart and ambitious man named York Scott. He was from the plantation of Muirhead's father near Georgetown, South Carolina, so he was not familiar with Edisto traditions or with the Murray plantation community. He probably also had limited experience cultivating sea-island cotton, because most plantations near Georgetown were rice plantations.

Soon afterward, Major Murray and his wife "Miss Liddy" (Lydia Clark Murray) went on vacation for a week, leaving the overseer in charge, and Mule Head told the new driver to use the whip liberally if the field hands did not obey him. York Scott not only did so, but also reassigned a young slave named Charles, who was Miss Liddy's gardener, to heavy duty as a field hand, and whipped him very severely when he could not complete the task he was given. Charles almost died. Charles's extended family, including his brother and three or four sisters, was horrified.

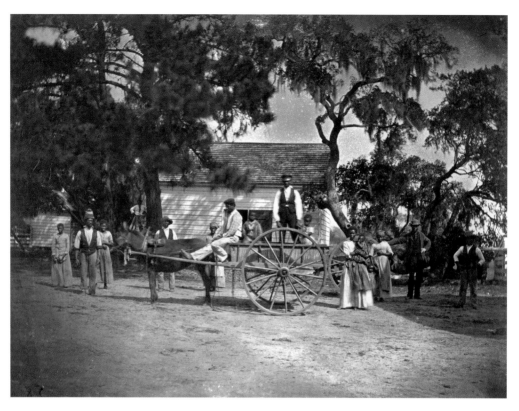

Figure 19. "Going to the Field," Edisto Island, 1862. Henry P. Moore posed these photographs (Figures 18–21) with people recently freed by Union army occupation. However, the clothing and equipment are accurate. *Courtesy of New Hampshire Historical Society.*

In the society of the Murray plantation, Charles's family was not just "any" slave family. As the children of Kwibo Tom, they were high-status members of the slave community. (See Chapter 3, "An Edisto Family from 'Angola.'") In addition, they were actually the property of Miss Liddy, not Major Murray, so they were under her protection but his management. Everybody but, perhaps, York Scott knew that.

Charles's sister Jane was especially angry. The first morning Major Murray was back at home she went straight to him and told him what had happened. She also told him that if Charles got whipped again, Master Murray had better prepare for a funeral, for she personally would kill York Scott. Major Murray not only took this threat seriously, but he evidently cared enough about the welfare of his and his wife's slaves that he immediately instructed Muirhead to stop all whippings. He told Muirhead that if any field hands failed to complete their tasks, they should go to Jane. She would get them to work. And she did. After that, Jane was the driver, and York Scott was not. Charles was retrained as a high-status carpenter, was taught to read and write by Miss Liddy and eventually became a literacy teacher to the other slaves on the same plantation.[179]

Just under the driver in status on each plantation were the slave craftsmen, sometimes called mechanics, who had been taught a skilled trade valuable to the community, usually by apprenticeship to an older slave who was an expert. The most common craftsmen on an Edisto plantation were the carpenters, who built all the new structures and repaired or improved the old ones.[180] Other craftsmen were the blacksmith or farrier and the brick mason. A planter who owned one of these men could also hire him out to neighbors, and the monthly wage went to the owner, not the slave. However, slave craftsmen also had many opportunities to barter their skills for extra material privileges from an owner's family and within the community of slaves.

Next in the social hierarchy of the slave community were the house and yard servants, both men and women. Some were highly skilled cooks, seamstresses, butlers, gardeners, coachmen and nurses; others were lower-status, but skilled, chambermaids, laundresses, stable hands and livestock and poultry tenders. Even the apprentices and helpers around the house and yard, usually boys and girls between six and fourteen, had higher status than the field hands and their children, who occupied the bottom of the social scale.

Finally, each fieldworker was rated as a "hand," based on how much work he or she could actually do, and this status also was known to everyone. The strongest adult men and women who could put in a whole day's work were full hands. Adults with any physical or mental handicap might be rated three-quarter hands. Aging men and women who tired more easily but could still work might be half hands. Three-quarter or half hands, including the aging, might also be reassigned to fill vacancies in the house or yard staff, where work was easier. Boys and girls usually entered the full-time field workforce at age fourteen, but they might start as quarter hands, then move up the rating scale as they gained skill and endurance.[181]

From the perspective of the plantation owner, looking for the maximum work from his or her slaves, these ratings were used to plan a workday, a workweek or the planting year based on how many "taskable hands" he could put in the fields; that is, how many "full-hand" equivalents he had at his disposal. This number varied from year to year, and also changed from week to week as slave workers became ill or injured, recovered or shifted status because of pregnancy, disability or age.[182] Some evidence from the sea islands suggests that a ratio of one field hand to three other (1:3) slaves in the plantation population probably was common on large Edisto plantations in the 1800s. Small plantations might have had a ratio closer to one to two (1:2).

Besides the ever-shifting number of taskable hands, planters or managers also calculated the rough annual "cost per slave" and thus the potential for gross "income per slave" at the end of each year. Slave labor costs were calculated like any other production costs, including work animals; seeds, tools and equipment; an overseer's wages (typically $1,000 a year); payments on debt; transportation of cotton to market; and the factor's (broker's) commissions on cotton sold.[183]

For plantation owners, every planting year was a gamble on weather, cotton prices and other conditions. Only the careful managers among Edisto plantation owners actually paid off all their debts and banked money in the good years; most just paid the interest annually. An unnamed Edisto planter who lived into the twentieth century once said that his family had lived in "bondage" to Charleston factors for more than one hundred years.[184] The circumstances of everyone on a plantation were affected by the overall economic situation and management skills of the plantation owner.

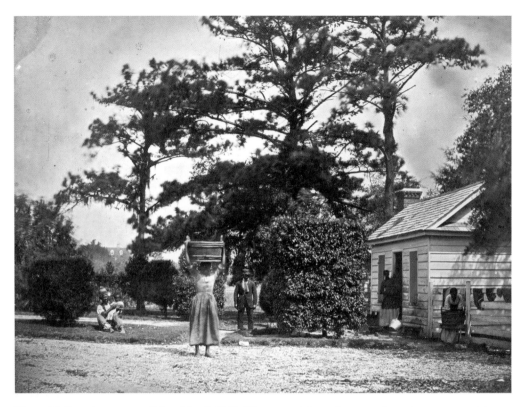

Figure 20. Laundry women, Edisto Island, 1862. Woman on left carries a wooden tub; woman at right scrubs clothes; woman in doorway may have hot water. Clean clothes dry on the fence. *Henry P. Moore photo, courtesy New Hampshire Historical Society.*

## The Sea Island Task System[185]

From the owner's point of view, work that did not get finished in time meant fewer acres planted, smaller yields per acre, crops ruined by rain before harvesting and delays in delivering the product to market, which all led to potential loss of income. From the slaves' point of view, although they might have been agricultural or pastoral people in Africa, work on a plantation was an unending task, and generally there was no advantage in finishing it faster.

Slave management by threat and punishment persisted on the majority of plantations and farms across the South until emancipation. But a different system, which at least from today's vantage looks more mutually beneficial to owner and slave, was invented on the Carolina rice plantations in the 1700s. A "task" was both a measure of land, one quarter of an acre, and a flexible daily work assignment, depending on the season of the year and the type of work. Both concepts were carried over intact to the nearby sea-island cotton plantations starting about 1790.

The task system in its simplest form was a daily contract between a supervisor and each slave. Each slave had to finish a clearly defined amount of work in a day, and when

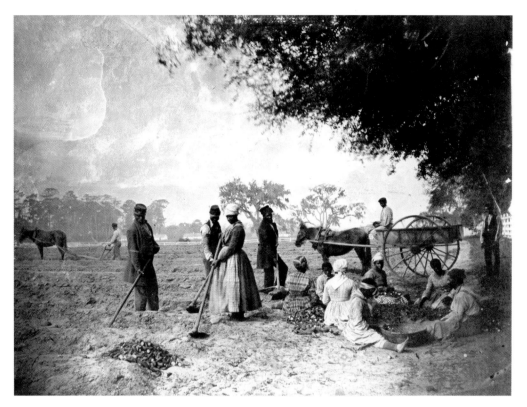

Figure 21. Sweet potato planting, Edisto Island, 1862. Note the typical broad, heavy hoes and handmade coil baskets. Sweet potatoes were a staple food for slaves. *Henry P. Moore photo, courtesy New Hampshire Historical Society.*

it was finished, *no more work would be assigned that day*, and the slave was free to use whatever time remained for his or her own benefit.

For owners, the task system made farm management easier because, weather permitting, all tasks got finished each day. Work could be planned days ahead and priorities could be shifted if weather or other conditions changed. For slaves, it offered a positive incentive to work hard, complete the task early and have time for their own pursuits—such as tending their own gardens and livestock, earning money or exchanging work with each other, spending more time with their families or resting, fishing and crabbing.

That was the basis of the task concept, but Edisto and other sea-island cotton planters developed it, over the years from 1790 to 1861, into a highly complex management tool. The quarter-acre task was the basic reference point. Listing[186] a quarter acre of cotton field (Figure 18) was a task for a full hand. Simple cultivating with the hoe was easier, so that work task might be hoeing half an acre. Seeding cotton was easier still, so the task might be seeding three quarters of an acre. Each day's task was reduced proportionately for people rated as three-quarter hands, half hands and quarter hands.

Some work tasks were not measurable by land area, but they nevertheless became somewhat standardized on Edisto plantations as the functional equivalent of a quarter acre of listing. On a nearby sea island, splitting one hundred fence rails twelve feet long was a day's task, as was cutting a cord of firewood, plowing three acres of corn or digging six hundred cubic feet of ditch. A task of digging and hauling pluff mud from the marsh to the field was a specified number of cartloads.

By all accounts, African-descent slaves on Edisto plantations took full advantage of the task system. Strong field hands were sometimes able to complete their tasks by midday and use the entire afternoon for themselves. It was not uncommon for members of the same family to work their tasks cooperatively by choice. Those who finished first would pitch in and help their parents, grandparents or children finish their tasks so they could spend their remaining time together.[187]

However, it is well to remember that this less inhumane work system might have been the norm but was not applied uniformly on all Edisto plantations, nor was it applied at all in some work situations, such as housework. And even with a smoothly functioning task system in the fields, plantation slavery still allowed arbitrary work assignments, favoritism or hostility between drivers and certain slaves, and some harsh punishment and cruelty by owners, overseers and drivers, if they were so inclined.

## Food, Clothing and Housing for Slaves

The following description is again taken from the more complete records on a sea island near Edisto, with anecdotal corroboration from Edisto records.[188]

In addition to cash crops, such as cotton, slaves also grew staple foods for the entire plantation community. These were then given out as standard rations each week to each slave, based on an adult's work rating, with children receiving proportionately less of each food. Families prepared and cooked their own meals. The foods rationed out by owners changed with the seasons, and the amounts varied from one plantation to another. The basic rations on a well-run Edisto Island plantation would have been potatoes, dry shelled corn or rice, depending on the time of year. Rations also normally included bacon or salt pork; fresh meat, usually beef, could be a supplement for periods when the fieldwork was the hardest, and a special addition for holidays, such as Christmas. Most Edisto planters also oversaw the cultivation of large quantities of cowpeas and sweet potatoes by the slaves, which were then distributed as supplements. These foods became part of the characteristic dishes of the Gullah people. Salt, molasses and smoking tobacco also were doled out regularly on most plantations. At least one Edisto planter gave each field hand a quart of vegetable soup every day during hard labor, and twice a week the rest of the year.

Each slave family was also allowed to cultivate a piece of land, typically a quarter acre near their cabins, for a kitchen garden where they usually raised corn and potatoes to supplement the rations. Slaves were usually allowed to raise a pig and a flock of chickens per family. Chicken was a luxury food that they rarely ate themselves, but sold both eggs and poultry to the owner's family, or at island markets. They might spend the cash on tobacco, coffee, refined sugar and specialty items of clothing that their owners did not provide.[189]

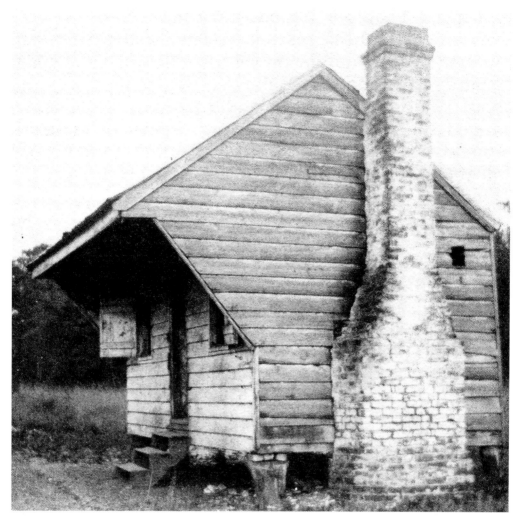

Figure 22. Former slave cabin, Edisto Island, about 1940. Roof overhang sheltered the front steps. Other cabins were more basic. Some poor Edisto families lived in former slave cabins until after World War II. *Photo courtesy of Clara C. Mackenzie.*

Slaves on Edisto also supplemented their diet with seafood all year and were free to take crabs and oysters from the creeks that bordered almost every plantation on Edisto Island. They also fished, but the better quality fish, such as whiting, and all the shrimp that they caught usually had to be delivered to the owner's kitchen.[190]

A recent medical anthropological study of slave nutrition on the sea islands concluded that corn and pork, supplemented by foods available to most slaves—vegetables, fruits, nuts, berries, game, fish and shellfish—"would have provided a well-balanced and ample diet for even the hardest working prime hands."[191] But it is well to remember that this diet describes only the ideal, for even on prosperous plantations some slaves had better access than others to all parts of this diet, and presumably only in years of ample harvests.

Slaves were also issued clothing by their owners, usually twice a year, and again some provided better than others. One or more slave seamstresses, depending on the size of the plantation, worked full time under the supervision of the plantation owner's wife to make clothing for the rest of the slaves from cloth bought at wholesale.[192] (During the rest of the year the seamstresses made much more elaborate clothing for the white family.)

Housing for slaves varied by plantation as much as did rations and clothing. A few cabins usually stood in the yard of the owner's house for the house servants, but those for the field hands were located outside the fenced yard, some distance away. They were typically arranged in a row or double row, called "the street," with their own small gardens. Both the main house and the slave cabins had privies nearby. The quality of the slave cabins ranged from "wretched hovels" with dirt floors, cooking fire in the middle of the floor and no toilet facilities, to relatively well-built wooden duplex cabins for two families, with plank floors, brick chimneys, shuttered windows, sleeping lofts for children and clean privies nearby. The single cabin pictured here (Figure 22) was fairly common on Edisto Island, though by no means universal. At the better end of the spectrum, an English visitor to Edisto in 1827 wrote that the "cottages" he saw compared favorably to the dwellings of white peasants in some countries he had visited, e.g., they actually had interior rooms, built-in beds and a few had windows. There were, on the average, five persons to a cabin.[193]

## Health and Medical Care of Slaves on Edisto

All large plantations, and many medium sized and smaller ones, had a slave woman who doubled as a nurse and midwife for the plantation community. Both African American and white women on Edisto Island before the Civil War routinely gave birth at home attended only by the midwife. Several doctors lived on Edisto Island at any given time, but they were not summoned for childbirth unless there were severe complications. A pregnant female slave usually worked at her assigned task, even fieldwork, until labor began. On a well-run plantation she was allowed complete rest for one month after delivery, then half her usual task for seven months. After eight months babies were usually started on cow's milk, molasses and solid food while the mother returned to full-time work. Women too old to work, assisted by young girls, supervised all the infants and children of slaves up to six or seven years of age, during work hours, sometimes in a plantation nursery.[194]

Despite this reasonably progressive day care and sanitation (on prosperous plantations) for babies and small children, the mortality rate for both African American and white children was high. The deadliest childhood diseases were tetanus and whooping cough, which was fueled by cold, damp, poorly ventilated cabins in the winters. Other killers were diarrhea, pneumonia, "debility" and fevers.[195]

The planters themselves often studied medical books and kept supplies of basic medicines to administer to their slaves when needed. Quinine, calomel, paregoric and Epsom salts were commonly used; planters might buy castor oil by the gallon as a preventative supplement for their slaves. Most planters left orders to call a doctor to diagnose and treat seriously ill or injured slaves, and large plantations might have a "sick house" with separate rooms for men and women. Prospect Hill Plantation (Chapter 7) had a brick hospital.[196] However, the level of medical care would have been below what was available to whites.

Some Edisto Island physicians treated both African American and white patients on a fee-per-visit basis. Planters James Hopkinson of Cassina Point and E. Mikell Whaley of Little Edisto (Windsor) each documented extensively in their plantation accounts the fees they paid to doctors to treat their slaves. Hopkinson paid over $670.00 in one year, 1854. When Whaley evacuated his slaves to Georgia in 1862, he paid a local doctor on a fee basis a total of $329.50 to treat them for the year.[197]

The deadliest diseases for adults who were slaves on Edisto Island apparently were cholera, peripneumonia and dysentery. Peripneumonia was a painful combination of pleurisy and pneumonia, and was nearly always fatal. Dysentery, called "bloody flux," might or might not be fatal, depending to some extent on the quality of medical care and nursing and the age and underlying health of the patient. Smallpox and yellow fever also caused some deaths among slaves. Progressive owners were having all the slave children on their plantations vaccinated against smallpox before the Civil War.[198]

Africans and African Americans were susceptible to malaria, but they contracted the most deadly form only a third as often as whites. The sickle-shaped red blood cell trait in some Africans from areas with malaria, especially "Angolas," made carriers of this trait resistant to malaria, but also susceptible to a painful form of anemia.[199]

## Religion among Slaves on Edisto

Virtually nothing is known about religious beliefs or practices in slave communities on Edisto Island in the 1700s. Statistically, it is very likely that most Africans who arrived as slaves brought with them animist or ancestor spirit-worship beliefs, and some probably were also from Muslim communities in West Africa. But we simply don't know for sure how many generations these beliefs survived and were practiced or how they were transformed on plantations in an overwhelmingly Christian white culture.

A few historians of slavery have suggested that some of the slaves arriving in America, especially from the Bight of Biafra (see Chapter 3), were already Christians. Certainly European Christian missionaries were active in some parts of coastal Africa by the late 1700s, but little systematic research has been done. Whether or not any of Edisto's African captives had previous experience with Christianity, both the Presbyterian and Episcopal churches on Edisto Island began to welcome them to their Sunday worship services about 1800, at the time of a growing national movement to provide Christian instruction to slaves (Chapter 6).

This is first mentioned in the records of Trinity Episcopal in 1809, when the Reverend Joseph Warren was rector. Four special benches were built to accommodate the African slaves, probably at the rear of the original, small sanctuary. In 1812 the tiny congregation listed 12 white and 3 "colored" communicants. In 1814 the bishop visited Edisto and confirmed "13 whites and six negroes." The new, much larger church dedicated in 1841 was built partly to provide balconies that could seat 200 slaves. By 1842 the Sunday school had 47 white and 125 slave "scholars" (in separate classes), and the Reverend Charles Leverett was conducting an occasional wedding or funeral for Christian slaves. He was also preaching every other Sunday afternoon to the slaves on several plantations. In the late 1850s the Reverend William Johnson "had services for the colored people, at the church on the Island every Sunday during the Winter, except Communion Sundays, and on every Sunday afternoon at different plantations. A principal part of the exercises at the plantation [was] to teach catechetically."[200]

A similar growth of slave participation took place in the Presbyterian Church on Edisto Island during those five decades, mostly under the pastorate of the Reverend William States Lee. A visitor described a communion service there in 1857 at which about one hundred white members took seats at the trestle tables down front, then retired and watched while two hundred slave communicants filed down from the galleries and took their places at the same tables. They were served the same elements by the same minister and elders. "The solemnity and decorum observed was alike throughout."[201]

Apparently, most of the slaves who attended the Presbyterian and Episcopal churches on Edisto Island were the favored few, mostly skilled servants, on each plantation. It was another situation, however, at Old First Baptist Church on Edisto.[202]

The Baptist Church was built and paid for by a white woman, Hephzibah Jenkins Townsend, in 1818. From the beginning, white and African American members worshiped together without formal separation. The white Baptists were always in the minority and were frequently all women. By 1845, there were 451 African American members and only 2 whites. When Hephzibah died in 1847, the church was owned by white trustees for an essentially African American congregation, and it kept going with a white minister until 1861. It has continued strong to this day. (This story is given in more detail in Chapter 6.)

Opportunities (or pressure) for all slaves to participate in Christian worship on the plantations also grew steadily during this period. By 1850 every large plantation, and some of the smaller ones, had a chapel large enough to accommodate all slaves who lived there, including the field hands and their families. Services were conducted every Sunday afternoon by a clergyman or missionary paid by the plantation owner. The owner's family usually attended when at home, and attendance for the slaves was compulsory. Methodism got its start on Edisto Island through missionary efforts encouraged by several planters, including William G. Baynard, in the 1840s.[203]

# Gullah Language and Culture

Over time the African American people of the South Carolina and Georgia coast evolved a unique subculture and a distinct language called Gullah that has survived into the twenty-first century. Gullah is much more than a dialect of English. It is a true blend

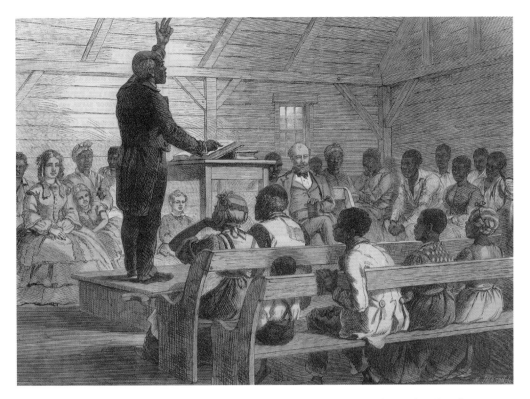

Figure 23. Sunday afternoon preaching in a plantation chapel, somewhere in South Carolina. Some Edisto plantations had chapels for slaves by 1850. Note the planter's family in attendance. *Engraving from* Illustrated London News, *1853, courtesy of South Caroliniana Library.*

of English and African syntax, vocabulary, intonation and speech patterns. It is "the only English-based creole known to exist in North America." A creole is a complete, distinct language derived from the mixing of two or more languages. Experts believe it evolved for a combination of reasons: the mixing of captives from several different African language groups, the population's relative isolation on large coastal plantations and their infrequent contacts with English speakers for long periods of time. Pure Gullah is still spoken today by a few people, and it is still completely unintelligible to those who don't speak it. Modified Gullah is spoken by many.[204]

Gullah has been carefully studied, described and explained by linguists and anthropologists only in the last sixty years, so a number of myths about it still survive in popular culture. One such myth is that Gullah people speak a corrupt form of English. They do not; they speak their own language. Another myth is that Gullah is a debased form of Elizabethan English. It is not; it has a few words from seventeenth-century English, but far more from African languages. Gullah, in short, is "a dynamic, coherent, and distinct language, one with an evolving, adapting, and patterned structure and a complex history of its own."[205]

Gullah, however, was and is much more than a language; it is also a complex cultural system with its own concepts, beliefs and behaviors, again blending African and Anglo-

American traditions. There are Gullah music, Gullah beliefs in the supernatural, Gullah medicine and Gullah folklore. All of these evolved on Lowcountry rice and cotton plantations, and provided the fabric of daily life for the slaves and, later, for the freedmen and women and their descendants on Edisto Island. No effort is made here to describe or even outline Gullah culture; that has been done by experts in a number of recent popular and scholarly books (see Selected Bibliography). But it is well to remember the complexity and pervasiveness of the Gullah language and culture as we follow the people of Edisto Island through time.

## Was Slavery on Edisto Island "Different"?

It was once very common to hear people (descendants of the plantation owners) assert that slavery as practiced on Edisto Island was not so bad, that it was in fact so benign that it was hardly slavery at all. That assertion is heard less often today, perhaps because it might sound insensitive or even racist. But the idea, or the question, still lives, and is spoken from time to time, privately. The following answers reflect the totality of the author's research, not any specific sources.

Was slavery on Edisto different? Yes and no.

Slavery in North America as a whole was far, far more humane than in the Caribbean Islands and South America, just in terms of the sheer numbers of slaves who survived and had descendants (see Chapter 3). Moreover, slavery on most medium and large plantations on the sea islands of South Carolina was at least materially better than on smaller, inland farms across the South, where there simply was not much money and conditions were harsher, for owners and slaves, and for small white farmers.

Was Edisto's slavery measurably better than on the other sea islands, say St. Helena or St. Simon's? Maybe, but it's hard to prove. Insofar as Edisto had a higher proportion of financially successful planters than some of the other sea islands, Edisto's average living conditions for slaves may have been slightly higher, but that would also depend on the inclinations of the owners.

Let us be clear, however, that even within the relative wealth of Edisto Island during its "Golden Age," there were still some plantations where slaves were routinely mistreated in addition to the oppression of the institution of slavery itself, where some were hungry day after day, where diseases and injuries were inadequately treated, where slaves aged quickly and died young, where they were not allowed to practice any form of worship or have their own praise houses on the plantation; where, in sum, slaves lived short and miserable lives.

Well, then, if we allow for some exceptions, wasn't slavery on the whole, as practiced on Edisto Island, really different?

In the deepest sense, no, slavery was no different on Edisto Island from anywhere else, because it was still slavery. The essence of enslavement is that someone else controls your life. You don't decide for yourself where to live, what kind of work to do, whom to marry, how to raise your children, etc. If you are allowed to make some small decisions in your life, such as how early to finish your task, where to sell your fish or whether to go to church, it is only a delusion, for even this limited freedom can be taken back from you tomorrow. Slavery is slavery, everywhere. Slavery is a daily offense against the human spirit and, in the aggregate, a transgression against a whole group of people.

## Resistance by Slaves on Edisto Island

All through the 1700s and 1800s, slaves on Edisto Island resisted slavery in any way they could. Chalmers Murray, a twentieth-century white islander and researcher, points out that some slaves saved up money and were able to purchase their freedom.[206]

In 1847 an old woman on Edisto Island, Maum Bella, was offered her freedom as reward for a lifetime of uncomplaining and highly skilled service as a baker. She refused, but asked for freedom for her grown son, Lewis, and her plea was granted. Lewis opened a large carpenter shop in Charleston, ran a successful business, bought and repaired houses and became quite prosperous.[207]

Beyond "earning" freedom, there are many hints in the scholarly literature, based on twentieth-century ex-slave interviews and other sources, that slaves sometimes broke plantation tools and machines not by accident but as a form of protest. It was nearly impossible for the driver, overseer or owner to prove intent, even if he suspected it. Slaves did not share in the profits, so they had no stake in greater productivity.

As for freedom, since Edisto was an island, surrounded by rivers, running away was not easy: if a slave stole a boat to get to the mainland, he or she might be spotted. Still, slaves did run away from time to time, as documented in planters' correspondence. In one dramatic incident, seventy-four slaves, more than half of them women, ran away from the James Hopkinson Plantation (Cassina Point) in January 1861.[208]

The ultimate act of resistance against slavery was defiance in the face of death. Three slaves died on Edisto Island in 1862 in such an act of defiance. That story is told in "The Confederate 'Expedition' of January 1862," in Volume 2, Chapter 1 of this history.

## CHAPTER 6

# EDISTO'S "GOLDEN AGE"

The period from 1790 to 1861 was one of steadily rising prosperity on Edisto Island, and the last half of the period, from about 1820, generated so much wealth for a few families that it drew attention to Edisto from places near and far.[209] The source of that wealth, of course, was sea-island cotton, a product for which Edisto Island was particularly suited, even compared to some of the other sea islands. This chapter quantifies that wealth and sketches, in broad terms, the material, social and religious life that the wealthy planter class created for itself. Chapter 7 locates, names and describes each of the sixty-two plantations on Edisto Island, their early histories and the planter families that occupied them during the last decade before the Civil War. As explained in the Preface, "Golden Age" is always in quotation marks in this book since it was golden mainly for the planter aristocracy and their creditors. Similarly, discussing the economic value of slaves describes the reality of the economic and social system on which this wealth was based.

## Sea-island Cotton Was King

The federal agricultural census of 1860[210] provides a good idea of the wealth on Edisto Island, including Jehossee, at the apex of its "Golden Age." There were about 29,000 acres of "improved" land, and probably virtually all of it was under cultivation. In the aggregate, the planters estimated their land was worth $2.1 million. Disregarding the unimproved land (another 18,000 acres, mostly marsh), this suggests that prime corn and cotton land on Edisto Island was worth, on the average, $72 an acre, which was no mean sum in 1860. The other major source of wealth, of course, was in slaves, of whom there were 5,082 on Edisto in 1860. To calculate this wealth in dollars, scholars have assumed a (conservative) average market value of $300 per adult or child, so Edisto's enslaved Africans represented at least another $1.5 million of assets to their owners.[211]

Edisto's plantations had about 1,200 draft animals: horses, mules and oxen—a surprisingly small number for the 29,000 acres under cultivation. (Most Edisto planters did not use the plow at all: see Chapter 4.) Edisto had about 4,100 cattle, more than half for beef, and about 3,500 swine, counting only what the planters owned. (Slave-owned pigs probably would have doubled that figure.) There were also 2,000 sheep on the island, raised both for wool and for meat.

Huge quantities of food crops were grown to support the large population of Edisto. For example, the 1859 harvests included 44,000 bushels of corn, 7,800 bushels of peas and 125,000 bushels of sweet potatoes. (Only 335 bushels of white potatoes were produced, and those were entirely for the planter families' own tables.)

The big money, of course, was in sea-island cotton, but the yield varied dramatically from one plantation to another. Of forty-six planters, ten sold fewer than 20 bales in 1860. (The census specified a bale of four hundred pounds.) Twenty-one planters produced between 20 and 60 bales of ginned long-staple cotton in 1859–60, and thirteen produced more than 60. The largest producers that year were J. Evans Edings (104 bales on two plantations), Edward M. Whaley (112 bales), John Jenkins (127 bales), John Townsend (150 bales on three plantations), Ephraim Baynard (150 bales on four plantations) and I. Jenkins Mikell (175 bales on four plantations).[212]

In the aggregate, Edisto Island produced in 1859 and sold in 1860 2,208 bales of sea-island cotton. At 400 pounds to the bale, that was 883,200 pounds of cotton. How much was it worth? The prices varied, of course, from year to year, and for each bale it depended very much on its cleanness, fineness and length of staple. But 1859–60 was a well-documented year, and most Edisto planters got around $0.60 a pound.[213] At that price, Edisto cotton may have earned its planters $530,000 in 1860. That is almost exactly a quarter of the aggregate value ($2.1 million) of all the plantation land on the island, including Jehossee, in the same year. It is also nearly 15 percent of $3.6 million, the estimated total worth of the primary assets of land and slaves on the island. By either measure, that was a pretty good monetary return on investment for one year.

## Edisto's Building Boom

As sea-island cotton gained momentum and planters began to pay off debts and accumulate money in the early 1800s, much of the new capital went into more land and more slaves. But an additional asset was in buildings. The planters (and their wives) began to think of greater comfort for their families. Many planter families were still living in relatively small, plain, boxy houses that had been built in the early to mid-1700s. (See Old House, Figure 14) Some of the old houses were too small even if they had been well maintained. The ones that were large enough still lacked modern conveniences, such as indoor kitchens, multiple fireplaces, large rooms, brick-floored basements and piazzas. And perhaps most important, the old houses were out of style. Edisto's new generation of prosperous planters had traveled, had seen Federal-style and Neoclassical buildings in Charleston, Philadelphia, New York and Newport and were no longer satisfied with just a roof over their heads.

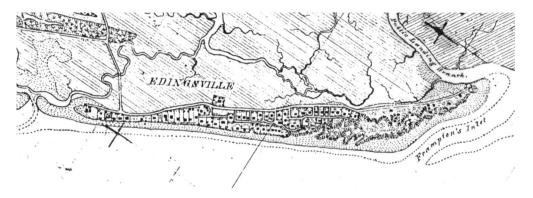

Figure 24. Edingsville Beach, 1852, from U.S. Coast Survey map. Jeremy Inlet and Edisto Beach are at far left. Causeway, top left, connects to Edisto Island. Square black dots are houses. A sheltered boat landing and "The Sands" are at right.

Dozens of planter residences on Edisto Island were completely rebuilt, expanded and modernized, or simply torn down and replaced with large new houses in the 1820s, 1830s and 1840s. Of those that have survived to the present, most were built during this period: William Seabrook House, Oak Island, Cassina Point, Seaside, Crawford, Peter's Point, Middleton, the Presbyterian Manse, Cypress Trees, Brookland and Frogmore.[214] Many more that have not survived were also built during this period. The "Golden Age" also brought new or improved cabins for some slaves and new barns, gin houses and wharves on many plantations. Roads were widened, graded and ditched, causeways were improved and bridges were strengthened or rebuilt. The entire infrastructure of the island benefited from the new wealth.

## Edingsville Beach

An integral part of this building boom on Edisto Island in the first half of the nineteenth century was the development of Edisto's first beach resort. Joseph Edings apparently started offering building lots on his private beach about 1800. His son William Edings (1809–1858) continued the practice, as did his grandson, J. Evans Edings.[215] By the Civil War there were about fifty private homes, two chapels and a billiard parlor in the village, and at least another ten cottages or fishing shacks among the dunes between the village and Frampton's Inlet.[216] Some of the planters, their widows and other professionals who owned beach houses at Edingsville just before and after the Civil War are listed in Table 6. Most of them are further identified by plantation in Chapter 7.[217]

*Table 6.*
*Edingsville Beach Homeowners in 1866*

| | | |
|---|---|---|
| Constantine Bailey | James Hopkinson | Ephraim Seabrook |
| Ephraim Bailey | Hamilton Jenkins | John E. Seabrook |
| Dr. William Bailey | John M. Jenkins | Mikell Seabrook |
| Edward Baynard | Col. Joseph Jenkins | William Seabrook Jr. |
| Thomas A. Baynard | Mrs. Seabrook Jenkins | William E. Seabrook |
| William G. Baynard | Rev. William Johnson[1] | Miss Minirva Street[5] |
| Theodore Becket | J. Berwick Legare[2] | Jabez Wescoat |
| Archibald J. Clark | Sydney Legare | John Wescoat[6] |
| L.R. Clark | M. Middleton[3] | Miss E.M. Whaley |
| J. Evans Edings | Thomas P. Mikell | Edward Whaley |
| William Edings | William Murray | Dr. James E. Whaley |
| James C. Hanahan | George Owens[4] | W. James Whaley |
| John J. Hanahan | Edward W. Seabrook | Col. Joseph Whaley |
| Dr. Ralph Hanahan | Miss Eliza Seabrook | William B. Whaley |
| | | Rev. Charles Wilson[7] |

[1] Episcopal minister on Edisto Island.

[2] The 1866 list actually shows James Legare, an older half-brother of John Berwick Legare. Berwick Legare owned plantations on Edisto Island but died in 1856, and his brother apparently inherited the beach house.

[3] The "M" may denote one of Oliver H. Middleton's daughters, although Middleton himself undoubtedly used the beach house.

[4] George Owens was an overseer in 1850 who by 1860 owned twenty-three slaves and called himself a planter. His real estate was worth only $5,000, approximately the value of his summer house on the beach, so he did not own a plantation. Perhaps he leased one, but its location has not been found. See 1850 and 1860 Census.

[5] Minirva Louise Street was a single woman living alone on Edisto Island with one slave. She was forty-eight years old in 1860. She had moved here with her mother from Connecticut before 1850, but her mother apparently had subsequently died. Her occupation was not specified on either the 1850 or 1860 census. She has not been further identified.

[6] John Wescoat owned two houses on the beach, one on each row.

[7] Methodist minister on Edisto Island.

The planter families moved to the beach in May and went back to the plantations in October. Multiple cartloads of furniture, furnishings, food and clothing preceded most families. The main reason for this annual white migration was to avoid spending nights on the main island during the fever season. The mosquito had not yet been identified as the vector for spreading malaria and yellow fever, but the correlation of beach life and good health was clearly understood. (Mosquitoes breed in freshwater swamps, ditches and ponds; there were none on the beach. Daily ocean breezes also kept insects away.)

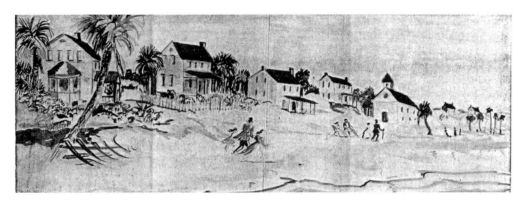

Figure 25. Edingsville Beach village. Note St. Stephen's Chapel, *right*, and vacationers promenading in dress clothes. Faith Murray based her 1955 sketch on a painting by Cecil Wescott, who enjoyed Edingsville as a youth. *Courtesy of the* Post and Courier.

Most slaves stayed on the plantations; only a few handpicked servants went to the beach. Work proceeded without interruption in the cotton fields (Chapter 4). Overseers stayed at home. If a planter had no overseer, he went personally to check on work every morning and returned to the beach every night. But the women, children and youth had a grand holiday for five months. It gathered momentum and traditions over the decades, and by the 1840s it had become an annual event that was its own justification, "summer at the bay."

Chalmers Murray, a twentieth-century Edisto journalist (below), wrote several articles about the Edingsville lifestyle and traditions based on interviews with old-timers, especially his bachelor uncle, Eberson Murray. No photographs of the village at Edingsville have been found, but artists' depictions are available (Figure 25).

Eberson told Chalmers Murray that

> *most of the cottages were substantial two-story buildings with wide verandas facing the ocean. They were spaced far apart and stood in two long rows: one row overlooking the ocean, and the other the marshlands…The houses were shaded by oaks and cedars. Behind the big sand dunes rose an impenetrable jungle…Although we had gardens in the village, much of the vegetables were brought from the plantations. Many hogs were raised* [at] *the beach.*

There was also a small store on the beach, but its location has not been found on the map. Boys went to school in the summer each morning, but were free to play in the afternoons; there was no school for girls. To a child, "life on Edingsville seemed one long happy holiday." Fishing, riding and swimming were their main sports.[218]

Cecil Wescott,[219] who had spent many summers at Edingsville as a youth and painted scenes of the village from memory later as an adult, told Murray that his family sat on their veranda on Sunday afternoons, enjoying the sea breezes and watching the "afternoon parade. I can shut my eyes now and see old gentlemen walking by, carrying gold-headed canes, young ladies in flowered muslins, arm-in-arm with their frock-coated escorts; old ladies out for an airing in their gleaming black carriages, and young men astride their prancing steeds."

Murray adds that "the villagers seemed to spend the greater part of their time on the beach or in the churches, ballrooms, or parlors of their neighbors." For the young adults, there were "riding parties, picnics under a grove of live oaks, surf bathing" and moonlight strolls along the beach. But "mixed bathing was not permitted…the beach was divided into two sections, with a forbidden strand between. The young ladies would race to the eastern end of the island, and the men would make off in the opposite direction. The young ladies never attempted to swim, that would have been very masculine indeed, but contented themselves with bobbing up and down in the breakers" and shrieking loudly for the fun of it.

The Presbyterians and Episcopalians were worshiping together once a week on Edingsville by 1821. They used an old, dilapidated schoolhouse for a sanctuary, and the two ministers alternated Sundays, preaching and using their respective liturgies. "Much harmony and kind feeling prevailed between the congregations." In 1824 they jointly built themselves a real chapel on the beach, which they planned to continue sharing. But a serious disagreement arose about "the internal arrangement of [the sacramental furniture in] the building," and unable to resolve it satisfactorily, the two congregations separated amicably. The Presbyterians sold their share in the new chapel to the Episcopalians and built themselves another chapel by the next summer. After that, they worshiped separately both on the island and on the beach.[220]

The Episcopal chapel was consecrated in 1826 as St. Stephen's Chapel. It stood on a high dune near the center of the village, and probably resembled the chapel in the drawing (Figure 25). The Presbyterian chapel was on the back of the beach, near the marsh. Both chapels were moved to Edisto Island in the 1870s and were given, or sold, to new African American congregations of their respective denominations.[221]

# The 1850s Mapping Project[222]

In the 1840s, the U.S. Coast Survey launched a major project to produce more accurate navigation maps for the entire Atlantic Coast of the United States (and later, the Gulf and Pacific Coasts). Agents went to selected places up and down the coastline to mark out new base lines parallel to the beaches, each several miles long. "Edisto's marvelous line" would be seven miles long, all on solid high ground, with no intervening marshes or hills, on farmland that would allow uninterrupted line of sight. With permission from the landowners and local labor, a field team cleared a twenty-foot-wide swath for seven miles in December 1849. The critical part, measuring exactly seven miles and placing permanent granite markers at each end, was done in January 1850 under the personal supervision of Professor Alexander Dallas Bache, a great-grandson of Benjamin Franklin, who was superintendent of the U.S. Coast Survey. They used a new device, a bimetallic rod six meters long, designed by Bache and a colleague, which automatically compensated for changes in air temperature, and hence was much more accurate than its predecessors.

The surveyors placed the eastern end marker of the seven-mile line in a field on John F. Townsend's Bleak Hall Plantation, which today is part of the privately owned Botany Bay Plantation. The western end marker stood in Spanish Mount field on William Edings's Locksley Hall Plantation, which is now in Edisto Beach State Park. Edisto Island's line was the third ever measured with the new device, and is the oldest now remaining with the original granite markers still in place after 150 years. When checked in 1992 by experts using the latest global positioning system (GPS) technology, the original seven-mile line was found to be off by only 2.4 inches.

The field crew then built temporary wooden towers over each end of their line. Standing on these towers, surveyors could see a third surveyor on the chimney of Governor Aiken's rice mill on Jehossee Island. They measured the precise angles at the three corners of this triangle, and then computed the exact length of the second and third sides, since they knew the exact length of the first side (seven miles). From this triangle they then selected tall structures, or built towers, at convenient places up and down the coast and created one triangle after another, each with one side of known length because it was part of the previously computed triangle. Figure 26[223] shows an official "sketch" that illustrates the trigonometry that put Edisto Island "on the map" of modern cartography, as it was already (and would be in the future) in several other respects.

For reasons that are not clear, the U.S. Coast Survey expanded the Edisto baseline project into a full field survey of the entire island, a huge undertaking at federal expense. It was done in three phases stretching over seven years: the corner of the island abutting the North Edisto River was first, in 1851; the southwest section abutting the South Edisto

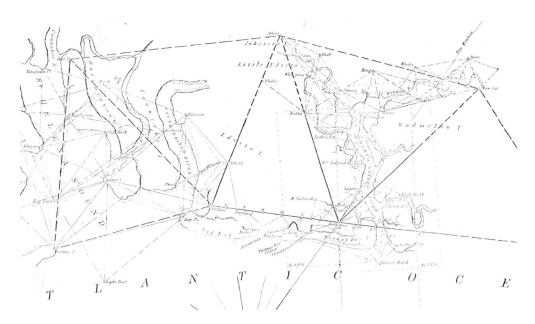

Figure 26. The U.S. Coast Survey's "Edisto Triangle." Base of middle triangle is Edisto's seven-mile line; its tip is on Jehossee. Top of right triangle is on Wadmalaw; left triangle crosses St. Helena Sound. *U.S. Coast Survey Sketch E, No. 3, 1851.*

River, from Edisto Beach up to and including St. Pierre's Creek, was done in 1852; and the interior of the island, all the way to the Dawhoo River, was done in 1856 and 1857.[224] The resulting map is the source of all the 1850s maps in this book, an incalculable boon to understanding the cultural geography of Edisto in its "Golden Age."

# The Presbyterian Church on Edisto Island

The Presbyterian Church was founded in the early 1700s, and had since struggled with a very small membership, scanty finances and some gaps in pastoral leadership during the remainder of that century. Still, it had survived, and its members had been extremely loyal. Things began to look up shortly after the end of the Revolutionary War.

The Reverend Donald McLeod, the church's third minister, was born in Scotland (but was no kin to the second minister, Reverend John McLeod). He accepted the church's call in 1793 and stayed until his death in 1821. He was succeeded almost immediately by the Reverend William States Lee, a Charlestonian who served the church for an amazing fifty-one years, from 1821 to 1872. Thus the Presbyterian Church on Edisto Island had exactly two ministers during the entire period considered Edisto's "Golden Age."[225]

In March 1784 the state legislature granted the congregation's petition for incorporation as the Presbyterian Church on Edisto. From then until the early 1900s, the church corporation, composed of all the male members over twenty-one, handled all the congregation's financial affairs, real estate, investments, affiliations with presbytery and even calls to the pastors.

When Donald McLeod came to Edisto Island in 1793 he was thirty-two years old.[226] There was a small one-story frame church building across the road from the present site on Highway 174, and a small shed room with benches was added to the meetinghouse in 1800 to accommodate slaves, who by this time were allowed to attend some services. A smaller, less comfortable parsonage existed on the site of the present manse. That parsonage burned in 1800 and apparently was not rebuilt until 1807. During the interim, the minister received a subsidy to pay for a rented house. The new parsonage was eighteen by thirty-seven feet on each floor, still considerably smaller than the present manse.

In early 1803 an unexplained, violent event shook members of the Presbyterian church. Apparently someone in the church physically attacked Reverend McLeod and then defamed his character. He resigned in March 1803 but returned a year later when the congregation issued him a new call, affirming their confidence in him with a 50 percent increase of salary, and appropriated funds to pay a lawyer to cooperate with the public prosecutor against "the perpetrator." There is no record of the name of the attacker, the reason for the attack or the outcome of the case.[227]

The Reverend Donald McLeod's pastorate saw a steadily gathering momentum in the Presbyterian Church on Edisto Island. There apparently was a sense that the church was entering a new era of growth and prosperity. But before he or the congregation could shape this potential into anything concrete, McLeod's ministry ended with his death at age sixty in January 1821.

He was much loved by the congregation, and they placed a memorial plaque on an inside wall of the meetinghouse that was later moved to the new sanctuary, and is still there today. It says, "He won and retained the respect, esteem and affection of the people…He was diligent in the performance of [his] duties…kind and friendly…to the poor; and compassionate towards the afflicted." In the absence of a candid character sketch by a contemporary, one may surmise, from what was said and not said, and what he is known to have done and not done in his twenty-eight years, that the Reverend Donald McLeod was a kind, gentle, easygoing Scot, prone to long, intellectual sermons, careful in the pastoral care of his flock, but something less than a visionary leader into the new age that people felt was dawning on Edisto Island.

William States Lee was an entirely different kind of minister, and the Edisto Presbyterians probably knew him by reputation and called him for that reason. Lee was twenty-eight years old when he came to Edisto Island in 1821. He was a graduate of Princeton College in New Jersey. He had studied theology and had been licensed to preach at Circular Congregational Church in Charleston, and he had already gained experience in parish ministry at the Presbyterian church at nearby Dorchester, South Carolina.

The Presbyterian Church on Edisto Island began to feel the effects of young Mr. Lee's energy, intellect and piety from the time of his arrival.[228] He instituted a formal records system for the church, including membership rolls; there were in 1821 only sixteen white and seven African American members baptized and in full communion. He increased the frequency of communion during the year from twice to four times, and increased the frequency of worship from once to thrice each Sunday during summer and fall on the beach. (That was not practical during winter and spring on the island because of the much greater distances people traveled to reach the church.) He initiated a Wednesday evening theological lecture series in parishioners' homes that was very popular for many years. He started a Sunday school for regular religious instruction of children during the summer and fall, a practice that did not become general among Presbyterians for another seventy-five years. He organized a lending library at the church, aimed at children and youth, to which members donated about eight hundred books, both religious and literary. He started a weekday women's Bible class and taught it himself. And those changes were just the beginning.

The most visible results of the ministry of the Reverend William States Lee are, of course, the buildings. The Greek Revival–style sanctuary still in use today was contracted in 1830, completed and occupied by the congregation in 1831 and substantially rebuilt in 1836 because of concerns about its structural integrity. The total cost, including modifications, apparently was $8,330, of which the prosperous planters pledged $3,000 in twelve days to the building fund, even though the corporation by then had more than $25,000 in reserves.

The contractor for the new church was a Mr. Pillans; for the 1836 repairs it was a Mr. Curtis, architect of Charleston. No other names are found in the church records associated with the new building. Nevertheless, recent research has raised the interesting possibility that the nationally renowned architect Robert Mills may have strongly influenced the design of this church.[229] In 1852 a new pipe organ was installed in the

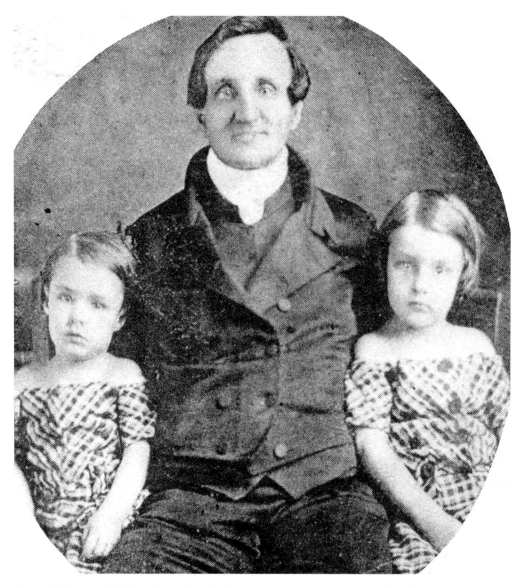

Figure 27. Reverend William States Lee, Presbyterian pastor, as a young man, with his two oldest daughters. *Courtesy of Clara C. Mackenzie.*

church. It was purchased for $850 from Henry Erben of New York City, who has been called the largest and most expensive organ manufacturer in the country at that time.[230] To accommodate the organ pipes, the rear section of the balcony was cut down in 1852 and reinstalled as a raised platform a few feet above the main floor. The combined organ and choir "loft" remained in this location for the next 150 years.

As soon as the new church was built, the old one across the road was torn down, but the lumber and timbers were saved and reused in 1838 to expand and rebuild the 1807 parsonage in the configuration seen today. An additional $3,000 was spent on labor and new materials. And a decade earlier (1826) the Presbyterian Church on Edisto Island had built itself a spacious summer chapel on Edingsville Beach, and had provided a comfortable summer house on the beach for the use of the pastor.

In 1831 and 1832, just after the new, much larger sanctuary was built, Mr. Lee organized two "protracted meetings" for evangelism, which both responded to and contributed to the powerful revival movement among Protestants that swept through South Carolina and Georgia in the early 1830s.[231] Between 1821 and 1858 Lee recorded adding ninety-seven adult white members to the rolls, but because many members also departed the island or died, the net increase during those thirty-seven years only doubled the meager rolls, from sixteen to thirty white members, men and women. Some of the most prestigious and wealthy families were Presbyterian, including most of the Baynards, Mikells, Murrays, Seabrooks, Townsends and Whaleys.

From his arrival on Edisto Island in 1821, the Reverend Mr. Lee also took a leading role in the growing movement across the South to actively evangelize slaves. The concept was not universally approved by slave owners, but Lee would not be deterred. Typically, he approached the task systematically, and in several ways. First, he continued to welcome the African-descent slaves to worship jointly with the whites; in the new sanctuary, they were allotted the entire balcony. They heard the same sermons, sang the same hymns, prayed the same prayers and—subject to the same conditions as whites—received the same communion at the same tables, after the whites had been served. Second, the slaves were encouraged to remain at church every Sunday after the whites departed, to participate in a second, more informal, more spirited worship that Lee termed "better adapted to their comprehension." Third, he encouraged the African Americans who were interested to go through the same process whites went through to join the church and be eligible for communion. He taught a separate catechism class for them every Sunday before worship. (They were, of course, with few exceptions, unable to read the Bible for themselves.) If they attended regularly for a year he would propose them for membership and the white elders would orally examine them to verify that they understood the catechism. The slaves would make their individual public professions of faith before the congregation on a Sunday, and Lee would baptize them into full communing membership. Lee recorded that in thirty-seven years he brought 352 slaves to full membership in the Presbyterian Church on Edisto Island, three and a half times more African Americans than whites.[232]

As the 1850s wound down, the Presbyterian Church on Edisto Island was at its strongest. During the turbulent events leading to secession, it was like a solid rock in the flood—for its white members at least—and a large part of that strength seemed to come from the Reverend William States Lee. In 1860 he had already been their pastor for thirty-nine years.

# Trinity Episcopal Church

Episcopalians also had lived on Edisto Island almost from the beginning of the colony, but for the first century they had been few in numbers and forced to travel off the island for formal worship. Between 1705 and 1734 Edisto Island was part of the Parish of St. Paul's, Stono, and the rector preached occasionally on Edisto. From 1734 to 1793, St. John's Church on Johns Island was the home church for Edisto Episcopalians. The Protestant Episcopal Church on Edisto Island (as it was first known) dates from 1774, when the islanders built themselves a small frame chapel on the eve of the Revolutionary War. Ten years after the end of that war, in 1793, Edisto Church was separated off as a parish and incorporated by the state legislature. In that same year the church called its first rector, the Reverend James Connor.[233] The Protestant Episcopal Church on Edisto Island came to be routinely called Trinity Episcopal Church in the late nineteenth century, but for simplicity we shall call it Trinity Episcopal Church from the beginning.

*Table 7.*

| | |
|---|---|
| Reverend James Connor | 1793–1796 |
| Reverend Edward Matthews | 1797–1799 |
| Reverend Joseph Warren | 1809–1811 |
| Reverend Andrew Fowler | 1813–1817 |
| Reverend Thomas Osborne | 1818–1819, 1822–1826 |
| Reverend James M. Gilbert | 1821 |
| Reverend Edward Thomas | 1827–1834 |
| Reverend Charles Leverett | 1835–1846 |
| Reverend W.H. Hanckel | 1846–1857 |
| Reverend William Johnson | 1858–1869 |

Trinity had difficulty obtaining and keeping a full-time rector for several decades, as Table 7 shows. Then, beginning with the arrival of the Reverend Edward Thomas in 1827, the church had an unbroken chain of full-time ordained leaders until 1869. So, as with the Presbyterian church, Edisto's "Golden Age" was, in very important respects, Trinity Church's "Golden Age" too.

Most of those early rectors had excellent preparation for ministry, judging from what we know. Edward Matthews (1797–99) was a member of the very first group of seven clergy ordained in South Carolina itself, by the diocese's first bishop, Robert Smith. Andrew Fowler (1813–17) was a Yale College graduate and a former Episcopal missionary who had founded churches in Columbia, Camden and Wadesboro, South Carolina, and St. Augustine, Florida.

The energetic ministry of the Reverend Mr. Fowler involved Trinity Church in an ecclesiastical first for the entire diocese of South Carolina. The ancient Anglican rite of confirmation to full communing membership by the hand of a bishop had fallen into disuse in the Carolina colony for want of bishops, and this lapse had carried over into the nineteenth century, to the dismay of many devout Episcopalians. In 1813, Mr. Fowler instructed a class of 20 adult and youth confirmation candidates at Trinity, wrote and published a tract on the importance of confirmation by bishops and personally visited Bishop Theodore Dehone in Charleston to persuade him to visit Edisto Island the following week (on a Tuesday) and administer the rite in person. The bishop agreed. Mr. Fowler then rode his horse back to Edisto Island, was delayed by torrential March rains and the absence of a reliable ferry at Dawhoo and arrived in the nick of time on Sunday morning to personally lead morning prayer and deliver the required formal announcement of the proposed confirmations. Everything went well after that, and the 18 parishioners present on the appointed day (Table 8) were the first-ever South Carolina Episcopalians confirmed by their bishop. The practice spread quickly among Lowcountry parishes, and within a year Bishop Dehone had been invited to many churches and had confirmed a total of 516 persons.

*Table 8.*

| | |
|---|---|
| Benjamin and Sarah Bailey | Martha LaRoche |
| Charles Bailey | William C. and Elizabeth Meggett |
| Edward Bailey | Edward Mitchell |
| Thomas Bailey | Sarah Patterson |
| Louisa Devaux | Ann Seabrook |
| Isaac Jenkins | Benjamin Seabrook |
| Joseph and Elizabeth Jenkins | Joseph and Martha Seabrook |

Thomas A. Osborne was born in Ireland about 1795 and came to America at an early age. He was educated at Union College in Schenectady, New York, trained for the Episcopal priesthood and preached in Ohio and elsewhere before coming to Trinity Church (1818–19).[234] He left Trinity to teach languages at the University of Cincinnati,[235] but then accepted a second call and served Trinity again (1822–26). It was during his tenure that Trinity Church acquired a rectory with thirty acres of land, far from the church, on the public road to Pine Landing.[236] About that time the church also built a summer rectory and a chapel for its congregation at "the Bay" (above, "Edingsville Beach"). Under the next rector, the Reverend Edward Thomas, Trinity in the late 1820s founded its own lending library and organized a Ladies' Working Society.

By the mid-1830s the vestry was actively discussing with a new rector, the Reverend Charles Leverett, the need for a new sanctuary building. They were still using the small, one-story frame church built in 1774, which, they noted, had "no proper sittings for the colored people," among other inconveniences. The cornerstone for their large, new church was laid in November 1840, and it was consecrated by the bishop in December 1841. The old church was torn down and sold for materials. During construction the congregation worshiped in the Baptist church (now Old First Baptist), just up the road.

The new Trinity Episcopal Church was forty-five feet wide and seventy-five feet long, including a portico. Its columns were brick, its steeple one hundred feet tall. Inside, it had a vestibule and a robing room. The semicircular chancel was beautifully decorated with religious paintings and inscriptions. The sanctuary was handsomely furnished with pews and sacramental furniture, and it had a gallery that would seat two hundred slaves. Before long they filled it on some Sundays. A new organ was installed in 1845.

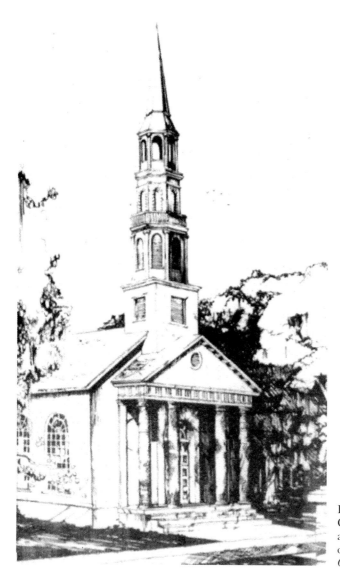

Figure 28. Trinity Episcopal Church, 1841. A twentieth-century architect's rendering of what the church may have looked like. *Courtesy of Trinity Episcopal Church.*

The new church cost $9,000, of which $6,400 was pledged before the construction began. The same Mr. Curtis who had extensively repaired the new Presbyterian church in 1836 was the builder for Trinity Church. The wardens at the time were William C. Meggett and James B. Seabrook. The vestrymen were Dr. Edward Mitchell, Joseph B. Seabrook and Jabez J.R. Westcoat. Joseph E. Jenkins chaired the building committee.

Nothing is known of the architect of the new church; apparently it was the builder himself, Mr. Curtis. Some people have remarked on the similarities, both external and internal, between this building at Trinity and St. Michael's Church in Charleston, which is a few years older, and is still standing today.[237] Unfortunately, Trinity's big new church burned down only thirty-five years later. (That story is told in the second volume of this history.)

The Reverend Mr. Leverett (1835–46) was just as active as his two predecessors in evangelizing and catechizing the slaves on Edisto. His 1842 report to the Episcopal convention in Charleston said Trinity had 41 white and 20 African American communicants, with another 55 white and 100 African American noncommunicants. The Sunday school had 125 African American and 47 white "scholars." During the winter season he was preaching every other Sunday afternoon on a plantation. In 1845 the rector wrote to a new *ad hoc* group in Charleston that was about to host a two-state "Meeting on the Religious Instruction of the Negroes in Georgia and South Carolina," that he now had 100 African American communicants at Trinity. "The Negroes are preached to and catechized every Sabbath by the Rector. He is, also, ready to engage the services of an assistant to visit the several plantations" and preach more frequently. There is no record, however, that Trinity actually hired such an assistant.[238]

The next fifteen years apparently were a time of calm, steady growth at Trinity Episcopal Church. The church sold its old parsonage, so distant from the church, and bought from Mr. Leverett his private home for its new parsonage in 1843. Its location is not documented. The Reverend W.H. Hanckel succeeded Mr. Leverett as rector in 1846, and the Reverend William Johnson succeeded him in 1858. Regular evangelistic work among the slaves continued. On the eve of the Civil War, Trinity Church had about $30,000 in cash reserves. "It was not to see that much money in any kind of dollars again for well over a hundred years."[239]

# Old First Baptist Church

The Edisto Island Baptist Church was built in 1818 under the auspices of the Charleston Baptist Association, but under the personal sponsorship and philanthropy of a most remarkable woman, Hephzibah Jenkins Townsend (1780–1847). She was the wife of Daniel Townsend, proprietor of Bleak Hall, one of the wealthiest planters on the island. He was a Presbyterian elder, but she was a devout Baptist, converted in 1807 by the preaching of the Reverend Richard Furman of Charleston. She struggled continually for the next ten years to realize her dream of a Baptist church on Edisto, and against considerable odds, she finally achieved it.[240]

That church continued to be called Edisto Island Baptist well into the twentieth century, but today it is called Old First Baptist Church. To avoid confusion with several Baptist churches now on the island, this one will be called Old First Baptist from the beginning.

The original part of Old First Baptist is the oldest church building still standing on Edisto Island today. It was a tall, square frame building about half the size of the present structure, and it stands on a tabby foundation. Originally, it may have had a small porch, but the two-story, pedimented portico and the square belfry existing today were added in 1880, some years after the size of the building was doubled. Inside, the original church had a platform for the pulpit, open pews and galleries on the two sides. Twin entrances flanked a window on the front, as today, and entrances on each side of the building were

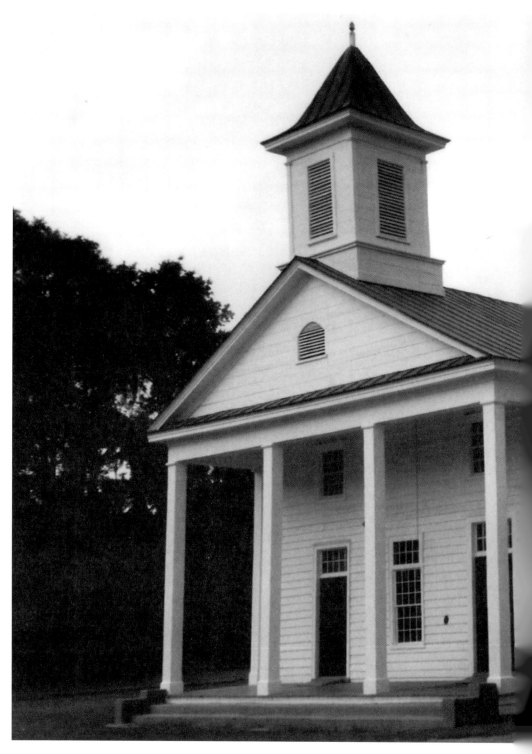

Figure 29. Old First Baptist Church today. The rear half, built in 1818, is the oldest surviving church building on Edisto Island; the front half is post–Civil War. Obelisk (right) marks the grave of Hephzibah Townsend. *Photo by the author.*

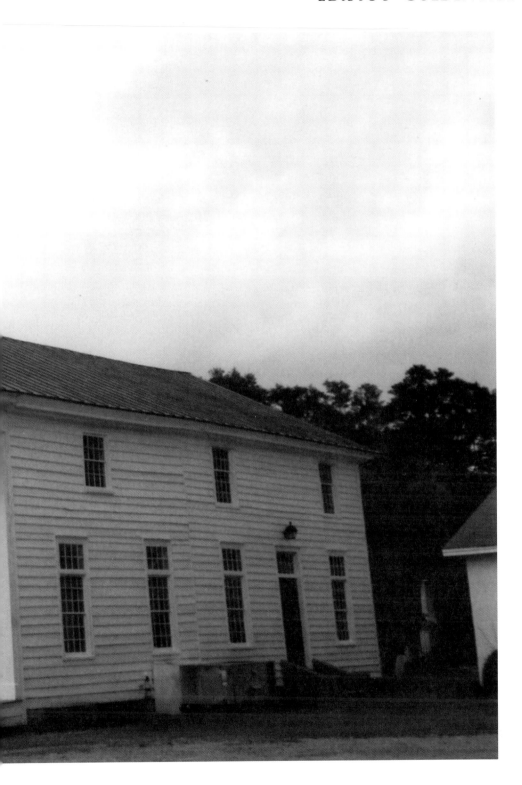

flanked by clear windows on the first-floor level. At the gallery level there were two more windows on each side and two on the front. Access to the galleries was from inside the sanctuary.[241] No image of this early structure has turned up, but it is easy to visualize it by viewing the rear half of the present building.

From the beginning, this church was controversial. A protracted legal struggle over the ten acres of land on which it stood lasted for many years. Both Trinity Episcopal Church and Euhaw Baptist Church (on the mainland in Colleton County) claimed ownership, at various times, under arcane state laws governing early land grants for churches. Even more controversial, there were never more than three or four white Baptist members, and for a time, all of them were female except the ministers assigned by the Charleston Baptist Society. But the slaves on Edisto Island responded well to the Baptist preaching. They attended in large numbers, and many were baptized into full membership. Hephzibah Townsend and two of her daughters were regular attendees, along with a few white visitors, and racial separation during worship apparently was never as strict as in the Presbyterian and Episcopal churches, which also made some slave owners uncomfortable. But Hephzibah Townsend withstood all the criticism and persevered, deriving great satisfaction from the success of her beloved Baptist faith among Edisto's African Americans. When she died in 1847, the church had good momentum, and never faltered.

All the Baptist ministers before the Civil War were white. The noted Reverend Richard Furman himself apparently preached on Edisto Island as often as he was able to get there. The church became an independent congregation in 1829, and its first called pastor was the Reverend Peter Ludlow (1829–37), but he probably did not live on the island. More likely he traveled from Charleston to Edisto to preach a few times a month. Ludlow was succeeded by the Reverend William McDunn in 1838, and records show he was still pastor in 1845. In 1850 the Reverend Daniel Shepard, a native of New Jersey, was living on the island with his family. In 1860 the resident Baptist minister was the Reverend Thomas Dawson, also with a family.[242]

In 1845 Reverend McDunn reported 461 baptized, communing African American members of Old First Baptist Church. That was more African American members than the Presbyterian and Episcopal churches combined. Moreover, the Baptist church was the only one that allowed those members to attend congregational meetings and to exercise some authority within the congregation, although under the supervision of the white minister. African Americans were deacons and they assisted with religious instruction. They were encouraged to monitor the morals of other members, and to report misconduct to the church for public censure.

Hephzibah Jenkins Townsend was such a central figure in the life of Old First Baptist Church, and she was so successful as a nonconforming white woman in a male-dominated society, that she has ever since loomed larger than life in the folklore of the Edisto white community. Very likely many of the stories told about her flaunting of her husband's orders are exaggerated: a recent scholarly study of her life, based on previously unpublished correspondence, reveals that Daniel Townsend (and later their son John F. Townsend) proved flexible under pressure and usually ended up giving her the support, both legal and financial, that she asked for in her many public endeavors.[243]

There is no doubt, however, that she was greatly loved and respected by her fellow Baptists, and most of all by the African American members and their descendants. She is buried, as she wished, in the cemetery behind her beloved Old First Baptist Church.

# Early Methodism on Edisto Island

The South Carolina Lowcountry was from an early date a focus of the Methodist movement. Both John and Charles Wesley visited Charleston in 1736. John Wesley passed twice between Savannah and Charleston in 1737, and left behind persistent traditions that he once stopped on Edisto, or even founded a church there. But no document has been found to lend any support to those legends. In Charleston and elsewhere, though, the Wesleys were offered pulpits in Episcopal churches, including St. Philips in Charleston, and preached resoundingly to receptive audiences. Other important early leaders of Methodism, including George Whitefield, Bishop Coke and Bishop Asbury, visited and preached in Charleston in the 1700s. The first permanent Methodist church in Charleston was established in 1785.[244]

In 1791 the Reverend Beverly Allen was appointed as Methodist missionary to Edisto Island, and the ensuing events would not be credible if they had not been recounted several times by Methodist clergy in Methodist publications. Mr. Allen was a very persuasive preacher, "a man of elegant manners and brilliant parts," and had married into a prominent Lowcountry family. We don't know where he preached on Edisto—perhaps in homes, perhaps as a guest in Trinity's pulpit—but he soon had a "flourishing society" that included some of the "first men of that region." Alas, not for long. Suddenly he was accused of crimes "of a foul nature," which were investigated by a Methodist committee in Charleston and found to be true. He was expelled from the Methodist Church, but he returned to Charleston and defended himself by writing letters to John Wesley and Bishop Coke in England, attacking the character of Bishop Asbury.[245]

It got worse. Allen fled Charleston when a U.S. marshal tried to serve a writ on him. The marshal followed him to Augusta, Georgia, where Allen pulled a gun and shot him dead. Allen then disappeared into the Western frontier, and was never caught. But the backlash against Methodism on Edisto Island and the Lowcountry was devastating. As late as 1947 a Methodist historian saw a connection between the scoundrel, Beverly Allen, and the fact that there was not yet a single white Methodist church on James, Johns or Edisto Island.[246]

But the key word there is "white," because in less than sixty years Methodism was making many converts among African Americans on Edisto Island. The Reverend Charles Wilson was a Methodist missionary living on Edisto with his wife and six children in 1850. A younger Methodist minister, the Reverend Henry Bass, was also living with the family. Wilson may already have been on Edisto for five years or more, because an 1845 report by the Episcopal priest, the Reverend Charles Leverett, credits the Methodists with a very active program of evangelism that year. "The Methodist minister visits eleven plantations: there are 345 church members and 180 children catechised."[247] The Methodist mission continued actively until the Civil War, for in 1860 the Reverend Charles Wilson was still living on Edisto with his family.

Where did all these African American Methodists go to church between 1845 and 1861? Perhaps in eleven plantation chapels. No evidence has been found that the Methodists built a church on Edisto Island before the Civil War.

# Edisto's Tiny Middle Class

Edisto Island had perhaps twenty plantations without a resident proprietor. Most of these were owned by a planter who lived elsewhere on the island, and who was able to drop by and check on things as often as he liked. A few had absentee owners—lawyers in Charleston, politicians in Columbia—who might visit only a few times a year, and who relied on a relative or neighbor to keep an eye on things. But no planter would leave a plantation even for a week without a resident white manager or overseer. Some wealthy planters even had overseers to handle day-to-day operations for the places they lived on (Chapter 5). Most of these overseers were the planters' own sons or nephews, in training for plantations of their own. But a few were under annual, renewable contracts and were paid between $1,000 and $2,000 a year, plus house and all the homegrown food they wanted.

Most paid overseers were Upcountry men who came to the island for a salaried job. Most left after a few years, discarded by the proprietors who evaluated them quickly through the "old-boy network" and found them lacking. The few who were good at it could make a career of it; planters felt that there were never enough tried and trusted overseers to meet demand. The most successful ones saved their money, bought land and slaves and became planters themselves, either on Edisto or elsewhere.[248]

Overseers' families typically lived in a small house of four or five rooms with a narrow porch,[249] set apart some distance from that of the proprietor and his family, if indeed the proprietor lived there at all. Socially, the overseer was a member of the minuscule white middle class of the island. He and his family, if he had one, were awkwardly suspended between the African American slaves and rich whites, largely unwelcome in the parlors of the plantation owners, though they did attend the same churches. Their children were more likely to have playmates from the slave community than from the proprietor's family.

In the 1860 census there were fewer than twenty white heads of household on Edisto Island who were not landowners, physicians or clergy. All but a few were overseers and managers of plantations, and those men were primarily young. For example, W.L. Chitty, twenty-nine; E. Dawson, twenty-six; John Lancaster, thirty-seven; Benjamin B. Martin, twenty-eight; J.J. Mitchum, twenty; B.F. Rice, twenty-eight; and S.W. Salisbury, twenty-three, were plantation overseers. Each was married and had several children, but owned no slaves and no land. Three other overseers were single men: J. Salisbury, twenty-five; G.W. Rudd, forty-three; and William Humbert, sixty. Two plantation managers were men of some means, for they also personally owned a few slaves. They were Thomas A.

Ham, forty-eight, and M.J. Rice, thirty-seven. Both were married with children. Ham was the resident manager of William Aiken's huge Jehossee Island rice plantation. None of the others has been identified by plantation.[250]

Also in 1860 S.H. Jenkins, thirty-one, owned a store near the Episcopal church and a few slaves. He had a wife and two children, and probably was related to the landowning Jenkinses of Edisto Island. Thomas Black, fifty-eight, born in Maine and living alone on Edisto Island, was a carpenter. He owned no slaves. M.L. Street was a forty-eight-year-old woman born in Connecticut who lived alone with one female slave. She owned no real estate except a house at Edingsville, and had no occupation listed in the census, so it is not clear why she was on the island.[251]

William E. Deleshine, seventy-two, was a former boat builder, but the census taker listed him and his wife, Elizabeth, as paupers. Their son William T. Deleshine, twenty-eight, lived next door and supported his parents and his own family as a boat builder, probably with his father's help. The remaining working whites were immigrants from Ireland. George R. Clark, forty-six, and his wife Catherine, thirty, both born in Ireland, had three children born in South Carolina. Clark was a blacksmith. Bridget Fields, a forty-year-old Irish woman, was a nanny in the home of Isaac Jenkins Mikell. Jane Vince, thirty-six, was a nanny in the home of J.E. Edings. Hester O'Neale was an eighteen-year-old nanny in the home of Thomas P. Mikell; she had been born in New York, but probably was second-generation Irish.[252]

At the very bottom of the white-dominated social scale on the island in 1860, just above slaves, were four free African Americans. Mary J. Maxwell, eighty-six, supported herself and fourteen-year-old Lizzie Maxwell (possibly her granddaughter) as a mantua maker. Martha Alston, fifteen, lived in the home of a young white couple with a baby, perhaps as a housekeeper. William Perry, forty-five, lived alone and supported himself as a carpenter.[253]

## CHAPTER 7

# EDISTO'S PLANTATION ARISTOCRACY

## What Constitutes a "Plantation"?

In this book, a full-fledged plantation was one that (A) had clearly defined boundaries, (B) had been traded or inherited for some time as a discrete entity, (C) had enough high land (140 acres was the smallest) to support a planter's family and their workers if well managed and (D) had its own distinct worker (slave) community. The author relies heavily on the yeoman work of David Lybrand of Edisto Beach in the 1990s. He matched archival plantation plats (shapes) with plantation boundary lines on the 1851–57 U.S. Coast Survey map. The author also cross checked plantation names, locations and owners against other available documents from the period, including federal censuses, "Losses Claimed" in 1862 and lists compiled by the Freedmen's Bureau in 1865.

Edisto had sixty-two full-fledged plantations in 1850, if we include Jehossee Plantation.[254] Each had its own history, traditions and subculture. Yet each was linked through the owner's family ties to most of the others. The white planter families of Edisto Island were remarkably inbred, even by South Carolina Lowcountry standards. On the whole, these families valued education, at least for their sons. Most of them were sincerely devout, even pious, in their Christianity. Overwhelmingly, they were conservative in their politics: they believed in a strict interpretation of the Constitution, and states' rights and slavery. They also valued family honor, money and a good time.

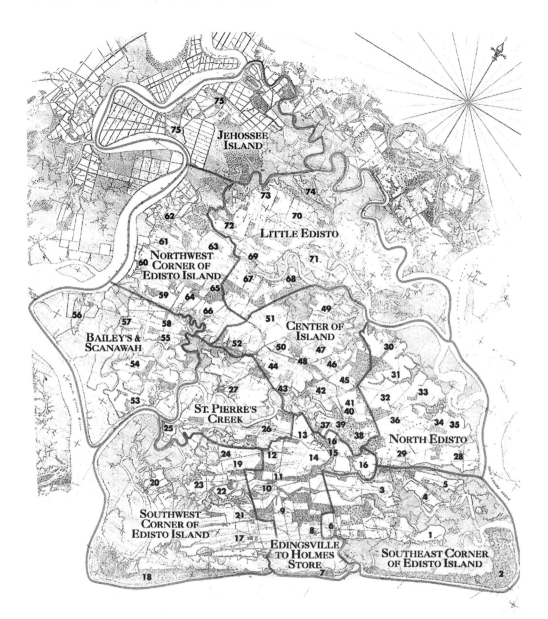

Location of Edisto Island
Plantations and Landmarks in the 1850s

*Numbers in the map are keyed to the accompanying list.*

Figure 30.

*Table 9.*

*Location Key: Edisto Island Plantations and Landmarks in the 1850s*

*The map shows the location of each place, keyed by number to the following list. Locations on the map are approximate. Family names after plantation names refer to owners in the "Golden Age." For more detail see the sector maps.*

| | | | | | |
|---|---|---|---|---|---|
| Ash's (Mikell Whaley) | 71 | Frogmore (Mitchell) | 64 | Palmetto (Con Bailey) | 21 |
| Bailey's Island, Bailey Pl. | 54 | Governor's Bluff (Fuller) | 37 | Peter's Point (Mikell) | 25 |
| Bailey's Island, Mikell Pl. | 53 | Green's Point (Whaley) | 5 | Pine Barren (Whaley) | 26 |
| Baptist Church | 40 | Gun Bluff (Seabrook) | 66 | Point of Pines (Bailey) | 28 |
| Baynard's Little Edisto | 72 | Hanahan (John J.) | 46 | Presbyterian Church | 48 |
| Baynard's Old Place | 67 | Hanahan's Little Edisto | 73 | Presbyterian Parsonage | 43 |
| Bayview (Edings) | 8 | Holmes's Store | 15 | Prospect Hill (Baynard) | 60 |
| Beckett's | 23 | Home Place, Whaley's | 63 | Rabbit Point (Baynard) | 49 |
| Berwick Legare | 9 | Hopkinson's (Cassina Pt.) | 34 | Raccoon Island | 56 |
| Betsy Seabrook's | 65 | Jack Daw Hall (Murray) | 6 | Ravenswood (Baynard) | 44 |
| Bleak Hall (Townsend) | 1 | Jehossee (Aiken) | 75 | Red House | 11 |
| Blue House (Con Bailey) | 47 | Jenkins Hill (de Lasteyrie) | 32 | Riverside (Bailey) | 61 |
| Botany Bay (Townsend) | 2 | The Launch (Middleton) | 27 | Seabrook's, Betsy | 65 |
| Brick House (Jenkins) | 68 | Laurel Hill (Seabrook) | 55 | Seabrook Tract | 12 |
| Brookland (Seabrook) | 58 | Locksley Hall (Seaside) | 17 | Seabrook's, William | 30 |
| Cassina Point (Hopkinson) | 34 | Mary Seabrook's | 45 | Sea Cloud (Townsend) | 3 |
| Cedar Hall (Whaley) | 51 | Maxcy Place (Dr. Bailey) | 50 | Seaside (Baynard) | 10 |
| Chaplin's Gardens | 31 | Meggett Place (Dr. Bailey) | 57 | Shell House (Baynard) | 24 |
| Charles Bailey's | 29 | Mitchell Place (Windsor) | 69 | Shergould | 22 |
| Chisolm's (Middleton) | 27 | Mitchell's Little Edisto | 70 | Sunnyside (Mikell) | 13 |
| Clark's | 35 | The Neck (Whaley) | 20 | Swallow Bluff (Bailey) | 4 |
| Crawford (Whaley) | 19 | Oak Island (Seabrook) | 33 | Tom Seabrook's (Whaley) | 52 |
| Cypress Trees (Clark) | 42 | Old Dominion (Dr. Bailey) | 62 | Trinity Episcopal Church | 39 |
| Dill Farm (Westcoat) | 16 | Old Hill (Jenkins) | 41 | Whaley's Home Place | 63 |
| Edingsville Beach | 7 | Old House (Whaley) | 36 | Whaley's Little Edisto (Windsor) | 69 |
| Edisto Beach | 18 | Old Place, Baynard's | 67 | Whooping Island | 74 |
| The Farm (Salt Landing) | 59 | Orange Grove (Mikell) | 14 | Windsor (Whaley) | 69 |
| | | | | The Woods (Westcoat) | 16 |

The following, then, were the families and the plantations during Edisto's "Golden Age," from about 1820 through 1861. They are described in a geographic sequence, starting with those nearest the beach, then the middle of the island and finally the landward side of the island. At the beginning of each cluster of plantations, a sector map shows the detailed geography of that part of the island. In the text, numbers in parentheses after the name of each plantation correspond to the plantation locator

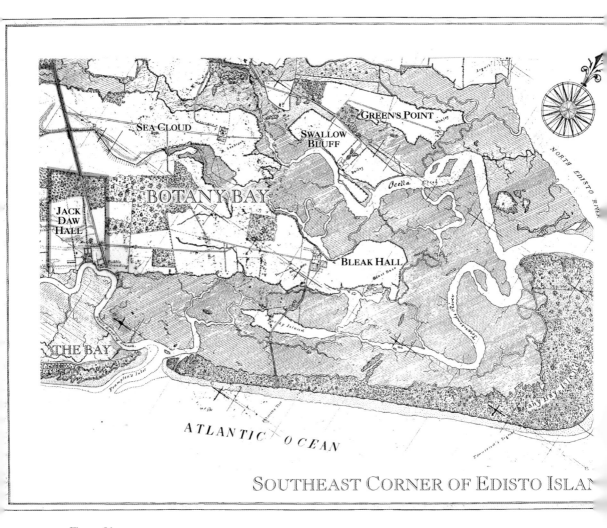

Figure 31.

map. A large-scale mini-map is shown for a few of the individual plantations, to illustrate different layouts of plantation communities, including the location of slave cabins. (Mini-maps for the remaining plantations are reproduced in *Documents on Edisto Island History*.) The mini-maps are oriented north-northwest, identically with the sector maps.

All of these maps derive from the one large map described in Chapter 6 ("The 1850s Mapping Project"). Maps with this degree of cultural detail are extremely rare for a rural area in the United States before the Civil War. Edisto Island is fortunate indeed to have these little windows into its past.

## Southeast Corner of Edisto Island

The Townsends of BLEAK HALL (1), BOTANY BAY (2) and SEA CLOUD (3). By 1859 the Townsend family had assembled 3,779 acres (including marsh) on the southeast corner of Edisto Island, by far the largest cotton plantation on the island. Its proprietor, John Ferrars Townsend, was noted for the quality of cotton he produced.

John Townsend's Edisto empire had been assembled mainly by his father and grandfather, Daniel Townsend II and Daniel Townsend III. It comprised twelve parcels, none of which was granted originally to a Townsend.[255]

The heart of Bleak Hall, where Townsend had his great house, was a 460-acre parcel of high land granted to James Bullock in 1749.[256] Bullock probably never occupied this site because he sold it within two years to Richard Jenkins and his wife Ann, who had other land nearby. Jenkins recorded his ownership of the tract in 1754.[257]

The Bleak Hall tract is shaped like a strong finger of land pointing northeast into the marshes of Ocella Creek. It had navigable creeks on three sides that connected with the North Edisto River, making it very accessible to early transportation. The grant document calls this tract Indian Point, and an adjoining grant document refers to it as "Indian settlement." If Indians were living there or actively using the land, the Proprietors may have delayed granting it for several decades. No record has been found of what happened to these Indians or their settlement after 1749.

A 360-acre tract adjoining Bleak Hall on the southwest was granted in 1710 to John Frampton. He still owned this tract in 1733, including the future public landing on Frampton's Inlet Creek.[258]

A 164-acre triangular sliver of land was part of a larger, 400-acre grant in 1707 to Dorothy Ogle (Hamilton).[259] (The larger section of that tract, 236 acres, became Jack Daw Hall. See below.)

Five hundred acres of high land immediately northwest of the Frampton and Ogle tracts was granted to John Hamilton in 1695. These five hundred acres were eventually acquired from the Hamiltons by the Townsends after 1733.[260]

Sea Cloud comprised two parcels to the northwest of Bleak Hall that, combined, formed a peninsula that also jutted northeast into the marshes of Ocella Creek. The larger parcel, 170 acres, where the Sea Cloud house and slave quarters were later built, had been granted to Christopher Linkley in 1695 and conveyed by him in 1727 to Paul Hamilton Sr. Paul Hamilton Jr. recorded his ownership of it in 1748.[261] A 21-acre parcel at the very tip of the Sea Cloud peninsula was held back by the colonial government and granted to Normand McLeod after independence. By the middle 1800s both parcels were fully integrated into the Townsend plantations, although a Seabrook family was living at Sea Cloud. A third parcel of perhaps 50 or 100 acres is sandwiched between the Frampton tract and Sea Cloud.

Old Edisto people have an enduring legend that the house at Sea Cloud was given that name because the couple who built it in the early 1800s was a Seabrook woman who married a McLeod (pronounced McCloud). No such couple has been identified with a clear link to this plantation, and it seems more likely that Ephraim Mikell Seabrook simply chose a romantic name when he built the house about 1825.[262]

The house was abandoned in the early 1900s and finally demolished about 1930, but was said to have been quite elegant. Its foundations are still visible in a protected area beside the farm road at Botany Bay Plantation.[263]

Pockoy (Pocky, Porky), a 60-acre island in the marsh between Bleak Hall and the beach, had been granted to John Frampton in 1710, at the same time as his 360-acre tract, above.[264] Townsend apparently planted Pockoy in cotton, and it served for many generations as an anchor for the causeway out to Botany Beach, which Townsend also owned. It had been granted in 1711 to John Frampton, who still held it in 1733.[265] Townsend did not clear the woods from the beach or build on it, but hunted and fished there with his guests.

The much larger barrier island that, then as now, turned the corner of the Atlantic Ocean into the North Edisto River was known as Watch Island. Its five hundred acres had been granted in 1711 to one William Green, who shortly disappeared completely from Edisto's history.[266] Watch Island also eventually became part of Bleak Hall plantation. Today it is separated by an inlet from Botany Beach (which has mostly disappeared under the waves), and Watch Island is known as Botany Bay Island. It is not part of modern Botany Bay Plantation.[267]

Townsend also owned Pig Island (Fig Island), which lies more than a mile north of his house in the large marsh between Ocella Creek and the North Edisto. This thirty-eight-acre marsh-locked island cluster was then, and is now, widely noted for its very large Indian shell ring and mound (Chapter 1). It was first granted to Jeremiah Fickling in 1752, three years after Bullock obtained Indian Point.[268] Very likely it was important to the people on Indian Point—economically, ceremonially and ancestrally—and was long exempted from grants for that reason. There is no record that John Townsend used Pig Island as anything other than a curiosity.

In addition to these ten parcels of high land, John Townsend also owned two enveloping tracts of marshland. The first, 154 acres north of Sea Cloud, was granted in 1735 to Paul Hamilton, and in 1748 was still owned by his son, Paul Hamilton.[269] The high flats of this marsh connect with those at the headwaters of Store Creek where, on a high spring tide, the waters of the North Edisto meet those of the South Edisto. A 1734 plat suggests that this strip of marsh was valuable as rice land, and that may explain why Hamilton bothered to seek a grant of it. The plat shows two dikes that could shut out the salt water from both Store Creek and Ocella Creek. The eastern dike apparently doubled as a wagon causeway north out of Sea Cloud. A third dike between the other two, allowing even greater control of water in those fields, is shown on a master plat of Sea Cloud and Bleak Hall drawn in 1855 by John Seib.[270]

Townsend's second marsh tract lay between Bleak Hall, Botany Beach, Watch Island and the North Edisto River, and was estimated by surveyors at 876 acres. It had been granted to Samuel Fairchild by the State of South Carolina in 1800.[271] Acquisition of these two marshes gave Townsend effective control of all the marine resources and waterways surrounding his large plantations and connecting them to the North Edisto River.

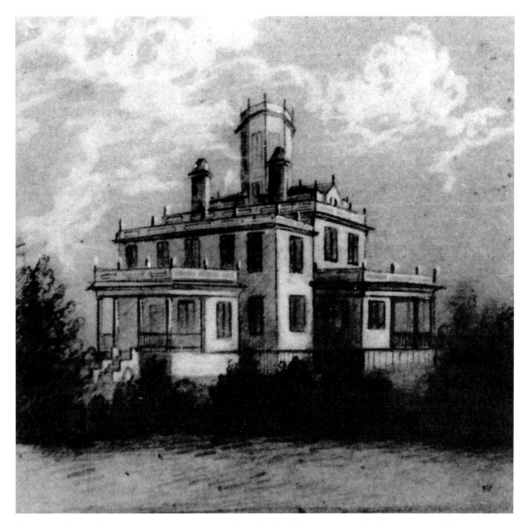

Figure 32. Daniel Townsend's widely admired first Bleak Hall, painted in 1861 by a family friend, Karoline Sosnowski. This house burned during the Civil War, probably in early 1865. *Photo courtesy of Mary M.W. Townsend.*

The big house at Bleak Hall reportedly was built by Daniel Townsend III (1759–1842). In 1796 he married Hephzibah Jenkins (1780–1847); he was thirty-seven and she was sixteen. They probably built the legendary first Bleak Hall in the early 1800s. It was a large, almost exuberant three-story house with a tall cupola on the roof, which was used later by Union troops as a signal station to "speak" to ships at sea.[272]

Hephzibah Jenkins Townsend gave birth to fourteen children, worked hard all her life for causes she believed in and is remembered as a formidable character and community leader. It is said that when her husband wrote a will leaving most of his vast estate to their oldest son, Hephzibah opposed him on principle and moved out of

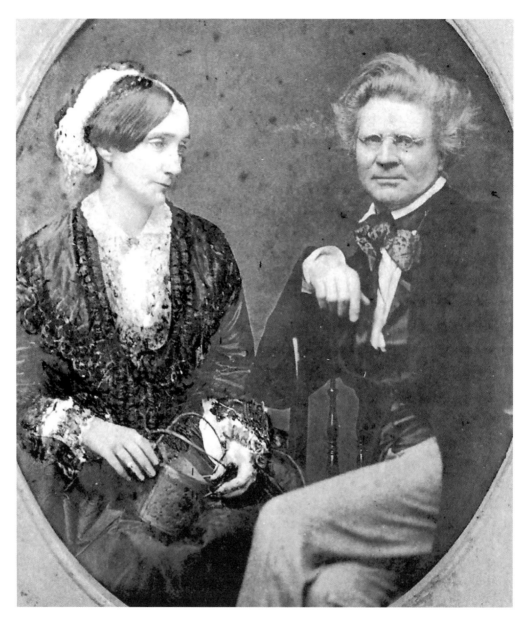

Figure 33. Mary Caroline Jenkins and John Ferrars Townsend, mistress and master of Bleak Hall, about 1850. *Photo courtesy of Mary M.W. Townsend.*

his house until he reconsidered. She also acted independently of her husband on religious matters, since he was a Presbyterian elder and she was a dedicated Baptist, responsible for founding and building Old First Baptist Church in 1818 (see Chapter 6).

John Ferrars Townsend (1799–1881) was Daniel and Hephzibah's oldest surviving child. He married Mary Caroline Jenkins, inherited Bleak Hall from his father and was its proprietor in the "Golden Age."[273]

Paul Grimball appears to have received a grant in 1734 for all the land south of Point of Pines and north of Ocella Creek, about 730 acres. Of this land, 500 acres appears to be the plantation known during the "Golden Age" as Bailey's[274]—today's SWALLOW BLUFF (4).

The house on a strong bluff overlooking navigable Ocella Creek was approached on a lane flanked by landscaped gardens and ponds shaped like the wings of a butterfly. This lane branched off the Point of Pines road near today's Clark Road, making Bailey's completely separate and private from neighboring Green's Point. Their shared approach road was not created until the twentieth century, when both plantations came under a single owner.[275]

Bailey's was an old name for this plantation by 1851. It was occupied, if not owned, in 1851 by William Edings Seabrook (1828–1889), grandson of the legendary William Seabrook of Edisto Island and son of William Seabrook Jr. of Oak Island.[276]

No record has been found of when the house was built or what it looked like. (The Swallow Bluff house we know today came later, and is discussed in the second volume of this history.) William E. Seabrook married Esther Marion Mitchell in 1856, but the landscaping and the house clearly date from 1851 or earlier.[277]

In 1750 Paul Grimball conveyed the remaining 230 acres of his Point of Pines grant directly to his grandson Joshua Grimball, who recorded ownership a year later. This land appears to be today's GREEN'S POINT (5). By 1789, the Grimballs apparently had sold this small plantation to Josiah Mikell.[278] The name of Green's Point most likely goes all the way back to William Green, who owned nearby Watch Island (Botany Bay Island) in 1711.[279]

During Edisto's "Golden Age," Green's Point was a satellite plantation owned and planted by Joseph Whaley of Pine Barren. He probably had a white overseer there, but otherwise it was occupied by slaves.[280]

In the 1850s a modest plantation called JACK DAW HALL (6) adjoined the vast lands of Bleak Hall on its west side. It was owned by Major William Meggett Murray, who also owned another small plantation near the center of the island, and a very large one on Fenwick Island. Jack Daw, however, had a big house: family tradition says it had twenty-one rooms, but no image of it has been found.[281]

Two very early Jenkins plantations were situated on this side of the island. In 1744, William Jenkins (circa 1704–1758) paid for a survey of 236 acres facing Frampton's Inlet Creek (then called Clark Inlet). This tract was part of the 400 acres that Dorothy (Ogle) Hamilton had purchased in 1710 from the Proprietors for eight pounds sterling, and that she had deeded that same year to John Jenkins.[282] William had a home there that he called Cedar Grove, probably on the same high bluff where Jack Daw stood later.[283]

William Jenkins's daughter, Abigail, was born in 1749, and between 1765 and 1769 she married James Murray, a newcomer to the island. Cedar Grove apparently went with her, for Murray was buried in 1779 in the Jenkins Family Cemetery at Cedar Grove. James and Abigail Murray's descendants have lived there continuously until the present day. By the middle 1800s, and perhaps much earlier, the Murrays were calling the old William Jenkins place Jack Daw Hall.[284]

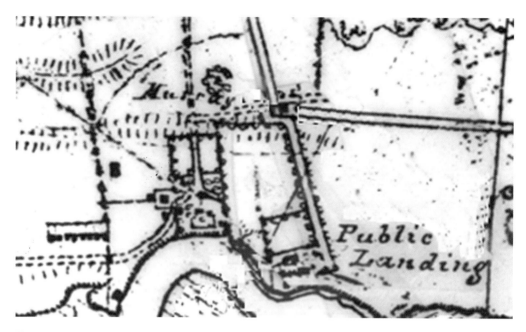

Figure 34. Jack Daw Hall in 1851. House faced Frampton Inlet Creek, inside large rectangular garden and branched driveway. Circular shape at top is Jenkins Family Cemetery. Slave quarters, *lower left*, line the back road to Bayview and Edingsville.

Family tradition, first recorded in 1886, says that James Murray was "killed by the explosion of a cannon while defending the Island from the [British] enemy, leaving one child."[285] That child, Joseph James Murray (1770–1818), married another Edisto planter's daughter, Martha Mary Meggett (1771–1818), and became a successful cotton planter on a modest scale. He also had a scientific bent, keeping a journal of weather, agriculture, vital statistics and community events for sixteen years, which was later summarized in a published history of South Carolina.

Joseph James and Martha Mary Murray's six daughters married into the Mikell, Hanahan, Clark, Seabrook and Meggett families. Their older son, the Reverend James Joseph Murray, was at one time assistant pastor of the Presbyterian Church on Edisto Island. He died in 1838 along with his wife and two children, when the steamer *Pulaski* sank thirty miles off North Carolina, drowning more than half the crew and passengers.[286] That left one son, William, to carry forward the Murray name on Edisto Island.

William Meggett Murray (1806–1866), among other pursuits, raised and commanded a militia company on Edisto, authorized by the state legislature, which he named the Calhoun Artillery after his political hero, John C. Calhoun. By the 1850s he had been promoted to the rank of major of militia, and was thereafter known as Major Murray.[287]

Major Murray's first wife, Lydia Eaton Clark (1804–1845), had twelve children, and his second wife, Martha Caroline Swinton (1820–1894), had six more. Two daughters

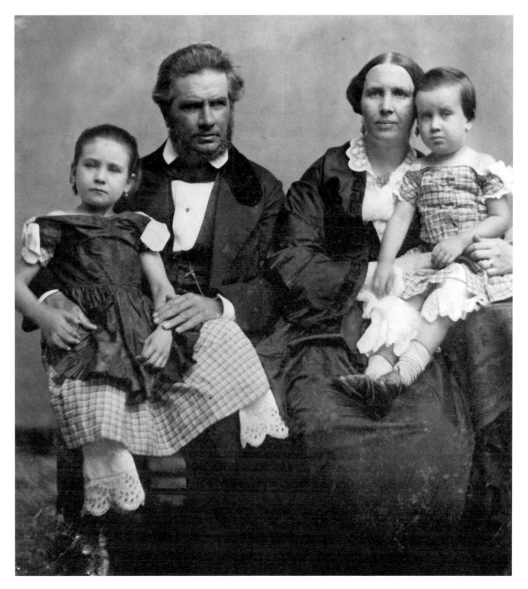

Figure 35. William Meggett Murray with his second wife, Martha Caroline Swinton, and two of their children, Caroline (born 1849) and Thomas Chalmers (born 1853). *From an 1856 ambrotype, courtesy of EIHPS.*

married into the Jenkins family and a third into the LaRoche family. A son from the first marriage, Dr. Joseph James Murray, is the progenitor of the descendants named Murray still living on Edisto Island and elsewhere in the early twenty-first century. A son from the second marriage similarly founded the Chalmers Murray branch of the family.[288]

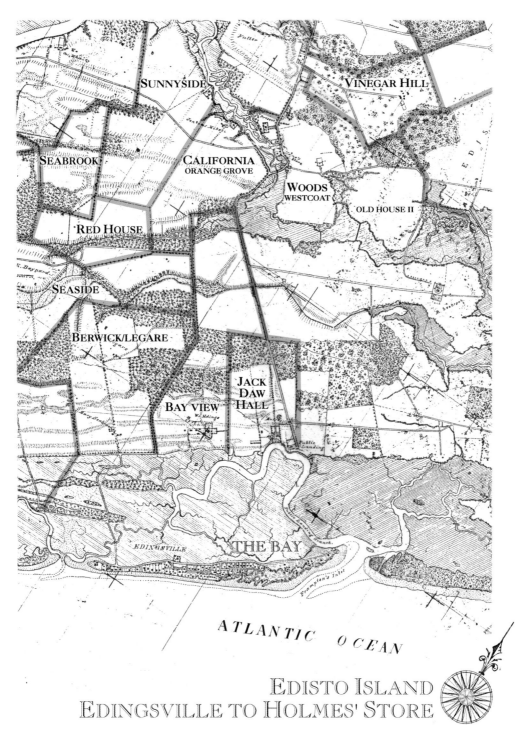

Figure 36.

# Edingsville to Holmes's Store

West of Jack Daw Hall was the much larger BAYVIEW PLANTATION (8), situated squarely facing the back of Edingsville Beach or "the Bay," as it was known in the 1800s.[289] Its owner, William Edings, also owned the beach resort itself and other plantations. When he died in 1858, his widow took over management of his considerable holdings. She was the widow of William A. Mikell (below, "Crawford") before she married Edings. Twice widowed by the age of forty, Hess Edings did not marry again but finished educating two sets of children, managed her extensive farming operations and sent two sons off to the Confederate army in 1861. Hess Marion Waring Smith (Mikell) Edings (1818–1904) was a very powerful and resourceful woman in a man's world.

Bayview included five hundred acres that apparently had been granted in 1709 to Henry Bower. In 1733, an earlier William Edings had registered the land as a gift from Henry Bower, and in 1769 it was registered again by Benjamin Edings.[290] It had no deep water access for shipping cotton, but the Edingsville Beach Road along Bayview's western boundary led up to the middle of the island.[291]

A fifty-seven-acre island in the marsh between Bayview and the beach, called Cowpens, had also been granted in 1736 to William Edings I and registered in 1769 by Benjamin Edings.[292] Apparently it had always served as a large wooded pasture for livestock. The causeway crossed Cowpens on its way from Edisto Island to the beach.

In 1769 Benjamin Edings also registered the 150-acre barrier island[293] EDINGSVILLE BEACH (7), which had been granted to "Captain Henry Bowers" in 1709. Like Botany Bay Beach, Edingsville was a long strip of forested sand dunes, considered worthless for farming and accessible only by water until the causeway was built, probably around 1800, when Edings began selling or leasing the lots on the beach. Planter families built summer houses, and by the 1820s the beach was a thriving resort (described in more detail in Chapter 6).

BERWICK LEGARE (9) was the next plantation along the seaside of Edisto Island. It was owned by John Berwick Legare (1819–1856), the husband of William Seabrook's youngest surviving child, Julia Georgiana Seabrook (1829–1852). No other Edisto plantation has a direct association with the Legare (La-GREE) family, but this couple was part of the extended Seabrook clan during the "Golden Age." Berwick and Julia had no children, so the Legare name disappeared from Edisto with Berwick's death in 1856.[294]

Berwick Legare was actually a double plantation, with two residences, for reasons that are not clear. The eastern section was called Berwick, and the western section was called Legare. In 1852 the U.S. Coast Survey mapped the western half as property of Mary Seabrook, an unmarried half-sister of Julia Seabrook Legare (below).[295]

SEASIDE (10), nearby, was a plantation shaped like an hourglass on its side. Seaside was a name used for several different Edisto plantations at different times, as well as a shorthand name for the entire half of the island closer to the ocean. But in the 1850s this apparently was the only Seaside Plantation. Its proprietor was Ephraim Baynard, who apparently lived several miles north, at Rabbit Point.[296]

Two small, irregularly-shaped tracts of cotton land lay just north of Baynard's Seaside. RED HOUSE (11), despite its name, does not appear to have had any residence for a white family in the 1850s. The origin of the name is obscure. The other small tract, perhaps two hundred acres, called the SEABROOK TRACT (12), also had no house for a white family in the 1850s. Apparently one or both were owned and planted by I. Jenkins Mikell of Peter's Point (below).[297]

Most of SUNNYSIDE (13), two hundred acres, had been granted to Lawrence Dennis in 1705, and by 1733 that part was owned by James Lardant.[298] Later it became part of the extensive holdings of the Mikell family. Sunnyside had no manor house at all, and probably had no name during the "Golden Age," although there was a small slave

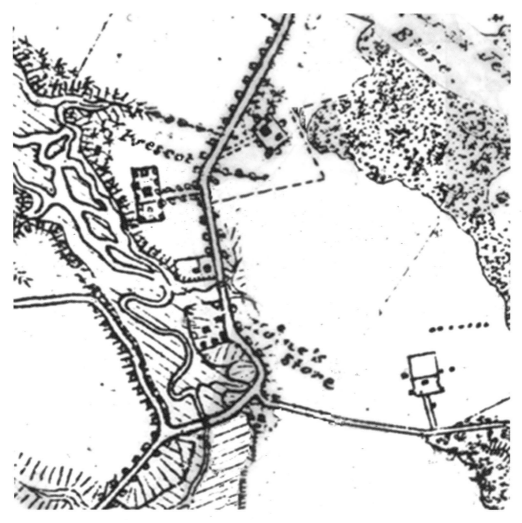

Figure 37. In 1852, Holmes's Store and a public cotton gin were clustered between road and creek. Jabez Westcoat's home faced Store Creek, *upper left*. His Woods Plantation straddled Point of Pines road. Seven slave cabins stood in an open field.

community on its northeast corner. It was still one of Isaac Jenkins Mikell's satellite plantations, but after the Civil War Sunnyside would be identified with Townsend Mikell.[299]

Isaac Jenkins Mikell gave ORANGE GROVE (14), a slightly smaller plantation adjoining Sunnyside, to his son Thomas Price Mikell, MD, older half-brother of Townsend Mikell. Thomas married Rebecca Moses, and they had children. Orange Grove (later called California) had a modest residence facing Store Creek near the public highway. The details on the U.S. Coast Survey map strongly suggest that, as late as 1852, Orange Grove and Sunnyside were still being planted as one plantation.[300]

The most important general store on Edisto Island was always, at least until the mid-twentieth century, in the center of the island where the main public road crossed Store Creek. A Scottish merchant named Mungo Mackay (pronounced MACK-ey) apparently had a store there as early as 1793, before there was even a bridge across the creek.[301] In

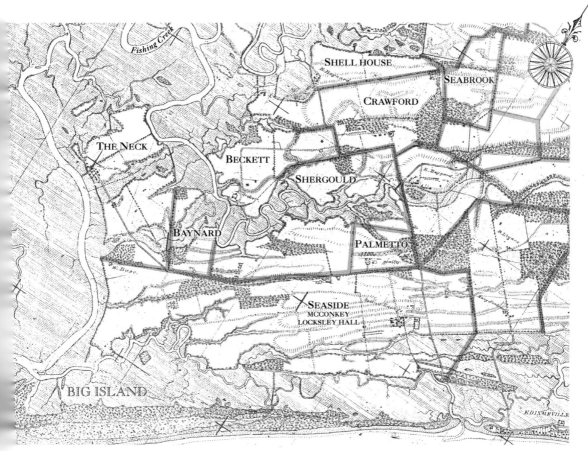

SOUTHWEST CORNER OF EDISTO ISLAND

Figure 38.

the 1850s, the store still operated out of a home and was called HOLMES'S STORE (15), although it is not clear who the owner then was.[302]

Just north of the store, on the same side of the road, was DILL FARM (16), the home of Jabez J.R. Westcoat, surrounded by a formal garden and fifteen acres of farmland. He called his 315-acre plantation directly across the public road THE WOODS (16). It apparently lay both north and south of the road to Point of Pines. Westcoat, a vestryman in Trinity Episcopal Church, also operated a public cotton gin on the creekside behind Holmes's Store.[303]

## Southwest Corner of Edisto Island

The southwest corner of Edisto Island was anchored by a very large plantation, including EDISTO BEACH (18). During the "Golden Age," it was called LOCKSLEY HALL (17), which was the name of a popular narrative poem published in 1842 by Alfred Lord Tennyson. Later the place was called simply Edings, after the owners. The handsome stucco house now known as Seaside is the old Locksley Hall, built by William Edings apparently between 1800 and 1810.[304] In the 1850s, John Evans Edings, son of William Edings, claimed three thousand acres, more than half of which appears to have been high land.[305] Edings and his wife, Josephine Seabrook, actually lived in her grandfather's great house on Russell Creek after 1854 (below), and they belonged to the Presbyterian Church on Edisto Island.[306]

W. James Whaley, called Major Whaley even before the Civil War, owned both CRAWFORD (19) and THE NECK (20). The Neck's three hundred acres of high land consisted mainly of two large islands and several smaller ones surrounded by one

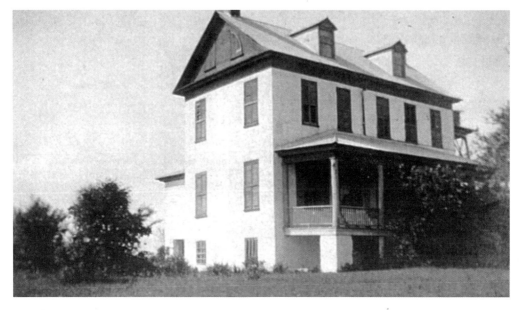

Figure 39. Seaside house, then called Locksley Hall, was built by William Edings in the early 1800s. Its construction is stucco over brick; its style is Federal. It still stands today. *Photo courtesy of EIHPS.*

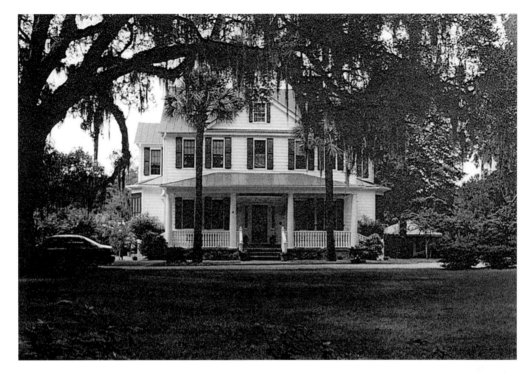

Figure 40. Crawford house as it looks today. During the "Golden Age," Crawford sheltered two prominent families. Built around 1838 by William A. Mikell, it was purchased in 1847 by William James Whaley. *Photo courtesy of EIHPS.*

thousand acres of marsh, between Big Bay and Fishing Creeks. The islands were connected, then as now, by causeways from Palmetto Road. Almost all the land was cleared for cotton, and a house and wharf stood on a bluff facing Big Bay Creek and St. Helena Sound beyond.[307] It was John Raven Mathewes (see below, "Ravenswood") who apparently pieced together this plantation around 1821.

Crawford, named for an early owner of one tract, included 434 acres of high land. It was a large rectangle with a thumb extending southwestward into the marshes of Fishing Creek, essentially landlocked and dependent on the goodwill of neighbors to load its cotton onto barges for transport to a gin or to market.

The plantation had been in the Mikell family for two generations when William A. Mikell, a brother of Isaac Jenkins Mikell, built the present house for his bride, Hess Marion Waring Smith, between 1835 and 1838. But William Mikell died in 1840; his widow remarried and relocated (see "Bayview," above); and Crawford was sold to James Whaley in 1847.[308] The house at Crawford was still owned and occupied by Whaley descendants well into the twentieth century.

A small plantation with 206 acres, called PALMETTO (21), belonged to Constantine Bailey, who apparently made his home at his larger place, Blue House, on the north side of the island. Palmetto (also called Rescue in some documents) was landlocked, but lay only a couple of miles from Edingsville Beach.[309]

SHERGOULD (22) was a small plantation with perhaps two hundred acres of high land stretching along the upper bank of Fishing Creek. Shergould apparently never had a white residence and it is not clear who owned it during the "Golden Age." Probably it was a satellite planting area for a more important plantation elsewhere on Edisto.[310]

Cato Beckett had a compact, two-hundred-acre plantation north of Fishing Creek, always called simply BECKETT'S (23). His modest house stood in a grove of trees facing the creek.[311] Apparently it had been in the Beckett family for several generations without making any of them particularly wealthy. Cato's son, Theodore A. Beckett, inherited the place as a very young man when his father died just before the Civil War.[312]

Wedged between Crawford and the upper marshes of Sandy Creek was a triangular tract called SHELL HOUSE (24) or LaRoche. It had 142 acres and a small slave community facing the marsh with a view all the way to the South Edisto River. Ephraim Baynard of Rabbit Point, one of Edisto's largest planters, was its owner.

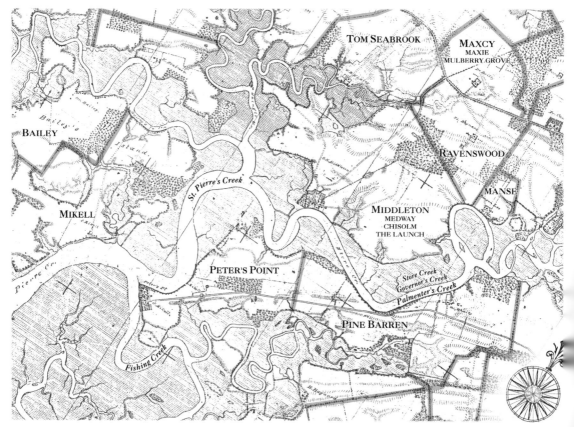

EDISTO ISLAND: ST. PIERRE'S CRE...

Figure 41.

Shell House apparently took its name from the tabby walls of a small house that probably was already quite old in the mid-1800s. Some tabby walls still stand today in the woods near Shell House Road. Whether the old house was occupied by a resident manager or was already a ruin during the "Golden Age" is not clear.

Baynard had an extensive system of dikes connecting small islands in the marsh at Shell House, probably for growing rice (see Chapter 4). A cart track atop the dikes also gave Baynard access to deep water on Sandy Creek. Big Island (today's Sandy Creek Point), nestled in a fold of the creek half a mile west, probably was part of this plantation. Big Island was completely cleared by 1852, suggesting that it too was planted with cotton, even though its only access then was by boat.[313]

# St. Pierre's Creek

St. Pierre's Creek itself was an important transportation artery for freight and passengers in the middle of Edisto Island. PETER'S POINT (25) (Point St. Pierre) was a small peninsula at the confluence of St. Pierre's Creek and Fishing Creek. It was one of the most dramatic plantation seats anywhere on Edisto Island, commanding 180 degrees of unobstructed views for miles across rivers and marshes: north up St. Pierre's Creek, past Middleton to Gun Bluff; west, past Bailey Island and Fenwick Island, across the South Edisto and St. Helena Sound to St. Helena Island; and south, past the Neck and Bay Point on Edisto Beach, to the wide Atlantic Ocean.[314]

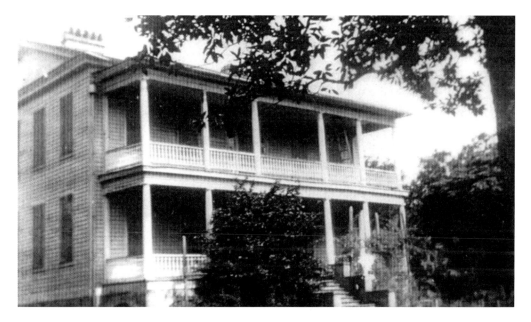

Figure 42. Peter's Point house about 1960. Isaac Jenkins Mikell built this house during the "Golden Age." Empty and badly dilapidated in the late twentieth century, it was being restored in 2004. *Photo courtesy of EIHPS.*

Peter's Point was the seat of Isaac Jenkins Mikell (1808–1881), another of Edisto's legendary figures. Its five hundred acres had been granted in 1707 to Joseph Sealy. Christopher Jenkins owned the land and already had a house on the bluff in 1821. Jenkins Mikell inherited it from his father, Ephraim Mikell II, in 1838.[315]

Jenkins Mikell built his house about 1840, a large, rectangular two-story structure set on high brick foundations, with four rooms divided by a central hall on each floor. Across the front were identical upper and lower piazzas, each with Tuscan-style columns. Wide, brick steps with treads of brown sandstone led up to the center of the front porch.[316]

Jenkins Mikell was one of that handful of Edisto planters wealthy enough to leave a plantation to each of his sons and considerable money to each of his daughters. He married four times (Emily Price, Amarinthia Townsend, Martha Pope and Sarah Lee) and had sixteen children. His town house on Rutledge Avenue in Charleston was large enough to serve as the county library a hundred years later, and still stands today.

This pillar of the Presbyterian Church on Edisto Island[317] and family man apparently also had a secret life. It has recently been asserted that, about 1840, Isaac Jenkins Mikell had a son with a woman who was one of his slaves, and still has living African American descendants.[318]

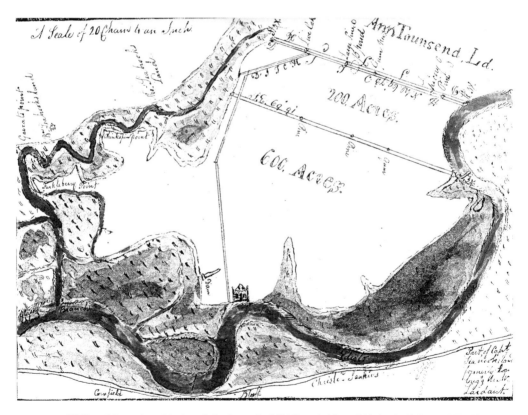

Figure 43. William Norton's 1786 plat of the Launch (Middleton). Note Chinkapin Point and Farkleberry Point, *left*. "Branch of So. Edisto River" is St. Pierre's Creek. House symbol represents Joseph Jenkins's small, early house. *Courtesy of Caroline Clarkson Boineau.*

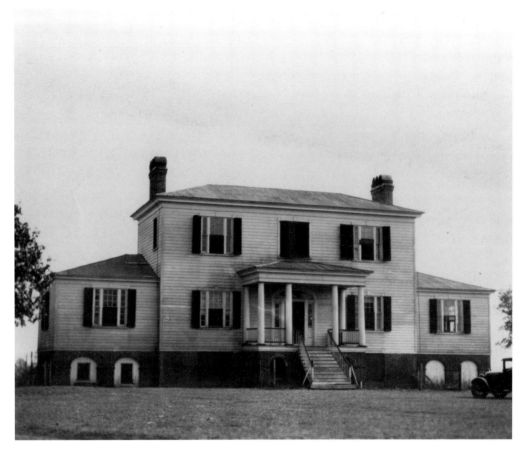

Figure 44. Dr. Chisolm's house, built in the 1820s and reputedly designed by Robert Mills, as it looked about 1930. Oliver H. Middleton owned the property during the "Golden Age" and it bears his name today. *Photo courtesy of The Charleston Museum, Charleston, SC.*

Joseph Whaley's PINE BARREN (26) was a six-hundred-acre plantation on Store Creek, named for the longleaf pine flat woods that existed on some parts of Edisto Island before European settlement. This land had a high water table and was less fertile than other parts of Edisto (see Chapter 1), but with careful drainage it would grow cotton.

Pine Barren, in two tracts, stretched almost two miles along the Peter's Point road, and included some of the best deep water access on the entire length of Store Creek. Whaley's house stood on the site now occupied by an early twentieth-century house, also called Pine Barren. This homeplace, with 234 acres, had been granted in 1703 to Lawrence Dennis, sold to Edward Rippon in 1730 and eventually conveyed to the Whaley family. The second tract had been part of the grant that became Peter's Point, but Christopher Jenkins sold 263 acres of it to Joseph Whaley in 1821.[319]

Joseph Whaley (1789–1872) was called Colonel Whaley well before the Civil War, and claimed to have lived at Pine Barren continuously from 1806, when he was seventeen.[320]

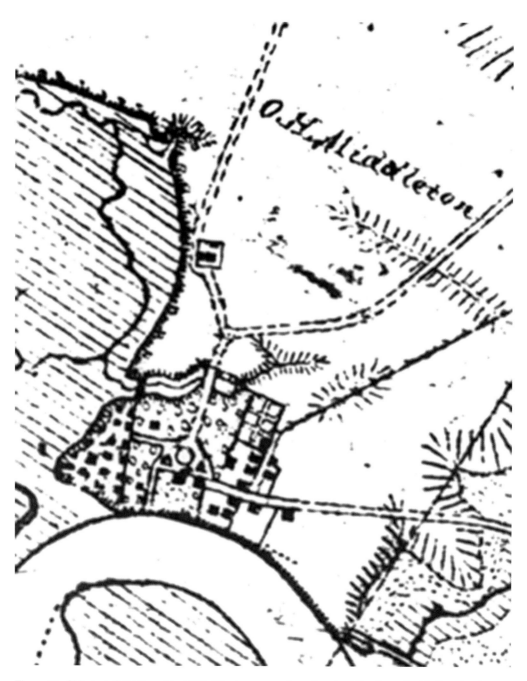

Figure 45. Chisolm's (Middleton) in 1852. The house stood two hundred feet from the bluff, a circular drive behind it and a large park surrounding it. Farm buildings clustered on the right. Five slave cabins lined the bluff at bottom.

He was the sixth of thirteen children of Thomas Whaley III, a veteran of the American Revolution and the progenitor of all the Whaleys of Edisto Island. Joseph's mother was Mary Ann Seabrook. He married his first cousin, Louisa Barnwell Seabrook, and they had eight children, who thus were related to the entire prolific Seabrook and Whaley clans. Louisa died in 1822, and Joseph then married Ann Jenkins, but they had no children.[321]

Just across Store Creek from Peter's Point and Pine Barren lay a large plantation, called CHISOLM'S (27) during this period, with a long history involving many different families. It comprised two very early grants to John Whitemarsh, the eastern three hundred acres in 1695 and the western five hundred acres in 1700. These eight hundred acres formed a wide peninsula facing a broad, deep curve of St. Pierre's (Store) Creek.[322]

Between 1700 and 1750 this plantation passed through at least six owners. John Whitemarsh Jr. inherited the land from his father in 1718. John Jr. died childless in 1723 and his wife Margaret Barnwell Whitemarsh inherited it. She then married Richard Stevens, who recorded his ownership in 1733. Between 1733 and 1750 title was transferred to Richard Ash, who sold the plantation in 1750 to Paul Grimball, son of Thomas Grimball and grandson of the first Paul Grimball.[323]

Frequent changes of ownership continued for another fifty years, involving several members of the Grimball, Calder and Evans families. In 1802 William Evans died and left the plantation to his twenty-four-year-old widow, Mary Elizabeth Edings Evans (1778–1848).[324] When she married Dr. Robert Trail Chisolm, a practicing physician, ownership stabilized in one family for the next hundred years. A written marriage settlement reserved "the Launch" (as it was then called) for Mary and her heirs. The Chisolms raised their one surviving child, Susan Matilda Harriet, on the plantation, and she eventually inherited it from her mother. In 1827 Susan married Oliver Hering Middleton (1798–1892), a son of Governor Henry Middleton of Middleton Place on the Ashley River near Charleston, and grandson of Arthur Middleton, a signer of the Declaration of Independence. Susan's mother, Mary Evans Chisolm, continued to live at the Launch until her death in 1848. It probably was because of Mary's more than fifty years of residence that the place became known as Chisolm's well into the twentieth century. (Oliver Middleton also called the place Medway in some documents.)

The Middletons lived mostly in Charleston, but Oliver managed the plantation and visited it frequently. Sometime between 1850 and 1860 Oliver and Susan Middleton moved with their unmarried daughters back to the island and were living at Chisolm's when the Civil War arrived. Susan died in 1865, but her daughters continued to use the plantation for many years. The fourth and current name, Middleton('s), obviously traces to this period.[325]

A residence, perhaps built by Joseph Jenkins (1761–1828), has existed on the dramatic bluff of St. Pierre's Creek at least since 1786 (Figure 43). The Chisolms presumably expanded or replaced that house in the late 1820s with one in the Neoclassical style and proportions that has survived to the present. There is circumstantial evidence, but no documentation, that the redesign was done by the nationally famous South Carolina architect, Robert Mills.[326]

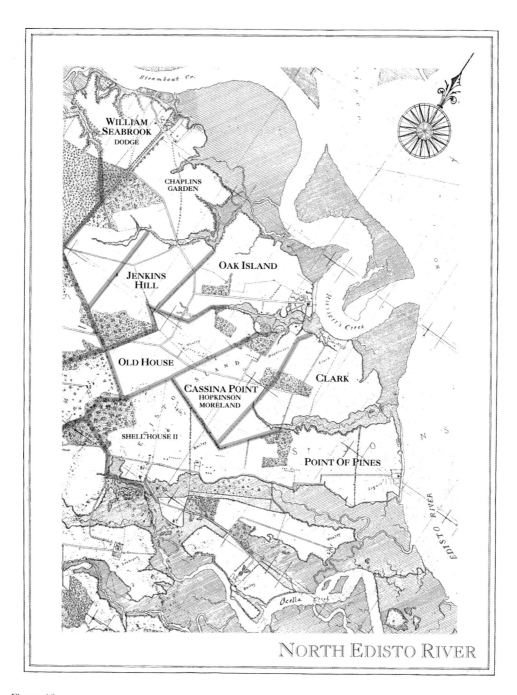

Figure 46.

# North Edisto

The earliest recorded land grant on all of Edisto Island is one for 1,590 acres on the North Edisto River to Paul Grimball in 1683. The document says the land was "already in his possession," suggesting he had claimed it even earlier. POINT OF PINES (28), then as now, has the best high ground access anywhere on the island to the deep water anchorage in the North Edisto, and for most of the next two hundred years the main shipping wharves of the island were located there.[327]

Point of Pines stayed in the Grimball family for several generations. Paul's son, Thomas Grimball, recorded ownership of the entire 1,590 acres in 1722, as did his son Joshua Grimball in 1751.[328] But by 1789 it was owned by Ralph Bailey and its size had shrunk to 1,124 acres. The difference apparently was the outsale of more than four hundred acres to James Clark (see below, "Clark's"). The 1789 plat of Point of Pines shows extensive diking of the upper marshes of Crooked Creek, probably for rice planting.[329]

Ralph Bailey's grandson, Charles Joseph Bailey, was the proprietor in the 1850s of Point of Pines and CHARLES BAILEY's (29) (then considered two adjoining plantations). Charles built himself a new house midway between Holmes's Store and Paul Grimball's old tabby ruin on the North Edisto. The Baileys of Point of Pines were a young family with more than their share of grief. Charles Joseph married his first cousin, Mary Elizabeth Bailey, about 1845. Within four years she had borne two sons and twin daughters, but she died in 1849. Charles then married Anne Manson Gautier and continued to live at Point of Pines, but in 1854 he died at age thirty, when the oldest child was only eight or nine. Jabez Westcoat and Thomas Baynard (of Dill Farm and Ravenswood, respectively) became guardians of the children and managed the plantations for their benefit until the Civil War.

The stepmother, Anne, struggling to keep the little family together, remarried in 1857 and brought the Bailey children into the household of Septimus H. Jenkins. That arrangement lasted four years, but when Edisto was evacuated in 1861, Jenkins went into the army, and Anne moved with her Jenkins children to her sister's home in Georgia and left all four Bailey children in boarding schools in South Carolina. Charles Henry was then fifteen, Edward Julian was fourteen and the twins, Mary Ellen and Martha Julia, were thirteen. Both boys went into the Confederate army when they turned seventeen, and both survived the war. How the four Bailey siblings made a new life for themselves after the war is another story, told in the second volume of this history.[330]

The patriarch of the Edisto Seabrook family was William Seabrook (1773–1836). He was rich by birth; his lands were extensive; his house was (and still is) impressive; and his lifestyle was lavish. Besides his extensive cotton lands on Edisto Island, he owned Seabrook Island and plantations on Johns, Wadmalaw and Hilton Head Islands.[331]

WILLIAM SEABROOK's (30) plantation was on the northeast side of the island where Russell Creek (later called Steamboat Creek) meets the North Edisto. Some 920 acres, granted originally to Henry Bower, appear to have been the core of this plantation. By 1728 Joseph Russell owned the tract, and he sold it that year to John Frampton, who recorded his ownership in a memorial in 1733. Ownership for the next seventy years is obscure.[332]

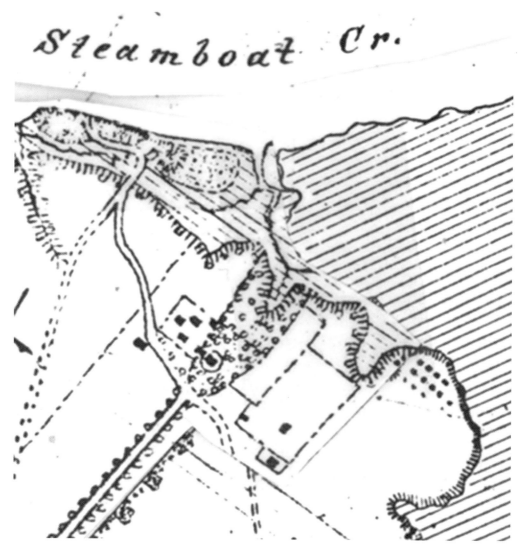

Figure 47. The William Seabrook Plantation in 1851. Note the oak-lined avenue, main house with formal gardens down to the river, triple row of slave cabins at right and Seabrook's private steamer landing at top left.

Today's oak-lined avenue from Jenkins Hill Road up to the big house is the only surviving portion of the original Seabrook lane.[333] William Seabrook probably built his mansion in the early 1820s, although one authority dates it as early as 1810. The house was still fairly new when General Lafayette visited in 1825. With its distinctive upper and lower piazzas front and rear, this is the largest and most elaborate house surviving on Edisto Island from before the Civil War.[334]

William Seabrook was a fourth-generation South Carolinian. His great-grandfather was Captain Robert Seabrook, a merchant from County Bedford, England, who arrived in Charles Towne in 1689. William's first wife was Mary Ann Mikell (1779–1818),

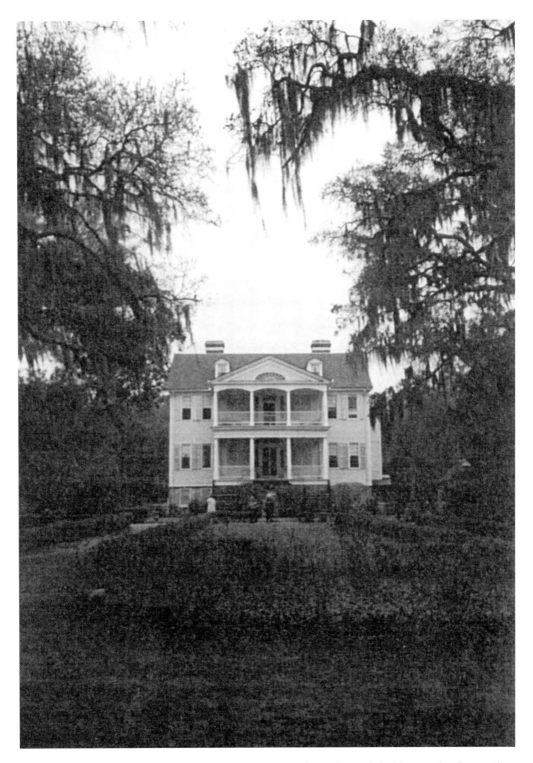

Figure 48. The William Seabrook House today. The large main section and double verandas, front and rear, make this the most impressive house surviving on Edisto Island from the "Golden Age." *Photo courtesy of EIHPS.*

daughter of Ephraim Mikell I and a descendant of Calders, Baileys, Splatts and Jenkinses. His second wife was Emma Elizabeth Edings, daughter of Joseph Edings and Sarah Scott. William and Mary Ann had five children; William and Emma had six. Seven of the eleven children married, and this extensive family, within two generations, bought land and planted all over Edisto Island.[335]

In 1825, forty-two years after the end of the Revolutionary War, the aging General Lafayette, beloved hero of that war and survivor of the French Revolution, returned to America for one last visit and a triumphal tour of each of the original thirteen states. While passing by boat between Charleston and Savannah, he was hosted overnight on Edisto Island by William Seabrook[336] and his second wife Emma. At their glittering reception attended by all of Edisto's planter families, a formal speech of appreciation for Lafayette's services to the new nation was delivered by Edisto Island's rising young politician and future governor, Whitmarsh B. Seabrook of Gun Bluff. During the festivities the Seabrooks had a minister to publicly christen their infant daughter, with General Lafayette standing as her sponsor and naming her Carolina Lafayette Seabrook.

William Seabrook apparently was one of those rare rich men who was generous to all his friends without being ostentatious, and was a strong and progressive force within his community without seeking the spotlight. An appreciation of his life published in an influential periodical, *The Southern Agriculturalist*, noted that William had been a diligent and open-minded planter of long-staple cotton, one of the first to improve yields by fertilizing with salt marsh mud. Three years before his death, he personally financed and managed the first scheduled steamboat service between Charleston and Savannah with intermediate stops at Edisto and other islands. He represented St. John's Colleton for a time in the state legislature. With his steadily accumulating wealth, he quietly lent money and mentored many younger men just getting started as planters.[337]

William Seabrook also was a loyal supporter of the Presbyterian Church and was an elder for many years. After his death, the congregation voted unanimously to place a permanent marble tablet on an inside wall of the sanctuary; it is one of only three ever placed there. It says William Seabrook was "Kind and Amiable...Enlightened and Patriotic...Humble, Full of Faith...[and] Belov'd...By Every Member of This Community."

When he died in 1836, William Seabrook was worth more than $375,000—a multi-millionaire in today's dollars. He left a will with various bequests. He left a tract southeast of his homeplace to his son, William Seabrook Jr. It already had a home on it: Oak Island (below). He gave 430 acres "bought of Ralph Bailey" to his other son, George Washington Seabrook. (This plantation has not been identified.) William Seabrook also willed a large tract to his daughter Mary. It is west of his homeplace and ends at Cypress Bottom. Today, Mary Seabrook Road runs through it and follows the route of the original private lane into William Seabrook Place.

Seabrook ordered his executors to spend $100,000 purchasing land for his other daughters, who then were minors. Those are detailed below.[338] William Seabrook also owned a large tract northwest of his homeplace that had belonged to his father, John

Seabrook. It has the original Lawton-Seabrook Cemetery on it. Later it was called Hanahan (below). Emma Seabrook apparently lived on in Seabrook House for some years after William's death; she herself died in 1856.

But in 1854 the homeplace, with its grand house, passed to one of William Seabrook's granddaughters, Josephine Edings Seabrook, and her new husband, John Evans Edings Jr. The Edings lived at Seabrook House until the Civil War, and afterward returned to live there until 1875. Edings was quite wealthy in his own right, having already inherited Locksley Hall Plantation and Edingsville Beach (above).[339]

Julia G. Seabrook, who married John Berwick Legare, inherited a tract called CHAPLIN'S GARDENS (31) from her father, William Seabrook. She and her husband were mostly absentee landlords (see "Berwick Legare," above), and there is no record of a big house at her plantation. It had its slave community, though, and grew cotton, which produced income for Julia. Little more is known about Chaplin's Gardens during the "Golden Age."[340]

JENKINS HILL (32) was the tract of land with its own slave community that William Seabrook's executors purchased for his daughter Martha Washington Seabrook. She married the Count Ferdinand de Lasteyrie, and they lived elsewhere, including Paris.

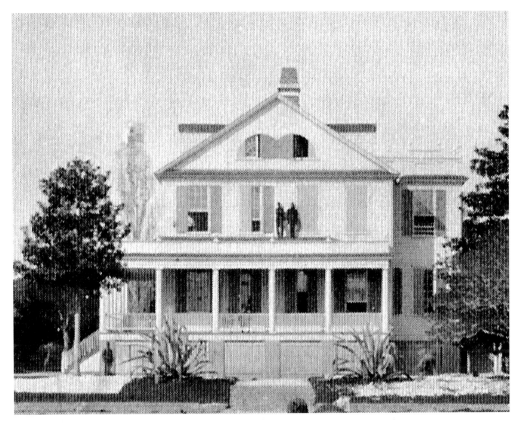

Figure 49. Oak Island house in 1862. Two Union soldiers pose on the porch roof. This side of the house faces east, toward the river. *Detail of photo by Henry P. Moore, courtesy of New Hampshire Historical Society.*

The plantation did produce income for them, and may have been managed for them by her brother-in-law, James Hopkinson, at nearby Cassina Point (below).

William Seabrook Jr. (1799–1860) inherited Oak Island Plantation (33) upon his father's death in 1836, but apparently had already planted it in cotton since his marriage to Martha Edings in 1822.[341] Their house probably was built around 1830. It was a big house, with twenty-one rooms, surrounded by elaborate formal gardens, a park with deer, a greenhouse, a free-standing library, a dairy house, serpentine walks of crushed shell, exotic plantings, 1,500 varieties of roses and a large saltwater fish pond with a "rustic bridge" to an island in the middle.[342] Oak Island today is one of Edisto Island's most beautiful surviving plantation houses.

William and Martha Seabrook had four children. Their eldest, William Edings Seabrook, lived at Swallow Bluff (above) after he married in 1856, but later inherited Oak Island. Their second, J. Edward Seabrook, owned Oak Island briefly at the time of the Civil War. Their youngest, Josephine E. Seabrook, became mistress of her grandfather's William Seabrook House (above) after she married Evans Edings in 1854.[343]

William Seabrook Jr. died in 1860, but his wife Martha lived on until 1892. Oak Island went to the eldest son, William E. Seabrook, and his direct descendants continued to own the property until 2003.[344] Using William Seabrook Jr.'s marriage in 1822 as the starting date, those 181 years of continuous ownership and continuous use (with brief interruptions) by the same family constitute one of the longest runs of any historic property on Edisto Island.

Carolina Lafayette Seabrook (1825–1879), who as an infant had been named by General Lafayette himself, married James Hopkinson in 1844. Her father's executors had already bought a plantation for her from A.J. Clark adjoining Oak Island, her older brother's plantation on Russell Creek. The Hopkinsons built a large, well-appointed house there, probably about the time they married, and lived there until 1861. The place was called simply Hopkinson's. Today it is known as Cassina Point (34).

James Hopkinson (1810–1875) was a grandson of Francis Hopkinson, a signer of the Declaration of Independence from Pennsylvania. Carolina Seabrook met him while studying in Philadelphia, and after their marriage they spent a lot of time there, as well as raising five children at Cassina Point.[345]

Part of the original Point of Pines grant to Paul Grimball was a large triangle on deep water at Russell Creek, a short distance from its mouth on the North Edisto. By 1789 this plantation belonged to James Clark III (1768–1819), and was known simply as Clark's (35). In the early days all shipping on Russell Creek passed Clark's house. Some time later Russell Creek cut itself a new entry into the North Edisto a mile and a half to the west, and the old stretch of river at Clark's was renamed West Bank Creek.[346]

James Clark III married three times: Sarah Grimball, Anna Scott Mikell and Sarah Webb Mikell; his second and third wives were sisters. He had nine children and was the progenitor of most of the persons named Clark on Edisto Island, as well as of daughters and granddaughters who married into the Bailey, Whaley, Jenkins, Murray, Seabrook, Mikell, Robertson and Hills families.[347]

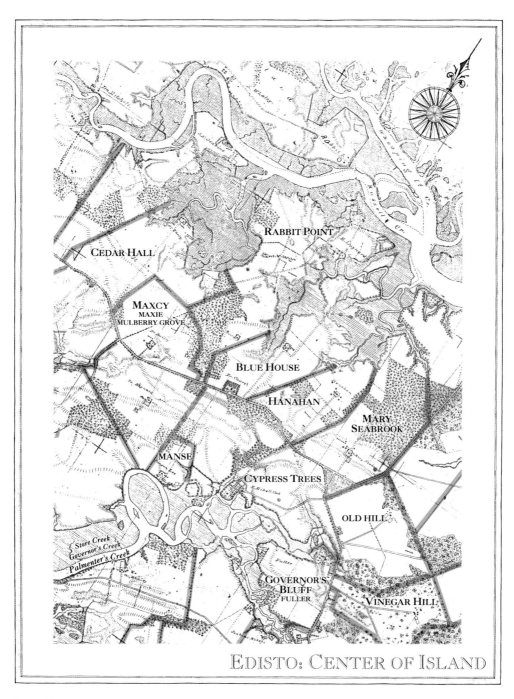

Figure 50.

When James Clark III died in 1819, at age fifty-one, ownership of this plantation apparently passed to William Mikell Clark, who was then living at Cypress Trees (below). So William probably planted both plantations and supported the extended family while his stepmother, Sarah, and her young children lived on at Clark's. When William Clark died in 1830, himself only thirty years old, ownership of Clark's apparently passed to his only surviving son, James Joseph Clark, who was then only six. His uncles by then were old enough and probably managed both plantations for the support of the extended family. When he came of age, James Joseph took over Clark's and lived there with his wife, Josephine Clark. James J. Clark then died in 1850, at age twenty-six, and Clark's was inherited by Josephine. She still owned it when the Civil War started.[348]

OLD HOUSE (36) was a 350-acre, landlocked plantation sandwiched between Oak Island and Cassina Point, near the North Edisto River. It was called Old House because in the "Golden Age," when so many new, larger and grander houses were being built all over the island, this modest but dignified house was one of a very few that survived from the mid-1700s still in use and not completely rebuilt (Figure 14).

Edward Charles Whaley (1826–1887) was the proprietor of Old House. His father was Benjamin Whaley. An uncle (and his father-in-law) was Edward C. Whaley of Old Dominion Plantation (below). Another uncle was Colonel Joseph Whaley of Pine Barren (above) and a first cousin was Dr. James E. Whaley of Cedar Hall (below). Edward's half-brother was William J. Whaley, the prominent attorney in Charleston and owner of Frogmore Plantation (below) after 1855. Edward married his first cousin, Abigail Mikell Whaley, whose father had exactly the same name as her husband. They had four children. Abigail died young, in 1862, but Whaley did not remarry.[349]

Besides planting cotton, Edward Charles Whaley was a politician. He represented St. Johns Colleton in the South Carolina Senate, and was still there when South Carolina seceded in December 1860.[350]

# Center of Island

GOVERNOR'S BLUFF (37) appears to be a very old name for the plantation behind TRINITY EPISCOPAL CHURCH (39). It faced Palmenter's Creek, later called Governor's Creek, St. Pierre's Creek and now Store Creek. There is speculation that the plantation took its name from one of the earliest governors of the Carolina colony, Joseph Morton I, who reportedly had his first home there about 1685, before he moved to the mainland near Wiltown. But only two written sources (1950 and 1960) clearly say that, and most likely it is not true. The fact is, no one really knows what the name means.[351]

In 1707 Edward Wayott (Wyott, Wyatt) platted a grant of four hundred acres on the north side of Governor's Creek. Wayott was still the owner when he registered it in 1733, but that same year he sold it to Joseph Sealy, who then sold it to Ephraim Mikell, a relative newcomer to the island.[352] At some point the four hundred acres were divided into more than one plantation. Also, probably about 1774, a large lot on the northeast corner of this plantation facing the Kings Highway was sold or donated for the site of the oldest Episcopal church on Edisto Island. In 1803 the plantation appears to have been owned by Joseph James Murray (1770–1818), but by 1852 it was again in the Mikell collection of plantations, now only two hundred acres.[353]

In 1839 Edward N. Fuller married Mary Ann Mikell, daughter of Ephraim Mikell and Providence Jenkins and sister of Isaac Jenkins Mikell of Peter's Point (above). The Fullers were a prominent Lowcountry family, centered apparently in the Beaufort area, but nothing else is known about Edward N. Fuller. He and Mary Ann raised children and cotton at Governor's Bluff, but did not return to Edisto Island after the Civil War.[354]

Across the public road from the Episcopal church was VINEGAR HILL (38), a small and completely landlocked plantation of 140 acres, without a white residence, but with a slave community. Its owner was Ephraim S. Mikell, who lived elsewhere.[355]

Near the BAPTIST CHURCH (40) was a three-hundred-acre plantation called OLD HILL (41). Its proprietor was John Micah Jenkins (1794–1854), a younger brother of Colonel Joseph E. Jenkins of Brick House (below).[356] Jenkins's wife, Elizabeth Grimball Clark, had inherited Old Hill from her father. She came into control of it when she turned

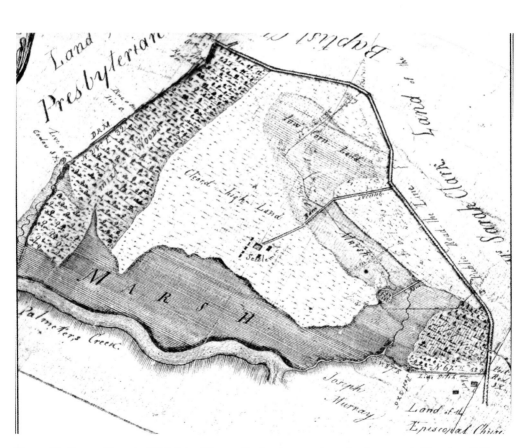

Figure 51. Cypress Trees in 1803. John Diamond's plat shows a plantation house and village in a field, with a creek, *right*, triple-dammed for planting. The promontory, *left*, where house stands today, was still wooded. *Courtesy of James C. Murray.*

twenty-one in 1824, the same year she married. Although they chose to live on Edisto, Jenkins also had a large plantation on Mussleborough Island, across the South Edisto River, and around 1850 he bought a third at Bennett's Point on the mainland.[357]

John Jenkins was a captain in the state militia and was elected to represent St. John's Colleton in the state senate from 1838 to 1841. John and Elizabeth raised three girls and three boys; the sons would later serve in the Confederate army with distinction. The youngest son, Micah, would become a general in Lee's Army of Northern Virginia at the age of twenty-six. (His military career is recounted in volume two of this history.)

Captain John Jenkins died in 1854 and his oldest son, John, executing the estate, was forced to sell Old Hill to pay the mortgage on Bennett's Point, a larger and more valuable plantation.[358]

In 1697 Joseph Palmenter was granted three hundred acres north of "Palmenter's Creek" (today's Store Creek). Sometime during the next thirty years this tract, CYPRESS TREES (42), passed into the Clark family, for Jeremiah Clark willed it in equal shares to his sons James and Jeremiah Jr. in 1726. James Clark recorded the two brothers' ownership in a 1733 memorial.[359]

The Clarks clearly were planting and living on this tract by 1790, if not long before, because that is the date of the earliest burials in the plantation's white cemetery. The 1803 plat by John Diamond (Figure 52) shows the size of the plantation as 233 acres and the owner as James Clark, a grandson of the first James Clark. With only 150 acres of cleared crop land, this was a small plantation in the middle of the island with no deep water landing from which to ship its cotton or offload its supplies. The Clarks apparently kept Cypress Trees occupied by in-laws and relatives while the really wealthy branches of the family lived elsewhere, at Clark's on Russell Creek (above) and on James Island.

William Mikell Clark, third of nine children of James Clark III, lived at Cypress Trees in the early 1800s, and two of his children are buried there. But his father apparently retained the title, and upon his death in 1819 left the place to his two youngest sons, Archibald Jeremiah Clark and Ephraim Mikell Clark. They added 121 acres on the west in two purchases in the 1850s to bring the total to 354 acres, including a deep water landing on St. Pierre's Creek. Both new tracts were bought from Thomas Baynard, who had bought them from the Presbyterian Church when its trustees decided the church did not need so much land. By 1859 Cypress Trees had become a medium-sized and efficient plantation.[360]

It had also acquired one of the island's most handsomely situated homes, for about 1830 the Clarks tore down their house in the middle of the fields and rebuilt it on a southern point facing the wide marshes of St. Pierre's (Store) Creek. Periodically rebuilt, restored and modernized in the twentieth century, Cypress Trees house still survives and is owned and occupied by direct descendants of the Clarks who built it.[361] In fact, using Jeremiah Clark's will in 1726 as a (conservative) start date, the Clark/Murray family had, by 2006, continuously owned and used Cypress Trees (with brief interruptions) for 280 years.

Henry Bower was granted three hundred acres on the north side of Palmenter's Creek in 1705 and gave it to the fledgling PRESBYTERIAN CHURCH ON EDISTO ISLAND (48) in 1717 as a glebe for the support of a minister. Bower is traditionally credited with

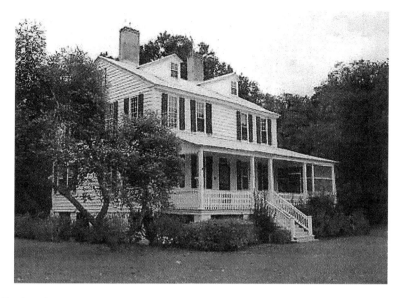

Figure 52. Presbyterian manse (parsonage) at end of the twentieth century. Built in 1838, this is the third house on the site. Several updates have left its appearance unchanged, and it still serves as the pastor's residence. *Photo courtesy of PCEI.*

generously contributing three hundred acres to help establish the Presbyterian Church. It now appears more likely that he was a conduit for land earmarked by the colonial government before 1697 as a subsidy to start a Protestant church on Edisto Island, which would have been consistent with the Proprietors' policy of encouraging settlement by religious dissenters. The trustees who received the gift in 1717 were Paul Hamilton, John Hayne, Joseph Russell, James Cockran, Ichabod Winborn and John Kennaway. In 1732 William Fry, on behalf of the trustees, filed a memorial on the property.[362]

As late as 1803 the church still owned all 300 acres, but between then and the 1850s it sold off 230 acres to the Baynards, its neighbors to the west. Thomas Baynard resold about 120 of those acres to the Clarks of Cypress Trees (above), and added the rest to his Ravenswood Plantation (below). That left ten acres of land for the church and its graveyard on the public road, and sixty acres nearby facing the marshes of St. Pierre's Creek for the parsonage and its farm.

THE PARSONAGE (43) farm during the "Golden Age" had a substantial two-story frame house that replaced an earlier residence in 1838 (Chapter 6). The shallow horseshoe creek under its bluff connected at both ends to the deep waters of St. Pierre's Creek. The house was practically surrounded by barns and outbuildings, and at least five slave cabins lined the bluff just east of the house.[363]

Most of the slaves who lived and worked at "Parson Lee" were owned by the church, not the minister. Their tasks were to feed themselves and the minister's family by growing the food crops and tending the livestock, under the minister's supervision, and to staff his house. The minister received a cash salary so he would not need to grow a cash crop such as cotton. This not only freed the minister to tend his human flock, it also freed the slaves who supported him from the unending drudgery of raising cotton. Even in the late twentieth century, the descendant of a slave elsewhere on Edisto Island remembered clearly that slavery at the parsonage had been about the lightest on the island. "They were slaves, but they didn't work like slaves. They worked more like free people."[364]

The Presbyterian Church on Edisto Island had only one minister for the half century from 1821 to 1872: the Reverend William States Lee. A legend in his own time, Lee's pastoral accomplishments are recounted in Chapter 6. He had seven adult children and a second wife by 1850.

RAVENSWOOD (44) was a plantation of perhaps three hundred acres that stretched for three quarters of a mile along the public road from the Presbyterian Parsonage farm to Middleton's lane. Shaped like a triangle, its point touched the old, shallow horseshoe of St. Pierre's Creek, but it was effectively landlocked. Its small settlement was in the middle of cotton fields, visible from the highway.[365]

William Bower obtained a grant of 270 acres in 1697, and that tract formed the core of this plantation. The Reverend John McLeod purchased it in 1744, and was still the owner in 1748. In 1786 Ann, widow of Andrew Townsend, was the owner. John Raven Mathewes apparently obtained the land before 1800, planted it until 1835 and was first to call it Ravenswood. Mathewes was a wealthy, restless and influential man, and Ravenswood was a relatively small part of his ventures. He also planted rice on a large scale at Chapman's on Bear Island, immediately west of Edisto Island. He probably lived there most of the time, and also had a house in Charleston.[366]

In 1835 Mathewes sold Ravenswood to William G. Baynard of Prospect Hill (below). Baynard kept the Ravenswood name and added to his income by planting cotton there. His son, Thomas A. Baynard, was the proprietor in the 1850s, and probably lived there with his young family.[367]

MARY SEABROOK'S (45) was a plantation of some four hundred acres, immediately west of her father, William Seabrook's. Except for a shallow branch of Blue House Creek, her plantation was landlocked, but as long as her father's place was owned by her mother or a close relative (above), she and her workers doubtless were welcome to use its deep water landing on Steamboat Creek.

Mary Seabrook was born about 1810 and was named for her mother, Mary Ann Mikell. She never married, but little else is known about her. Since the plantation carried her name, she probably lived on it. She may also have personally managed its planting. That would have been unusual for a woman, but not unique, in the mid-1800s.[368]

HANAHAN (46) lay immediately west of Mary Seabrook's along the main public road. Its three hundred acres were granted originally to Benjamin Wilman, who conveyed them by 1744 to William Tilley, who sold two hundred acres that year to Captain William Lawton.[369] Lawton was a planter from Johns Island who married Mary Clark of Edisto Island in the early 1700s. Their daughter, Sarah Lawton (1739–1798), married John Seabrook (1731–1783). Sarah and John were the parents of William Seabrook (1773–1836), who built Seabrook House nearby (above). Most of the Seabrooks on Edisto Island during the "Golden Age" were descended from William Seabrook, and thus also from Captain William Lawton.[370] He and his family clearly lived on this land, because the Lawton-Seabrook family cemetery is located there.

By the 1850s the place was called Hanahan and was occupied by a family of that name. The place was small and landlocked, about as far from deep water in every direction as one could be on Edisto Island. The Hanahans were not wealthy.[371] John James Hanahan (1821–1868), the proprietor, was a half-brother of Dr. Ralph B. Hanahan, a practicing physician who lived on a tiny farm directly across the public road from John. Their father's brother was James Clark Hanahan, a planter on Little Edisto (below). The Hanahans were close to the Clarks, whose family cemetery at nearby Cypress Trees holds several Hanahan graves. They also were close to the Murrays: John's mother was Martha Mary Murray, a sister of Major William Murray of Jack Daw Hall. John Hanahan's wife was Eugenia Galzer.[372]

The next plantation west from Hanahan was BLUE HOUSE (47). Its three hundred acres had been granted in 1701 to William Fry, and Ichabod Fry filed a memorial on it in 1733.[373] After 1733, the ownership of this plantation is obscure. During the 1850s Blue House was home to Constantine Bailey (circa 1829–circa 1884), who also owned Palmetto (above).[374] Con Bailey, as he was universally called, was a member of the large Bailey clan of Edisto and neighboring islands. Several planters were his first cousins, and another cousin, Mary Elizabeth Bailey, was the mother of his neighbor, Dr. Ralph B. Hanahan. Con Bailey married twice—Elizabeth LaRoche and Julia Loper—but he had no children.[375] He was a very successful middle-scale planter, and a strong supporter of Trinity Episcopal Church. When the Civil War came, he joined the Confederate army without hesitation as a private at age thirty-two.[376]

Ephraim M. Baynard was one of the largest landowners on Edisto Island. Besides Baynard's Seaside (300 acres, above), he also owned Shell House with its adjoining Seabrook Tract (about 350 acres, above) and a large plantation on Little Edisto (below). And then there was RABBIT POINT (49).[377]

This land originally was granted to Henry Bower in 1697, six hundred acres in a long strip that ran south from Russell Creek to what later became the public road.[378] His son, William Bower, split the six hundred acres in half and sold them as two tracts, in 1753 and 1754. Through subsequent transactions, however, most of the original grant seems to have been reassembled into one plantation by the early 1800s. In Ephraim Baynard's time, around 1850, Rabbit Point probably had about five hundred acres.[379] It was a relatively isolated, but apparently productive, cotton plantation.[380] When Baynard's executor reclaimed possession of his four Edisto plantations in 1865, he listed Rabbit Point first.

With his multiple plantations, Ephraim Baynard was reputed to be the wealthiest person in the parish,[381] but he was not a healthy man, and his poor health may have affected his disposition.[382] The people who worked on his plantations feared his wrath and compared the provisioning of his slaves unfavorably with practices elsewhere on the island. Behind his back they changed his surname to Binyard, and because his legs were spindly, they called him Pipe Shank. Sam Gadsden recalled in the 1970s that Emily Deas, whose ancestors were slaves at Rabbit Point, had told him,

*They work them from seven in the morning until noon with nothing to eat…[and]…then at two o'clock [they] go back to work until seven at night…They work right through with no Sunday off…Any place where Baynard owned land, that was a rougher place than the rest…He was a man who raised up slaves to sell…He marketed them…They say all of Baynard's people could stand more hunger than any other people, but that's just because he didn't feed them; they stole their rations from the other poor people…Pipe Shank Binyard, the stingiest man God ever let live.*[383]

One of Dr. William M. Bailey's many holdings on Edisto Island was a modest but conveniently situated plantation called MAXCY (MAXIE) PLACE (50). At the time of the Civil War it had 270 acres.[384] Its eastern section, perhaps 150 acres, appears to have been divided from 300 acres owned by William May in 1754. His memorial in that year named William Bower as the original grantee in 1697. The western section, perhaps 120 acres, may have been originally part of Cedar Hall.[385] To Dr. Bailey, who lived at the Farm and later at Old Dominion (below), Maxcy Place apparently was just extra income, and most likely he paid a resident overseer to manage it for him.

Dr. James E. Whaley, a practicing physician, owned CEDAR HALL (51), a plantation of 427 acres on the north side of the public road. It was a compact, medium-sized cotton plantation that could easily have supported the Whaley family comfortably if well run.[386] Born in 1825, the youngest son of the very wealthy Edward C. Whaley and Abigail M. Baynard of Old Dominion (below), all the other Whaley planters on Edisto Island were Dr. Whaley's brothers, cousins and uncles. In 1855 he married Jessie Randolph.[387]

Across the public road from Cedar Hall, and just west of Ravenswood, was a compact plantation of perhaps three hundred acres called TOM SEABROOK'S (52) but actually owned by another Whaley family.[388] No information has come to light about the original grantee or the early owners of this plantation. By the early 1800s it was owned and planted by Thomas Bannister Seabrook (1765–1839), an uncle of Governor Whitmarsh Seabrook, his neighbor to the west. Tom Seabrook probably built the house in the 1820s or 1830s, but unfortunately it burned in the early twentieth century.

When Tom Seabrook died in 1839, the place was purchased by Edward Whaley of Old Dominion, who deeded his son William a life interest in it, with actual ownership passing directly to his grandsons. William Baynard Whaley (1821–1857) married Martha Mary Hanahan (1823–1879), and in 1857 she became a widow with six young children. Old Edward Whaley then died in 1860. The grandsons, who would inherit equal shares of the plantation when they reached twenty-one, were William B., John C.C., Arthur M. and Percival H. Whaley. The executor was their uncle, the attorney Benjamin J. Whaley, who employed another islander, William Becket, to oversee the plantation for the widow and her children. The eldest son, William Jr., reached his majority in 1865.[389]

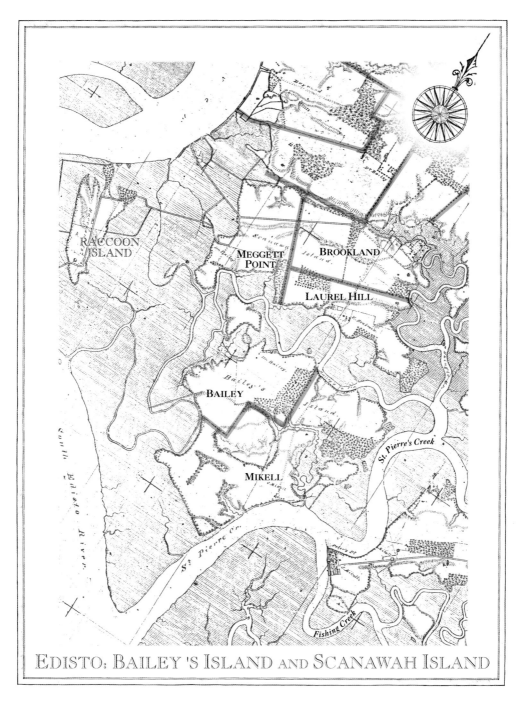

EDISTO: BAILEY'S ISLAND AND SCANAWAH ISLAND

Figure 53.

# Bailey's Island and Scanawah Island

Bailey's Island is the third largest of the constituent islands within the area normally considered Edisto Island. Shaped like a large heart, more than a mile and a half from bottom to top and the same across the top, Bailey's is separated from Scanawah by the narrow but deep Bailey's Island Creek, a branch of St. Pierre's Creek. On the south and east Bailey's Island has bluffs on deep and wide St. Pierre's Creek itself, making it one of the most water-accessible parts of Edisto Island. (The western side of the island faces the South Edisto River across one of the largest expanses of marsh anywhere on Edisto.)

Because it had no bridge, Bailey's Island had no resident planter families during the "Golden Age," and only briefly after the Civil War. Still, it was fully cleared for cotton planting except for two swampy pieces of woodland on the north side of the island. It had two plantations and two resident communities, with overseers' houses and slave quarters, in the 1850s.[390]

In 1695 the entire island then called Schenckingh's (Schinkins, Skinkins) Island and estimated at 802 acres[391] was purchased from the Proprietors by Christopher Linkley for one shilling an acre, a substantial sum. The plat that accompanied this initial grant divided the island with a straight east-west line into two tracts of 302 acres on the south and 500 acres on the north, to get around the Proprietors' rule that land grants should be 500 acres or less. This line was mostly ignored in subsequent conveyances and divisions of the island.[392]

Within fifty years Bailey's Island had been inherited or sold five times, ending with the purchase of all 802 acres in 1740 by Paul Grimball II (grandson of the original Paul Grimball). Rippon's Island, the 40-acre "steppingstone" between Scanawah and Bailey's, was now also part of the plantation.[393] Grimball's son, Paul Grimball III, was the owner in 1765.[394] But when he died two years later, the plantation (now called Grimball's Island) was sold at public auction to pay his debts, and the purchaser apparently was Joseph Edings.

In 1786 Joseph Edings sought and obtained ownership of the marshland adjacent to Bailey's Island. Four tracts totaling about eight hundred acres—all the marshes *inside* the river and creeks surrounding the island—were purchased from the state for about two shillings an acre, then a nominal sum.[395] Edings willed the plantation (now called Edings Island) to his son, Joseph Jr., in 1789, and the son may have kept it for ten years. It was during the Edings family ownership, if not earlier, that large sections of Bailey's Island probably were cleared for planting, for it was about this time that sea-island cotton was rapidly replacing other crops on Edisto Island.

Between 1789 and 1799, Edings apparently sold the plantation to the ancestor of Dr. William Bailey, and it has been called Bailey's Island ever since. A very detailed plat by John Diamond shows the island divided into three roughly equal plantations for the Bailey heirs. Rippon's Island was now called Crafford's (Crawford's), and was part of plantation (2) on the west side of the island.[396]

By the 1850s Dr. William Bailey, one of the largest landowners on Edisto Island, was planting the western side of the island, BAILEY'S PLANTATION (54). Isaac Jenkins

Mikell of Peter's Point was planting the eastern and southern portion, the MIKELL PLANTATION (53).[397] Neither was a resident of the island. Each treated it as extra acreage to plant in cotton. Bailey's settlement had five large structures and about fifteen slave cabins along northern bluffs. The large structures probably included an overseer's house and a cotton house, corn house and stables. The Mikell plantation had a larger house with five outbuildings and eighteen slave cabins on bluffs near the southeast corner of the island.

Peter's Point, the Mikell home plantation, was clearly visible across the creek and half a mile upstream. Mikell's Bailey's Island house was occupied briefly after the Civil War by one of Mikell's sons-in-law, but no record has been found that anyone other than an overseer occupied it during the "Golden Age."

Another of Edisto's large constituent islands, called Scanawah, lies just north of Bailey's Island. The name appears to be a corruption of Kennaway, one of the earliest settlers on this part of Edisto (Chapter 2). To reach Scanawah, one drove (then as today) down the public road beside Frogmore and crossed a short causeway over the marsh at the head of Shingle Creek. It held three plantations: Brookland, Laurel Hill and Meggett Place.[398]

LAUREL HILL (55) was a plantation of about three hundred acres on the southern side of Scanawah Island. Little is known of the plantation's early history, except that a John Stewart owned this land in 1733. That name, however, has disappeared long since from the history of Edisto Island.[399]

Laurel Hill house in the 1850s enjoyed a high bluff facing a perfect horseshoe loop of Bailey's Island Creek, but that house has not survived, and no image of it is available. The deep and sharp bend of Bailey's Island Creek has always presented an erosion problem at Laurel Hill. The main residence in the 1850s was situated fully one hundred yards back from the bluff. (A twentieth-century house on the same site actually collapsed down the bluff in the 1970s.)

Edward Whaley Seabrook (1824–1881) was "lord" of this small but elegant domain in the 1850s. His grandfather was Gabriel Seabrook (1765–1824), a lawyer and first cousin of William Seabrook of Edisto Island, so Edward was only distantly related to most of the other Seabrooks on Edisto. He graduated from Harvard College in 1845, returned to Edisto and commenced planting at Laurel Hill. He married Emma Dawson in 1854. By 1860 he was a very rich man.[400]

At the time of the Civil War, Seabrook also owned RACCOON ISLAND (56), nearly three miles away.[401] The island was never an independent plantation—too small—and traditionally, it had been part of Meggett Place (below), the nearest plantation.

Raccoon Island's one-hundred-odd acres were granted to Henry Bailey in 1698. Ralph Bailey sold the island in 1761 to John Calder, and his son Archibald Calder recorded his ownership in 1767.[402] The subsequent chain of ownership has not been found. In the 1850s almost the entire island was cleared for cotton planting. Two large rectangles of marsh east and west of the island were diked off, probably also for cotton planting. Raccoon Island has never had a large residence, but in the 1850s a small building stood beside the farm road in the middle of the island that could have housed an overseer, and a slave cabin or two dotted the shoreline.[403]

John Kennaway received 500 acres on what is now Scanawah Island from the Lords Proprietors in 1705. Ralph Bailey and William Scott assembled 1,090 acres, including Kennaway's 500 acres, and deeded all of it in 1719 to William Meggett, a newcomer to Edisto. Meggett may have been the first to actually live at Meggett Place (57), as evidenced by a Meggett family cemetery that still exists on Scanawah's southwestern point.[404] When William Meggett died, his son John, acting as executor, sold off parts of the Scanawah land (Laurel Hill, above, and Brookland, below) but kept the original 500 acres and the house where he had grown up, recording his ownership in 1733.[405]

This property apparently stayed in the Meggett family for more than one hundred years. A daughter of this plantation, Martha Mary Meggett (1772–1818), who is buried there, married Joseph James Murray and was the mother of Major William Meggett Murray of Jack Daw Hall. Other sons and daughters married into other Edisto and Lowcountry families. Later, a branch of the Meggett family was established on the nearby mainland at Archfield Plantation.

In the 1850s Dr. William Bailey, one of Edisto's largest landholders, owned Meggett Place Plantation. By then it was down to about two hundred acres. Bailey planted cotton on the land and probably installed an overseer in the old Meggett house. In 1858 Dr. Bailey sold Meggett Place to William Murray, who gave it to his son, Dr. Joseph James Murray, as a wedding gift. The land on Meggett Point, including the grave of Dr. Murray's grandmother, was back in the family.[406]

Brookland Plantation (58), with 370 acres, apparently was granted in 1705 or earlier to Walter Abbott, but the document has not been found. A 1733 plat says the owner then was John Megot (Meggett), who was about to sell to Archibald Calder. By the 1780s the property was owned by Joseph Jenkins, who is buried at Brookland. Next we find a 300-acre Brookland owned by Ephraim Mikell Seabrook and then by his youngest son, Henry Seabrook, who inherited it in 1846 but did not turn twenty-one until 1857.[407]

Henry Seabrook was a younger brother of Edward W. Seabrook, next door at Laurel Hill (above). Governor Whitmarsh Seabrook at Gun Bluff was their father's contemporary and second cousin. None of the other Seabrook planters on Edisto were close kin.[408]

There has been a residence at Brookland since before the Revolution, according to family tradition. Some time after he married Elizabeth Mary Hanahan, perhaps about 1840, Ephraim Mikell Seabrook built the present two-story house, two rooms wide and one room deep, with a one-room, one-story wing on each side. It had a two-story portico with four Corinthian columns, but only the two corner columns remain today. Many interior moldings and ornaments are lavishly detailed. This house has been well known and loved by many generations of Edistonians, even when—or especially when—its maintenance was beyond the means of its owners, as often happened in the twentieth century.[409]

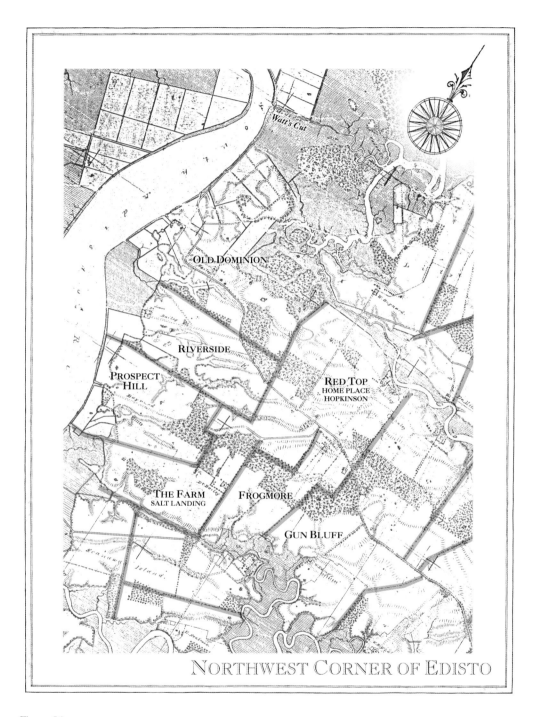

Figure 54.

## Northwest Corner of Edisto Island

One of Dr. William Bailey's four Edisto plantations, and the one he probably lived on in the 1840s and early 1850s, was called simply THE FARM (59). Later called Salt Landing, its three hundred or so acres probably had been assembled over the years by the Bailey family from parts of several small grants to Henry Bailey between 1695 and 1700.[410]

Dr. Bailey apparently lived in a house right beside the road to Laurel Hill. It stood in a small, fenced garden surrounded by four or five outbuildings and three slave cabins. Two more streets of slave quarters, totaling sixteen cabins, were three quarters of a mile west in the cotton fields.[411] It seems like a modest establishment for such a wealthy man. Perhaps he thought so too, for he bought and moved to Old Dominion Plantation shortly before the Civil War, leaving management of the Farm to a young relative or an overseer. His other two plantations were Maxcy Place and Bailey's Island (above).[412]

William Mikell Bailey (1817–1868) was a physician as well as a planter, at a time when that was not uncommon. His wife was Julia L. Graham (1821–1860). He served at one time as a vestryman of Trinity Episcopal Church. His medical degree was from the University of Pennsylvania in Philadelphia,[413] which may account for his unorthodox (by Southern standards) political views. How much medicine he practiced on Edisto is not clear, for Dr. Bailey was not a popular man. His politics made many on Edisto cordially dislike him, and others not so cordially: "[Dr. Bailey] was consistently opposed to secession, and made speeches in opposition to it, and…was threatened with personal violence by the Inhabitants of Edisto Island on account of [his] Union sentiments."[414]

Those sentiments also made Bailey a natural political ally of his near neighbor, Governor Aiken of Jehossee, and just as naturally the political opponent of other powerful men on the island, such as Governor Seabrook of Gun Bluff, Joseph Jenkins of Brick House and Major Murray of Jack Daw Hall. Surprisingly, in view of this increasingly polarized opinion, Dr. Bailey was elected to a two-year term in the state legislature in 1852, was reelected in 1854 and, after defeat in 1856, was elected to a third term in 1858. But his opposition to secession apparently ended his political career in 1860.[415]

PROSPECT HILL (60) is one of the best-known and most admired places on Edisto Island today because it has a very old and handsome house that, at this writing, is regularly open to the public. During Edisto's "Golden Age," however, Prospect Hill was one of dozens of reasonably profitable, medium-sized plantations on Edisto. William Grimball Baynard was the proprietor of Prospect Hill and of a satellite plantation on Little Edisto.[416]

Baynard's house faced south on a low rise of land, possibly an ancient sand dune, which commanded a view, or prospect, for several miles down the South Edisto River toward the ocean. Another unusual feature of Prospect Hill is that the entire strip of marsh between the high land and the river—some two hundred yards wide and three quarters of a mile long—had been diked for cultivation.[417] Rice may have been planted originally, but it is now well established that, during the sea-island cotton era, the Baynards (and several other Edisto planters) grew cotton on those reclaimed marshes.[418]

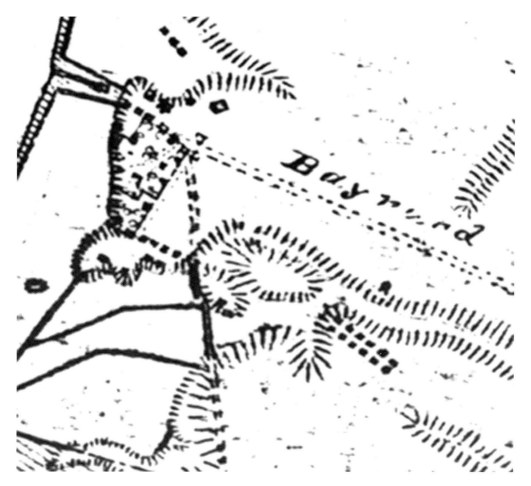

Figure 55. Prospect Hill in 1856. The house stood within a triangular park. Barns were near the bluff at top. Twelve slave cabins formed a double row at right. Extensive dikes, *top and bottom left*, created more cotton fields.

Who designed and who built Prospect Hill house are the subject of considerable speculation. One local historian, Clara Puckette, believed it was built by the first Ephraim Baynard. G.G. Johnson, a scholar at the University of North Carolina writing in 1930, states as a fact, but cites no authority, that it "was built about 1790 and was designed by James Hoban," the architect in 1791 of the White House in Washington, D.C.[419] Prospect Hill certainly is an excellent example of sea island style, with its full above-ground basement, central hall with two rooms on each side upstairs and down and full-width piazza on the front.

William Baynard was born in 1792, graduated from Princeton College in 1812 and was an elder in the Presbyterian Church. His first wife, Ann Jenkins, died young, and his second wife was Mary Bailey Swinton. When he died in 1861 he left Prospect Hill to his three sons, William G. Jr., James S. and Henry H. Baynard.[420]

The next plantation north of Prospect Hill was RIVERSIDE (61), the home of Ephraim Clark Bailey, containing 489 acres exclusive of marsh. The plantation had no deep water landing of its own, and probably carted its cotton two miles to Pine Landing. The house no longer exists, and no picture of it has been found.[421]

The southern section of Riverside, about 300 acres, had been in the Bailey family for at least three generations, and probably much longer. This land almost certainly derives from some of the small grants along the South Edisto to Henry Bailey between 1695 and 1700 (see above, "The Farm"). By 1804 Ralph Bailey IV owned the three hundred acres. His son, Charles Bailey, inherited the plantation, and on his death in 1836 passed it to his son Ephraim. In 1857, Ephraim Bailey substantially increased his planting by purchasing the 189-acre adjoining tract on the north from the estate of John Hanahan. On both this new tract and on part of the old tract, Bailey planted cotton on fields like Prospect Hill's, reclaimed from the marsh right out to the South Edisto.[422]

Ephraim Clark Bailey was born in 1832 and graduated from The Citadel in 1851. Like his older brother, Dr. William Bailey (above, "The Farm"), he was active in the Episcopal church. In 1854, Ephraim married Charlotte Porcher Edings (1834–1909) and settled in as a moderately wealthy planter. In time they would have five children.[423]

The last plantation in the northwest corner of Edisto Island proper was OLD DOMINION (62), home of another of Edisto's legendary characters, Edward Charles Whaley (1790–1860). Old Dominion had 950 acres of land and marsh, but only 350 of those acres were "arable land," and much of that was located on and between an archipelago of islands in the marsh, some cleared and linked by dikes, some not. Old Dominion was not a compact, efficient plantation, but it had excellent water transportation access and apparently was productive.[424]

Part of the good land of Old Dominion, 224 acres, derived from two small grants: 180 acres to Henry Bailey in 1698 and 44 acres to John Hayne in 1714. Bailey conveyed his grant to Mark Matthewes who sold it to John Hayne in 1706. Hayne combined the two tracts and sold them in 1736 to Ralph Bailey, who sold them in 1757 to John Calder, who willed them to his son Archibald, who registered them in 1767. These 224 acres probably are the southern side of the plantation, on the "mainland" of Edisto Island. The history of the remainder of Old Dominion has not surfaced.[425]

Edward C. Whaley married Abigail Mikell Baynard about 1820. She lived only ten more years, but she bore six sons and one daughter who lived to marry and have children. Tradition has it that Whaley was so wealthy that he was able to give each of his children a plantation when they married.[426] Whether or not that was literally true, it certainly helped to have a wealthy father. By the late 1850s, each child but one was comfortably situated on a different plantation.[427]

The Old Dominion settlement was on the south side of the plantation, near the public road. Slave cabins were scattered in twos and threes nearby. The big wharf nearby on the South Edisto River, called Pine Landing, was on Whaley's land but probably was used, by long custom, as a public landing for all the plantations on the northwestern corner of Edisto Island. Moreover, a causeway ran north along the river's edge from Pine Landing to Jehossee Plantation (below). This was in fact the only land approach that Jehossee Island has ever had, and it probably generated its share of human, animal and wheeled traffic up and down Pine Landing Road. Thus Old Dominion, which looks rather isolated at first glance, probably had steady traffic near its front door in all seasons.[428]

At some point in the 1850s, Whaley sold Old Dominion to a neighbor, Dr. William M. Bailey, who promptly moved his family there, for the federal surveyors put his name on it in 1856, and Bailey was living there when the census was taken in 1860. Whaley probably moved back to his Home Place next door, and he died in 1860.[429]

HOME PLACE (63) lay immediately east of Old Dominion Plantation. In 1700, Thomas Rake had been granted about three hundred acres, and in 1709 he got two hundred acres adjoining the first tract, both bounded on the north by Russell Creek. Thomas Rake Jr. registered ownership of these parcels in 1732.[430]

Ownership later passed to Archibald Calder, who owned Old Dominion and several other tracts from Bailey's Island to Little Edisto. Calder died in 1777 and left this plantation to his son Archibald John Calder, who sold it in 1798 to Thomas Crawford. John Diamond resurveyed the land for Crawford and found that the original 516 acres were actually 419 acres. Most of the land was still (or re-) forested, and no dwelling was shown. The Rakes almost certainly had lived there (Chapter 2), but their house was gone by 1799.[431]

When the federal surveyors came to this part of Edisto in 1856, they recorded the owner as "Whaley." The only road from Edisto to Little Edisto ran due north through this plantation. Edward Whaley of Old Dominion called this his Home Place; it may have been where his branch of the Whaley family grew up. (Later it was called Red Top and, still later, in the twentieth century, Hopkinson's.) When Edward bought and moved to Old Dominion, probably about the time he married in 1821, he continued to plant the Home Place for extra income. But when his son Benjamin J. Whaley married, about 1850, Edward apparently gave him the Home Place as a wedding gift. Benjamin became a successful attorney and lived mainly in Charleston, but the Home Place supplemented his income and provided a second home on the island, near all the relatives. At least three quarters of the land was cleared for planting in 1856.[432]

Edward Mitchell, MD, owned a small plantation of about 240 acres that he called FROGMORE (64). It lay immediately south of Whaley's Home Place and east of Dr. Bailey's Farm. It was all land he had bought from relatives of his wife, Elizabeth Grimball Baynard, shortly after he married into the family in 1812. By 1820 they had built their house at Frogmore.[433] It was an unpretentious but solid two-story frame house with cypress siding, which traditionally is left unpainted to weather to a deep gray. The house still stands today.

Edward Mitchell (1788–1855) was the son of a rice planter near Georgetown, South Carolina, and was a medical graduate of the University of Pennsylvania. "Eliza" was a sister of the prosperous and influential William G. Baynard of Prospect Hill. Her mother was a Mikell, her grandmothers were a Grimball and a Calder and one of her great-grandmothers was a Bailey. Edward and Eliza raised six children at Frogmore, effectively founding the Mitchell clan on Edisto Island, and were active members of Trinity Episcopal Church. (Both are buried there.) In the 1840s, Edward and Eliza

Mitchell moved permanently to Charleston, leaving overseers to manage Frogmore and two other plantations (below). When Dr. Mitchell died in 1855, his executors sold Frogmore to his son-in-law, William J. Whaley (1819–1888), who had married Rachel Mitchell. Whaley purchased the adjoining 100 acres called "Ballard's," which brought Frogmore up to the more efficient size of 350 acres. Ballard's apparently filled the angle between the public roads known today as Pine Landing and Laurel Hill Roads.[434]

William Whaley planted Frogmore beginning in 1858. He lived in Charleston, where he had a lucrative law practice, handling the land sales, wills and probates of the planter class on the nearby islands. When he bought Frogmore he paid cash to the Edward Mitchell heirs but mortgaged the land to a New Yorker, Mrs. Anna Newbould. And when he bought the Ballard tract, he borrowed the money from his sister-in-law, Abigail Baynard Whaley, who lent him the cash inheritance of her minor children, expecting to get it back with interest by the time the children grew up.[435] Unfortunately for both women, the Civil War intervened, all income from Edisto plantations stopped and lenders waited a long time for their money. But Frogmore stayed in the family, and in 2005 was still owned and occupied by a direct descendant of Edward and Eliza Mitchell. Using 1820 (conservatively) as the building date, Frogmore could claim 185 years of single-family ownership.

Eliza Ann Seabrook lived on a thirty-acre farm, called BETSY SEABROOK'S (65), facing the public road at the northwest corner of Gun Bluff, but closer to Frogmore house. "Miss Betsy" was a half-sister of Louisa, the wife of Colonel Joseph Whaley at Pine Barren (above). Born in 1774, she never married. She was already 76 years old in 1850, and would live on after the Civil War to the ripe old age of 102. Her thirty acres clearly had once been part of Gun Bluff Plantation (below). In 1818, John Raven Mathewes had sold the thirty acres to Trinity Episcopal Church; they had built a house on it and had used it as a parsonage for 25 years. Miss Betsy had bought the house and land from the church in 1843 for $2,010, and had lived there ever since.[436]

Miss Betsy apparently lived alone and contented, assisted by a few slaves who kept her house, tilled her garden and tended her animals. All of her thirty acres were cleared, and in 1860 she reported "raising" two bales of cotton.[437]

GUN BLUFF (66) was the next plantation east from Frogmore along the south side of the public road. With 450 acres of land and access to St. Pierre's Creek from both Shingle Creek and Milton Creek, it was a valuable plantation.[438] It was the seat (but not the only plantation) of Whitmarsh Benjamin Seabrook, who served as governor of South Carolina from 1848 to 1850. He is buried in a small family cemetery at Gun Bluff.[439]

Governor Seabrook was an ardent secessionist during his political career. While a few cooler heads were counseling caution, continued negotiation and political action to advance Southern rights within the Union, Seabrook and others urged decisive action, and preparedness to fight if necessary. Their campaign gradually won over the majority of the public in South Carolina, and when the Secession Convention met in 1860, there was no doubt that secession would result.

Gun Bluff was sold before 1852 to William Edings, a large Edisto planter whose holdings were mostly on the seaside of the island, including Locksley Hall and

Edingsville Beach. He bought Gun Bluff for his younger son, Joseph, since his older son Evans would inherit Locksley Hall. In 1860 Joseph Edings was planting at Gun Bluff, but he was only twenty-three and still unmarried.[440]

Immediately east of Whaley's Home Place along Russell Creek lay Edward Baynard's OLD PLACE (67). With 447 acres, it was about the same size as its neighbor. The 200 acres closest to the creek had been granted to Lewis Price in 1702. Nothing else is known about Price, nor has the original grant of the rest of this plantation been located. Federal surveyors in 1856 put "W. Baynard's" name on Old Place, but it probably was already being planted by his son by that time.[441]

Edward Mitchell Baynard (1830–1882) was a son of William G. Baynard of Prospect Hill and his second wife, Mary Bailey Swinton. Edward married his second cousin, Catherine A.M. Baynard, around 1850, and they probably lived at Old Place from that date. They had four children. Edward's father had bought Old Place "from the estate of J.C. Baynard" and willed it to Edward's children, but provided Edward a "life estate" in it. Edward and Catherine Baynard are buried at the Presbyterian Church on Edisto Island.[442]

BRICK HOUSE (68) on Russell Creek is one of a handful of Edisto places that is known and admired by everyone who is interested in Edisto plantations today. That is partly because of its handsome ruin of a very old brick manor house, shown on every old homes tour. It is also because Brick House has continuity: it has stayed in the Jenkins family—in fact it has symbolized the Edisto branch of the influential Jenkins family—for more than two hundred years.

Like many Edisto plantations, Brick House changed hands many times in the early years. Thomas Sacheverell conveyed it before 1726 to one John Williams, who sold it that year to Paul Hamilton, who registered it in 1733 among nine plantations he then owned on Edisto, James and Johns Islands. Hamilton sought and obtained a grant for the adjoining 181 acres of marshland east of Brick House. Paul Hamilton Jr. inherited both tracts when his father died, and sold them to John McLeod, who lived only a few years longer. McLeod's estate sold the plantation in 1769 to William Maxwell, who still owned it in 1773.[443] Joseph Jenkins bought the house and plantation in 1798, and it has been in the Jenkins family ever since. Joseph and his wife, Elizabeth Evans, lived there for several years, but by 1818 they lived on a much larger plantation near Beaufort. In that year he deeded his Edisto homeplace, now 530 acres, to his oldest son, Joseph.[444]

By 1818 Brick House was already a venerable old house. Its design and construction were unusual for the sea islands (Chapter 2 and Figure 13). Built in 1725 or earlier, it was a symmetrical two-story rectangle in brick with elaborate stucco trim, twin chimneys and a mansard roof. By the 1850s almost all the land was cleared for planting.[445]

Joseph Evans Jenkins (1793–1874) married his first cousin, Ann Jenkins Fripp of St. Helena Island, in 1816. They took over Brick House from his parents and raised eight children there. In 1829 they hosted the gala wedding of Abigail, Joseph's youngest sister, to George Chisolm Mackay. Their son Edward (who would later own Brick House) married Martha Murray, a daughter of Major William Murray of Jack Daw Hall. But Edward's sister Martha married a newcomer, John Cornish, who had moved from Michigan to South Carolina and later became an Episcopal priest.[446]

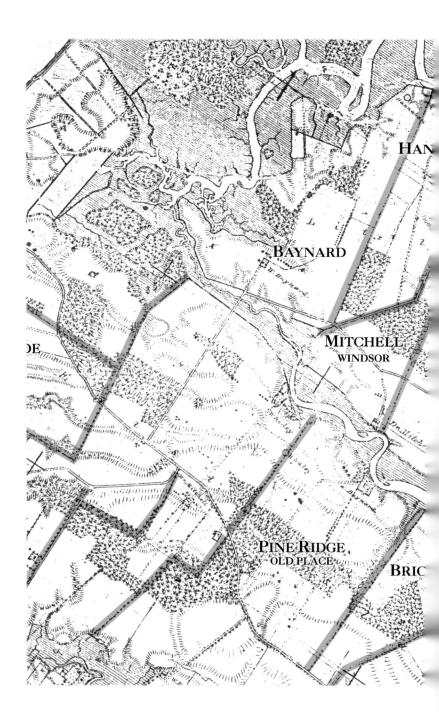

Figure 56.

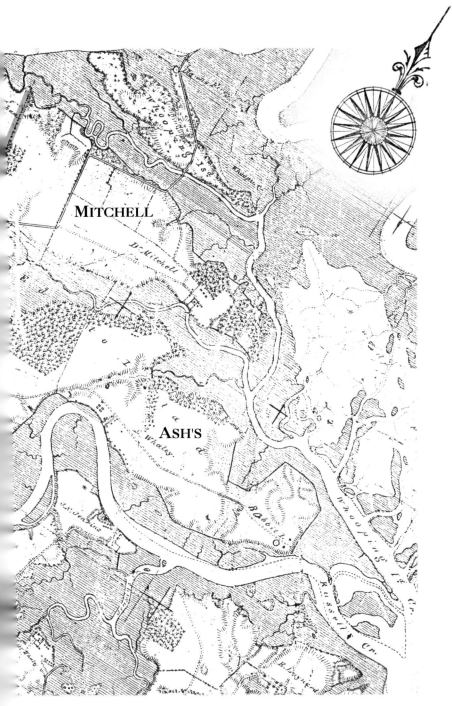

**MITCHELL**

**ASH'S**

LITTLE EDISTO

Joseph E. Jenkins was called Colonel Jenkins from his rank in the South Carolina militia. From 1834 to 1838 he was state senator representing St. John's Colleton, and was active and vocal in the states' rights and pro-secession movements. In 1860, clearly aging, he was a delegate to the South Carolina Secession Convention and signed the Ordinance of Secession (see volume two of this history).[447]

By the 1840s, Colonel Jenkins felt his planting land at Brick House was insufficient for his needs, so he bought Roxbury and neighboring tracts on the nearby mainland, eventually totaling 1,300 acres, and moved to Roxbury in 1845. He continued to plant cotton at Brick House, by then reduced to 325 acres of high ground, but the old house stood empty after 1845, and remained so until after the Civil War.[448]

# Little Edisto

Little Edisto is a two- by four-mile island immediately north of "Big Edisto" that usually is considered part of Edisto Island. The two are separated only by Russell Creek, which at its upper end is not even navigable at high tide. Little Edisto has been the main access route onto Edisto Island in recent history. But before the Civil War, most of Little Edisto was a sparsely populated backwater, valued mainly as extra cotton acreage.

Of the five plantations on Little Edisto and a sixth on Whooping Island, only two were home to a planter family during the "Golden Age." One of those was the MITCHELL PLACE (69). The place known today as Windsor started small. William Whippy was formally granted 140 acres in 1699. Records of intervening owners have not been found, but this tract probably passed through the hands of Archibald Calder in the 1760s, as did most of Little Edisto. Throughout the 1800s and, in fact, as late as 1933, land maps show the core tract still as the same truncated triangle of about 140 acres.[449]

William Whippy had a good eye for land. Like all of Little Edisto, this tract had a protected inland location, but unlike most of Little Edisto, it had a handsome homesite and twenty-four-hour water access on the deep section of Russell Creek.[450]

Though called "Dr. Mitchell" or "Mitchell Place" in at least two contemporary documents,[451] Dr. Edward Mitchell never lived there. He probably owned and planted the land for several decades while he lived nearby at Frogmore (above) and, later, in Charleston. When his son, William G.B. Mitchell, planted his father's extensive lands on Little Edisto in 1849, he may have lived in the overseer's house at Mitchell Place.[452]

Edward Mitchell died in 1855, and his wife Elizabeth died in 1857. Their heirs sold Mitchell Place to Elizabeth's brother, William G. Baynard, then at the height of his prosperity. This prime homesite became a wedding gift from the "squire" of Prospect Hill to his third daughter, Abigail, who had married E. Mikell Whaley just a few months before. The Whaleys built there in 1858, replacing the simple overseer's house with a handsome, two-story, sea island–style house. Later called Windsor, it would stay in the Whaley family until the late twentieth century, and still stands today, beautifully restored.

Meanwhile the groom's wealthy father, Edward Whaley of Old Dominion, deeded his son the adjoining southwest corner of the plantation called Ash's, and eventually bequeathed him all of it. The two plantations, Mitchell's and Ash's, made a natural combination, with a first-class homesite and extensive cotton lands.[453]

Ash's (71) also had a long history. Joseph Russell was granted 570 acres in 1710 on the large peninsula surrounded on three sides by "Marshes & Creeks out of N. Edistoe river." But Russell apparently settled the area even earlier, for his name is on the 1696 map (Figure 11), and the largest creek in that part of Edisto has had his name from the earliest days to the present.

Russell died intestate and his 570 acres "descended to Joseph Ash and Samuel Perronneau as joint tenants." Perronneau sold his half-interest in 1759 to Ash, who willed the entire plantation in 1767 to Richard Cochran Ash Jr., a minor and probably his grandson. The Ash family owned and planted this land for many decades, but in 1831 the estate of John Ash sold it to Edward C. Whaley of Old Dominion. Whaley added to his wealth by planting Ash's for twenty-five years, and then turned it over to his just-married son, Mikell.[454]

The cotton fields of Ash's stretched eastward from Mitchell Place for more than two miles to a place called Rabbit Island, with another deep water landing. Any planter residence the Ashes might once have occupied was gone before the federal surveyors arrived in 1856. About halfway out the peninsula, five barns and a dozen slave cabins were clustered along the banks of Russell Creek. Except for the occasional passing boat, Ash's was one of the most isolated plantations on all of Edisto: its only approach passed through Mitchell Place. But with its hefty size and no resident planter family to support, it may also have been one of the most productive.[455]

Dr. Mitchell of Frogmore also owned a medium-sized plantation on the northeast corner of Little Edisto where, then as now, the Dawhoo Ferry (Bridge) road crossed the last marsh to Whooping Island. Neither Mitchell nor the next owner appears to have given this plantation a name other than LITTLE EDISTO (70) (which was overused).

This solid chunk of land came down from a grant of 430 acres to William Whippy in 1698. In 1728 Whippy split it and deeded the two tracts as gifts to his brothers Joseph (200 acres) and Robert (230 acres), perhaps as encouragement for them to settle near him on Little Edisto. Five years later these lands were still in the Whippy family, but after 1733 the next confirmed sighting was in 1856, when federal surveyors mapped Little Edisto and wrote "Dr. Mitchell" on this plantation.[456]

It is doubtful that boats could get out of this part of narrow little Sand Creek except on a high tide, but so important was water transportation to plantation life in the "Golden Age" that this was better than nothing, and it justified placing the slave settlement in the remotest, most isolated part of the plantation.[457]

Dr. Mitchell probably made a significant portion of his income from this plantation. Ephraim Baynard of Rabbit Point (above) bought it from Mitchell's estate about 1857. Baynard planted it with his three other plantations until Edisto was evacuated in 1861, and he died in 1862.[458]

William Whippy was granted 212 acres on the west side of Little Edisto in 1702. No chain of ownership has been found from this grant down to the 1850s, but almost certainly this tract was the core of what William Grimball Baynard of Prospect Hill

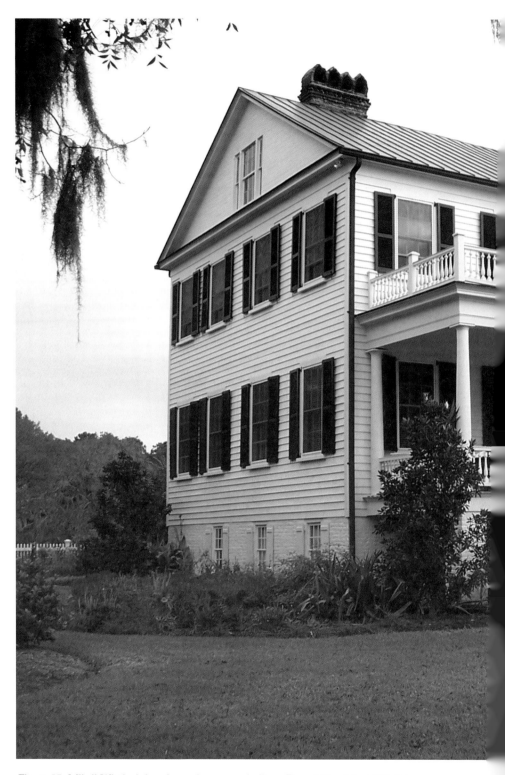

Figure 57. Mikell Whaley's handsome house was built on Russell Creek in 1858. It is now called Windsor. *Photo by Demi Howard, used with permission.*

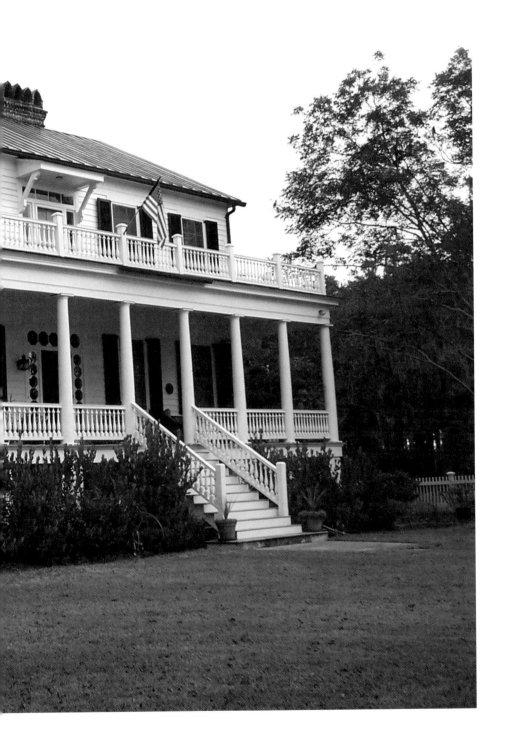

called his LITTLE EDISTO (72) plantation. It appears to have had at least 400 acres, but the history of the additional land is unknown.[459]

Baynard's Little Edisto apparently had a small house for an overseer and four or five barns. The plantation appears to have been L shaped, with several diked fields jutting into the marshes of North Creek. That fact, and sufficient quarters for up to eighty slaves, both suggest an intensive effort to maximize cotton production on this plantation. A cart road led to a deep water landing on North Creek, about a mile above the plantation village.[460]

The second resident proprietor on LITTLE EDISTO (73) was James C. Hanahan. He had a three-hundred-acre tract on which he resided "for very many years" before the Civil War. The land was granted first to Christopher Linkley in 1695, and regranted in 1700 to William Whippy, who paid the quitrent (unpaid taxes). Then this tract, like many on Edisto, changed hands repeatedly. Whippy sold it in 1754 to Ralph Bailey, who sold it in 1756 to Henry Bailey, who sold it in 1762 to John Calder, who willed it to his oldest son Archibald Calder, who registered it and recited all this history in 1767.[461]

No plat of this Hanahan plantation (nor image of the house) has come to light, but we know he had his home at the northwest corner of the tract where it touched deep water on North Creek (today's Intracoastal Waterway), about a mile from its junction with the Dawhoo. The house occupied a fenced garden or park perhaps 150 by 600 feet, which also contained several outbuildings. There was no lane from this settlement east toward the Dawhoo Ferry, which suggests that when Hanahan wanted to get to the mainland, it was simpler to use his own boat on North Creek and leave it at Dawhoo until his return.[462]

In March 1862, while Union troops from Pennsylvania occupied this plantation, they came under attack by Confederate forces, and the sharpest skirmish of the war anywhere on Edisto was fought on James Hanahan's land. (That story is told in detail in volume two of this history). When he died that same year, Hanahan left this plantation to his brother's six sons: Dr. Ralph Bailey Hanahan and J.S., James, H.D., W.S., and E.J.L. Hanahan.[463]

If Little Edisto is the steppingstone to Edisto Island, WHOOPING ISLAND (74) is the steppingstone to Little Edisto, the first high land one touches after crossing the Dawhoo River from the mainland on the way to Edisto.

Thomas Sacheverell sought and received in 1700 the grant of a 217-acre island "bounding on all sides by Creeks [and] Marshes out of Dahoe and North Edisto at their Confluence." Sacheverell kept it most of his life, then sold it in 1749 to Joseph Ash, who willed it to John Ash. In 1767 it was still in the Ash family and John was still a minor, so it was registered that year by his father, Richard Cochran Ash, a landholder on nearby Little Edisto.[464] There is a strong and consistent tradition down the centuries that Whooping Island takes its name from the ferry at Dawhoo River, whose attention one had to attract from the opposite shore, a quarter mile away, by sheer lung power. There is no reason to doubt that tradition.[465]

Whooping Island apparently never was planted during the 1700s and 1800s, because it is shown on the 1857 map as mostly wooded, with no houses and no owner's name.

The island's most important function was to support the road from Edisto and Little Edisto to the Dawhoo Ferry.[466]

# Jehossee Island

William Aiken's JEHOSSEE (75) was an enormous plantation; there is no other word for it. When fully developed with Pon Pon's vast marshes diked for rice planting in the mid-nineteenth century, it measured two miles from Watt's Cut on the south to the water mill on the northern edge, and four and a half miles from east to west. It contained 665 acres of high land, and more than 4,000 acres in all, including vast rice fields and salt marshes.

Jehossee was, of course, an island and, in many ways, a little world unto itself. A huge bowtie bend of the South Edisto River enfolds Jehossee on the west. The Dawhoo River separates it from the mainland on the north, and the meandering North Creek and Watt's Cut separate it from Little Edisto and Big Edisto on the east and south. There has never been a bridge to Jehossee from the mainland. Its only dry link to another community was a series of flimsy wagon bridges and pontoon bridges across Watt's Cut in the nineteenth century. Jehossee is included in this history of Edisto because of that tenuous land link and because, repeatedly, the fates of the two islands have been lumped together by politicians, generals and other historians.

The high land of Jehossee Island is relatively modest in size, but it caught the attention of settlers very early in Carolina's history, probably because of its location. Even before any of the land was granted, it appears to have been settled—possibly by Indians.[467]

Robert Fenwick was granted two parcels totaling 275 acres on "Jehossie Island" in 1694. Fenwick, however, was more interested in the much larger island west of Pon Pon River that bears his name to this day, and he sold his Jehossee grant within days to one Daniel Courtice (Curtis?). Three years later Courtice secured the grant of the remaining 390 acres "on Jehoshua," which included the old "Chehasah" settlement. The delay in granting the more valuable portion of Jehossee may have arisen, as with Bleak Hall (above), from a colonial policy of giving the Indians time to move, if in fact they had a village there. Courtice died shortly after receiving this second grant and his widow, Elizabeth, sold the entire 665 acres to James Cockran in 1701. Cockran's son, also James Cockran, registered his ownership in 1733.[468]

Cockran settled on Jehossee sometime after 1701, and for a long time the place was known as Cockran's Island. It was a well-known stopping place for inland waterway travelers during those pre-industrial times when slow communication made it socially acceptable to stop overnight without advance notice. If a place were isolated, as Cockran's Island surely was, the visitors also provided welcome relief from boredom, and news of the outside world.

We know of one such traveler who visited Cockran in 1733 because the traveler was famous. He was General James Oglethorpe, founder of the Georgia colony, which was just getting started then.[469] The following item appeared in the *South Carolina Gazette*, dated Charles Town, June 2:

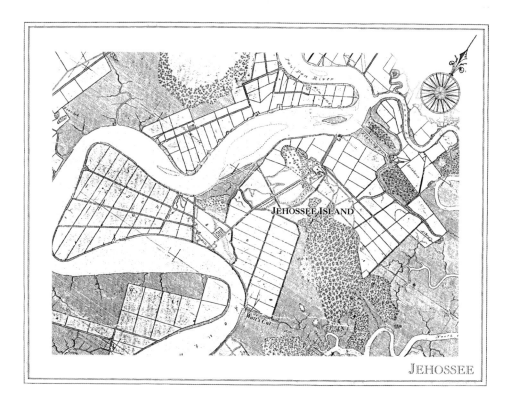

Figure 58.

*Mr. Oglethorpe, set out from hence on the 14th of May, and lay at Col. Bull's house on Ashley River, where he dined the next day…Mr. Oglethorpe, from thence, went by land to Capt. Bull's [at Toogoodoo], where he lay the 15th. On the 16th in the Morning, he embarked at Daho, and rested at Mr. Cochran's Island. On the 17th dined at Lieutenant Watts's at Beaufort, and landed at Savannah on the 18th, at ten in the Morning.*[470]

Cockran probably raised cattle at first, for islands were naturally suited and much coveted for that. Cockran also began actively developing and expanding his Jehossee plantation by diking the marshes, as the 1741 plat clearly indicates. He probably began to raise rice on a small scale, but that is supposition; his plantation records have not been found. The unusual river hydrology that favored rice growing at Jehossee was just being discovered in Cockran's time, and is described in Chapter 4.

James Cockran Jr. died in 1739 and his heirs sold the 665 acres. Meanwhile, in 1741, the crown granted 3,500 acres at Jehossee to one Paul Jenys, and each of his two sons inherited a moiety (half-interest) in this huge tract. It appears to have included all the remaining area not owned by Cockran. Thus, by the mid-1700s, Jehossee Plantation totaled more than 4,000 acres. Multiple conveyances of the Cockran and Jenys lands occurred between 1742 and 1830. Parts of Jehossee passed through the hands of owners named Ash, Peronneau, Gibbes, Middleton, Izard, Maxwell, Drayton and Milliken. By 1830, however, William Aiken Jr. owned all of Jehossee, which was then estimated at 4,700 acres.[471]

William Aiken must have worked himself and his slaves steadily for the next twenty-six years to improve and expand rice production at Jehossee, for in 1856 he presided over a huge, complex operation that simply had to be seen to be believed. Headquarters, including Aiken's house, a manager's house, a steam-powered rice mill and at least a dozen other farm buildings, were located on the high ground where Cockran's house had stood, near the north end of the plantation. A wooded park of several acres was set aside just for the pleasure of Aiken and his guests. A wheel turned by the water flowing in a canal could mill rice or grind cornmeal, but only when the gates were open to flood the rice fields. It was probably the oldest mill on the plantation, and became more or less obsolete when Aiken later installed two steam-powered rice mills, whose boilers were fired by wood.[472]

The plantation was so large and distances were so great that hundreds of worker hours could be saved each day just by reducing the distance that field hands had to walk to get to their "tasks." So Aiken had two separate slave villages, one for the eastern fields and one for those in the west. Most of the high ground was cleared for planting provisions, mainly corn and sweet potatoes. Pigs, cattle, poultry and a dairy herd certainly were provided for somewhere on the plantation. Perhaps two hundred acres of high ground on the southeast side of the plantation had been left in trees, for wood was an essential resource for heating the houses and cabins, and for firing the boilers of the two rice mills.

The road from Jehossee to Edisto Island ran southeast from the "summer house," along the top of a dike that separated rice fields from a bend of the South Edisto River. After three quarters of a mile it came to Watt's Cut, which was the plantation boundary. In those days the cut was neither wide nor deep. A light wooden bridge, probably wide enough for a carriage or cart, led across to another causeway down to Edisto Island's Pine Landing. At times during the Civil War and perhaps at other times as well, the bridge rested on pontoons that could be untied and pushed aside for a boat to pass, and then tied back in place. Even though the alternative route from North to South Edisto Rivers via the Dawhoo River remained available, it is clear that Watt's Cut was an active waterway as early as the 1700s. The 1741 plat of Jehossee labels North Creek "the thoro faire from Dawhoe river to Wat's Cut."

The amount of human labor that went into building and maintaining Jehossee Plantation was far greater per acre than on cotton plantations where, typically, one just cut down the forest, worked around the stumps and prepared the ground for planting. Once it was done, it was done. Here, one first had to build dikes around the perimeter—one basket- or cartload of earth at a time. After the salt water was drained out and the marshland dried somewhat, one had to dig the network of primary and secondary canals, piling the mud on both sides to keep the fresh water in the canals until it reached where it needed to be released on the fields. (Jehossee had at least two secondary freshwater intakes along the riverbank, in addition to the main one at the north end of the plantation.) Canals had to be fitted with brick or wooden gates called trunks, to channel the water where it was needed within the complex of canals. Finally, the broad fields between canals were further divided by interior dikes into a checkerboard of smaller fields or tasks, which could be selectively flooded and drained by opening trunks on the canals. It took months or years of construction work before a new section of marsh could be planted.

And when all this was done, there was constant maintenance. Canals periodically had to be drained and the silt dug out by shovel to keep them deep enough to flow well. Dikes and the roads on top of them were damaged by storms and had to be rebuilt. Bridges across the canals wore out and had to be repaired. Firewood had to be cut in the plantation forest and stockpiled at the mills to keep the boilers running during rice harvest season.

Jehossee repaid Aiken his large investments of money and slave labor many times over. Years later he told an interviewer that for several years before the Civil War he had grossed $70,000 a year from Jehossee's rice, of which $50,000 a year was profit. Those were huge sums for that period.[473]

William Aiken was born in 1806, graduated from South Carolina College in 1825 and married Harriet Lowndes in 1831. After terms in the South Carolina House and Senate, he was elected governor in 1844, but the rapidly growing secession sentiment during the 1850s limited his influence: Aiken defended slavery but opposed secession. He served in the U.S. House of Representatives from 1851 to 1856, but as opinion became increasingly polarized, his political career ended.[474]

Aiken lived in Charleston during the unhealthy summer months, but in the fall and winter he resided at Jehossee and personally managed the plantation. A Northern visitor in 1844, who preferred to remain anonymous, wrote a long description of a visit to Jehossee for the Charleston *Courier*, in which he gave a physical description of the plantation and commented on it, displaying the attitudes and prejudices of that time. Here is what he wrote about the accommodations and treatment of the seven to eight hundred slaves at Jehossee in 1844:[475]

> *The houses are of uniform size and contain four apartments* [rooms] *each; with double fireplaces of brick. Attached to every house is a small garden and yard in front. The slaves are required to cultivate their gardens—and in every yard there is a poultry house and other buildings. All the houses are kept neatly whitewashed inside and out, and the strictest and most constant cleanliness is required...*
>
> *The plantation has a commodious and well arranged hospital, to which every sick negro is carried, and attended to during his sickness....Nurses are always in attendance and a skillful physician is yearly employed...In the same building is a large hall for invalids...Care is taken that no negro is permitted to "play sick", while equal care is taken that every real ailment is promptly and kindly attended to...*
>
> *...Their weekly allowance is measured out to them, in the best, and most wholesome grist. This with other articles of food such as meat, potatoes, etc., they cook for themselves...The food of the children, however, is cooked for them by nurses, who attend them during the absence of the parents at a building called the nursery. I never saw a finer looking set of negroes anywhere.*

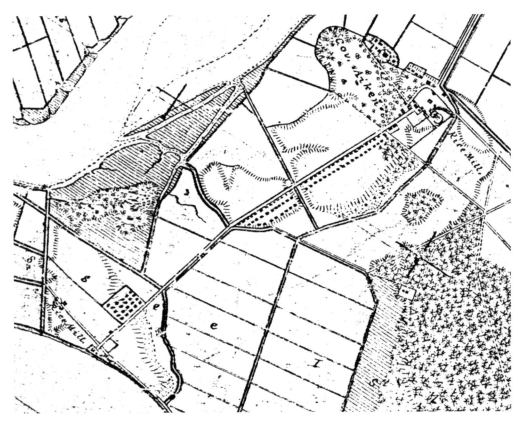

Figure 59. Jehossee Plantation in 1856. Black square inside a small circle near "Gov. Aiken" was his residence. Manager's house stood in open field near upper rice mill. "Summer house" faced the river inside the tiny square, *bottom left*.

> *...On his plantation* [Mr. Aiken] *has a neat chapel at which religious services are performed semi-monthly by a minister employed for the purpose. Every slave is compelled to attend and each is orally instructed and catechized by the minister. Marriages are performed according to religious rites, and a Christian code of morals is strictly enjoined upon the slaves in their intercourse with each other. More than one-half of the negroes on the place are communicants of the church...There is not to be found in all the country around, any body of negroes more orderly, well behaved, or contented. They look well, work well, and more than all, work with a cheerfulness which no one can fail to observe who visits the place.*

This visitor thought Aiken's good treatment of his slaves was good business: "For extent, excellent management, and productiveness, [Jehossee Plantation] is not surpassed by any other within the State." He also drew a patriotic conclusion: "[Mr. Aiken] has not talked of what he could do for Carolina but has done it."

Of course, since we do not have similarly recorded observations from the workers on Aiken's land, we do not know what their conclusion or commentary might have been.

# POSTSCRIPT

Not only Edisto Island's "Golden Age," but Edisto Island as all its people had known it for 168 years, ended abruptly in 1861. The Civil War changed almost everything.

The war itself did not catch anyone on Edisto by surprise. Planters, slave owners and their families followed the newspapers closely. Several were politically well connected. They knew a war was coming, and most of them welcomed it. The African American slaves, who outnumbered whites more than nine to one, had fewer sources of "news," but their informal channels of communication must have been humming with information, and they could discern major events in the offing. They, too, welcomed it, of course for different reasons.

It is safe to say, though, that everyone was taken by surprise at the way these events played out. Few whites had any inkling that their beloved Confederate government would decide, as a matter of cold military strategy, that it not only would not defend Edisto Island, but would force some of the state's richest and most influential planters to evacuate the island almost overnight. Few African Americans dared to hope that within a matter of weeks, they and their children and grandchildren would effectively be free of slavery for all time. No one could have foreseen the physical devastation that would come to Edisto's plantations and infrastructure, partly from wanton malice and greed, but mostly from neglect, during three and a half years as part of "no man's land." The long decades of Reconstruction and economic stagnation that followed the Civil War throughout the South, including Edisto Island, were simply beyond the imaginings of even the most radical Northern abolitionists.

The complete story of Edisto Island from South Carolina's secession in December 1860 to the end of the twentieth century is told in the second volume of this history. The History Press will publish it shortly after the release of this first volume. Its title is *Ruin, Recovery and Rebirth*. Here is the first page of that book.

# Chapter 1. The Civil War on Edisto

The war came late on Edisto Island, as the chill, wet winds in November 1861 began to blow across the marshes. By then the cotton crop—a good year for cotton, ironically—was mostly picked and partly ginned, baled and waiting in the barns for shipment to Charleston by steamer. The planters were pushing their slaves hard. They wanted that money in the bank, and they knew time was not on their side. The war had bypassed them for seven months, but they must have realized it could not do so much longer. Even so, when the war came home, the way it came was a shock.

## Secession "At Last"

The Edisto delegate, Colonel Joseph E. Jenkins, a white-bearded old curmudgeon, had stood up in the Secession Convention in Charleston and said, "If South Carolina won't secede, Edisto Island will."[476] This was not just rhetoric; it was a threat. Secession sentiment was not unanimous among planters on Edisto, but it was overwhelming, and most thought the state government had waited far too long already.

One famous holdout was former Governor William Aiken, the rice planter on Jehossee and owner of some seven hundred African slaves, who was wealthy beyond most people's comprehension.[477] People like him had no love for the Yankees but doubted the South could win a war, and he was willing to test Mr. Lincoln's implied promise that if the secessionists would give him time to work something out, he would not touch slavery in the Southern states.

South Carolina's politicians, in the end, needed no prodding from Joseph Jenkins. They voted overwhelmingly on December 20 to secede, followed shortly by Mississippi, Florida, Alabama, Georgia, Louisiana and Texas.[478] Despite secession and theoretical independence from the United States, life on Edisto proceeded for eleven months with only surface changes.

## The Drums of Not-So-Distant War

One thing led to another in slow motion after secession. Charleston eventually proved to be not only a hotbed of "fire-eaters" leading the way to secession, but also the tinderbox needed to start the conflagration.

U.S. Army Major Robert Anderson commanded the small federal garrison at Fort Moultrie on Sullivan's Island. Feeling beleaguered and vulnerable there, he moved his men under cover of darkness in late December 1860 out to Fort Sumter, an isolated island in the harbor. The South Carolinians promptly stopped his local supply boats. By early April the Sumter garrison was very low on food, but Major Anderson still refused to come out. Confederate General Pierre G.T. Beauregard, a Louisianian commanding in Charleston, finally gave the Federals an ultimatum: surrender Sumter, or he would force them out with artillery fire. They wouldn't, and he did.

Most Edisto planters and their families cheered when Citadel cadets and other batteries fired on Fort Sumter, and when, after a brave but brief resistance, the Federal garrison surrendered on April 13, 1861.[479] Virginia, Arkansas, Tennessee and North Carolina seceded after Fort Sumter.

On Edisto Island that summer, farming proceeded as usual. Owners and overseers rode horseback from field to field, day after day, checking on progress and urging greater activity. Corn, potatoes, yams, rice and other provision crops were harvested as usual. In August the cotton bolls began to split open, and whole fields began to show white.

# NOTES

CHAPTER 1

1. Laylon W. Jordan and Elizabeth H. Stringfellow, *A Place Called St. John's* (Spartanburg, SC: The Reprint Company, 1998), 5.

2. The following description of the formation of Edisto Island and Edisto Beach is based, except where otherwise noted, on Richard D. Porcher and Sarah Fick, *The Story of Sea Island Cotton* (Charleston: Wyrick Press, 2005), 1–24.

3. Thomas D. Matthews, et. al., *Ecological Characterization of the Sea Island Coastal Region of South Carolina and Georgia: Volume I, Physical Features of the Characterization Area* (Charleston: Marine Resources Division of the South Carolina Wildlife and Marine Resources Department, manuscript, 1980), 76.

4. Ibid., 67. These measurements date from 1980.

5. The erosion and narrowing of Edingsville Beach was noted by a naturalist as early as 1857. See Lewis R. Gibbes, "Botany of Edings Bay," in *Proceedings of the Elliott Society*, 1857, reprinted in *South Carolina Naturalists*, David Taylor (Columbia: University of South Carolina Press, 1998), 174.

6. Author interview with John G. Murray III, DVM, July 29, 2007.

7. Richard D. Porcher and Douglas A. Rayner, *A Guide to the Wildflowers of South Carolina* (Columbia: University of South Carolina Press, 2001), 11.

8. Ibid., 357.

9. *Cosmopolitan World Atlas* (Chicago: Rand McNally, 1987), 142–43

10. Porcher and Rayner, *Wildflowers of South Carolina*, 83.

11. Ibid., 352.

12. Telephone interview with Richard D. Porcher, February 6, 2004; Porcher and Rayner, *Wildflowers of South Carolina*, 89–90.

13. Porcher and Rayner, *Wildflowers of South Carolina*, 95.

14. Ibid., 102–04, 343–57.

15. Porcher and Fick, *Story of Sea Island Cotton*, 15.

16. Porcher and Rayner, *Wildflowers of South Carolina*, 356.

17. Ibid., 105–06, 361–64. Field botany on this site was done jointly by Porcher and Patrick McMillan, now curator of the Herbarium at Clemson University.

18. Robert Mackintosh and Tim Belshaw, "Big Game Hunting the Archival Way; Robert Mackintosh Uncovers a Goldmine of Prehistory at Edisto Beach," *Acid-Free News*, SCDAH Publications Division, Columbia, 1997. See also, *Encyclopedia of Prehistory*, London: The Diagram Group, 2002, 113.

19. John Lawson, "The Beasts of Carolina," in *A New Voyage to Carolina...* (London, 1709), excerpted in *South Carolina Naturalists*, 12–21.

20. John Edwards Holbrook, "Alligator Mississipiens," from *North American Herpetology*, 1842, excerpted in *South Carolina Naturalists*, 132.

21. This overview of South Carolina's indigenous people follows Charles F. Kovacik and John J. Winberry, *South Carolina: A Geography* (Boulder, CO: Westview Press, 1987), 51–63, except where otherwise noted.

22. Jordan and Stringfellow, *A Place Called St. John's*, 19.

23. Ibid., 61–62; Robert Sandford, "A Relation of a Voyage on the Coast of the Province of Carolina, 1666," transcribed and edited by A.S. Salley in *Narratives of Early Carolina*, 1911, reprinted in *A Place Called St. John's*, 293–303.

24. Jesuit Father Juan Rogel, who lived among the Orista (Edisto) in 1570, quoted in Jerald T. Milanich, *Laboring in the Fields of the Lord: Spanish Missions and Southeastern Indians* (Washington, D.C.: Smithsonian Institution Press, 1999), 103.

25. Sandford, "Relation of a Voyage," 301.

26. When the English first visited the Edisto village (Chapter 2), the first night's ceremonies were presided over by "a Female [probably the cacique's wife] who received them with gladnes and Courtesy." Sandford, "Relation of a Voyage," 300.

27. Ibid., 300.

28. Father Rogel's mission is summarized from Milanich, *Laboring in the Fields of the Lord*, 83–103.

29. William Hilton, "A Relation of a Discovery Lately Made on the Coast of Florida...1663," summarized in J. Ralph Randolph, *British Travelers Among the Southern Indians, 1660–1773* (Norman: University of Oklahoma Press, 1973), 29.

30. Randolph, *British Travelers*, 30–31.

31. Sandford's visit to Edisto Island is from his "Relation of a Voyage," 298–303.

32. Jordan and Stringfellow, *A Place Called St. John's*, 21.

33. Kovacik and Winberry, *A Geography*, 60.

34. Lawrence S. Rowland, Alexander Moore and George C. Rogers Jr., *The History of Beaufort County, South Carolina: Volume I, 1514–1861* (Columbia: University of South Carolina Press, 1996), 11.

35. This summary of Indian survivor communities in South Carolina is from Kovacik and Winberry, *A Geography*, 62–63.

36. Nicholas Lindsay, ed., *And I'm Glad: An Oral History of Edisto Island* (Charleston: Tempus Publishing, 2000), 81.

37. Herb McAmis, "Indian People of the Edisto River: A Brief History of the Kusso-Natchez Indians, Often Called 'Edistos'," pamphlet, self-published by Edisto Tribal Council, Inc., n.d. (circa 1990), 3.

38. Wesley DuRant Taukchiray and Alice Bee Kasakoff, "Contemporary Native Americans in South Carolina," in *Indians of the Southeastern United States in the Late 20th Century*, ed. J. Anthony Paredes (Tuscaloosa: University of Alabama Press, 1992), 91–95.

39. McAmis, "Indian People of the Edisto River," 25–33.

## CHAPTER 2

40. Walter Edgar, *South Carolina: A History* (Columbia: University of South Carolina Press), 1998, 21–34.

41. Events leading to the founding of Charles Towne are from Edgar, *South Carolina*, 35–48, except where otherwise noted.

42. "Charles II," *Encyclopedia Britannica* (Chicago: William Benton, 1960), vol. 5, 269–71.

43. Edgar, *South Carolina*, 47–51.

44. H.A.M. Smith, a noted scholar of early Carolina history, believed that Lord Ashley's plan to lay out a town on the landward side of Edisto Island, though never implemented, was the origin of the local custom of calling this neighborhood "The Borough." Henry A.M. Smith, "The Baronies of South Carolina," *The South Carolina Historical and Genealogical Magazine* 11, no. 2 (April 1910), 81–84.

45. Ibid.; S.C. Dept. of Archives and History, Columbia, Royal Grants, vol. 38, 204–06. Some historians have interpreted the 1675 treaty as conveying Edisto Island to the English for "a valuable parcel of Cloth, Hatchetts, Brads and other goods and Manufactures." The author doubts this interpretation, and believes Edisto Island was not "purchased" until 1683 (see below). "Cassoe" in the 1675 treaty was an alternate spelling of Coosah, a sub-tribe of the Cusabos then living on the mainland, not the islands (Figure 8). The confusion over the 1675 treaty seems to have arisen because of Lord Ashley's well-documented instruction to purchase a huge tract for his barony on Locke Island, and to treat the Indians residing there kindly and fairly. Andrew Percivall followed the spirit, but not the letter, of this instruction. The text of this treaty is in *Documents on Edisto Island History*.

46. The dowager "queen" and the young cacique of the Edisto Indians signed the treaty in February 1683 along with caciques and captains of eight related tribes in the Lowcountry. This treaty appears to have paved the way for Grimball's 1683 land grant, and the prospect of many more on Edisto Island. The Indians agreed to yield all their rights to the islands in perpetuity, in exchange for one hundred pounds in English money. A partial text of this treaty is in *Documents on Edisto Island History*.

47. Mabel L. Webber, "Grimball of Edisto Island," *The South Carolina Historical and Genealogical Magazine* 23, in three parts: no. 1 (January 1922), 1–7; no. 2 (April 1922), 39–45; no. 3 (July 1922), 94–101; SCDAH, Land Memorials, vol. 1, 62–63 (March 31, 1722, Thomas Grimball). See also "Abstracts of Land Memorials on Edisto Island in the 1700s" in *Documents on Edisto Island History*.

48. Tabby was made by baking or burning oyster shell to get lime, then mixing equal parts of lime and crushed shells with water. (*Standard Dictionary of the English Language, International Edition*, New York: Funk and Wagnalls Co., 1960.) It made a surprisingly hard and durable masonry.

A portion of Grimball's walls have been destroyed by river beach erosion, but about half were still standing in 2003, after more than three hundred years. The ruin is on private property, and can be visited only with permission of the owner.

49. Jordan and Stringfellow, *A Place Called St. John's*, 30.

50. Edgar, *South Carolina*, 58.

51. While Morton clearly had a close association with Edisto Island, the author is inclined to doubt that he ever had a home on the island. The evidence, pro and con, is summarized in *Documents on Edisto Island History*.

52. Occupying the land before acquiring a grant was fairly common. Robert K. Ackerman, *South Carolina Colonial Land Policies* (Columbia: University of South Carolina Press (published for the South Carolina Tricentennial Commission), 1974), 96.

53. Charles H. Lesser, "Secretary Paul Grimball, The Sothell Coup D'etat, and the William Dunlop Papers," in *South Carolina Begins: The Records of a Proprietary Colony, 1663–1721* (Columbia: SCDAH, 1995), 143.

54. Isabella G. Leland, "Ancient Seal All That Remains of 1685 Colony of Stuart Town," *Charleston News and Courier*, March 29, 1985.

55. Leland, "Stuart Town"; Jordan and Stringfellow, *A Place Called St. John's*, 31.

56. Leland, "Stuart Town."

57. This sketch of Paul Grimball's life in South Carolina is drawn from Lesser, "Paul Grimball," 138–48, except where otherwise noted.

58. Paul Grimball was both secretary of the colony and receiver and escheator. (Lesser, "Paul Grimball," 138.) The latter two positions dealt with real estate and tangible property that reverted to the state under certain circumstances.

59. By tradition, Paul Grimball was buried by his family on the southern section of his Edisto plantation, the part now known as Swallow Bluff. The exact location has been lost. Chalmers S. Murray, "Side Tour of Edisto Island," unpublished Federal Writers Project manuscript, circa 1936, in his Papers (1178) at the South Carolina Historical Society.

60. Lesser, "Paul Grimball," 146.

61. Webber, "Grimball," 3–7, 39–45.

62. Lesser, "Paul Grimball," 139, 147.

63. Webber, "Grimball," 3–4; Joseph L. Rivers, *Seven South Carolina Low Country Families: Bailey, Clark, Grimball, Jenkins, Seabrook, Townsend, and Whaley* (self-published, revised and reprinted 1999), G-1. Rivers says Hamilton's service in the SC Commons House of Assembly began in 1697; Webber says 1695, which is consistent with Lesser.

64. See, for example, Clara Childs Puckette, *Edisto: A Sea Island Principality* (Cleveland, OH: Seaforth, 1978), 4; Jordan and Stringfellow, *A Place Called St. John's*, 31. The latter say this Paul Hamilton was Paul Grimball's son-in-law, but Mabel Webber, whom this writer relies on, makes clear he was Paul Grimball's grandson.

65. Webber, "Grimball," 3.

66. Governor Paul Hamilton wrote that his uncle "built a Mansion House on Edisto Island on his Upper Plantation (now in possession of Joseph Jenkins)." The quotation about the earlier Paul Hamilton's character is from the same source, quoted in William G. Albergotti III, *Abigail's*

*Story: Tides at the Doorstep: The Mackays, LaRoches, Jenkinses, and Chisolms of Low Country South Carolina, 1671–1897* (Spartanburg, SC: The Reprint Company, 1999), 361.

67. Albergotti, *Abigail's Story*, 359–65. His analysis of the available documents on the early ownership of Brick House and its land is meticulous and cautious. His "posit" is moderately persuasive to the present writer, but it remains to be proven. Another expert also states that Brick House was built prior to 1703: Harriet K. Leiding, *Historic Houses of South Carolina* (New York: Lippincott, 1921).

68. The 1732 tax list is transcribed in *Documents on Edisto Island History*. The original is at the New York Public Library, and a copy is at South Carolina Department of Archives and History, Private Papers, Box 8.

69. Archibald Calder's several plantations are catalogued in "Edisto Island Land Memorials."

70. *Biographic Directory of the South Carolina House of Representatives, Volume II, 1695–1775* (Columbia: University of South Carolina Press, 1977), 133. The Watt or Watts for whom the cut was named remains obscure. The 1715 map (Figure 12) shows a settler named Watts, but he has no identified land grant. He may be the "Lieutenant Watts" in Beaufort in 1735; see "William Aiken's Jehossee Plantation," Chapter 7.

71. This sketch of the Rake family of Edisto Island is based largely on "Thomas Rake," an unpublished but carefully researched manuscript by Gary Rake, 2005 (copy in the author's files).

72. A.S. Salley Jr., "Stock Marks Recorded in South Carolina: 1695–1721," *South Carolina Historical and Genealogical Magazine* 29 (1912), 128.

73. David McCord Wright, "Petitioners to the Crown Against the Proprietors: 1716–1717," *The South Carolina Historical Magazine* 62 (1961), 88–95.

74. "An Account of the Appraisement of the Estate of Thomas Rake…1762," Inventory Book 87-A (1761–1763), 195, Charleston County Probate Court.

75. Land tax calculations are by the author, extrapolated from values shown in the "1732 Tax List."

76. Ibid.

77. The grievances that led to the "Revolution of 1719" were both substantive and procedural. See Edgar, *South Carolina*, 102–08.

78. William A. Fickling III, comp., et. al., "The First Ficklings in America: George Fickling of South Carolina [and descendants]," www.ficklin-fickling.org, accessed August 13–19, 2001; Joseph Fickling in "Edisto Island Land Memorials"; "Muster Roll—1775" and "Roster and Regulations of Edisto Island Company, 1776," in *Documents on Edisto Island History*.

79. Puckette, *Sea Island Principality*, 4.

80. Events of the Yemassee War are summarized from Edgar, *South Carolina*, 98–102.

81. *South Carolina Gazette*, December 10, 1753, cited in Jordan and Stringfellow, *A Place Called St. John's*, 51.

82. This account of the Stono Rebellion draws on Edgar, *South Carolina*, 74–78, except as otherwise noted.

83. Duke University historian Peter H. Wood, quoted in Roddie Burris, "Failed Uprising Resulted in Harsher Life for Slaves," *State* (newspaper), Columbia, SC, February 2, 2003, page B1.

84. Edgar, *South Carolina*, 76–77; *State*, "Uprising." The location of the decisive battle is believed to be on Battlefield Plantation at Parker's Ferry, which is private property. A historical marker is on U.S. Highway 17 near SC Road 38.

85. Edgar, *South Carolina*, 161; Jonathan Mercantini, "The Great South Carolina Hurricane of 1752," *The South Carolina Historical Magazine* 103, no. 4 (October 2002): 351–65.

86. Guion G. Johnson, *A Social History of the Sea Islands; With Special Reference to St. Helena Island, South Carolina* (Chapel Hill: University of North Carolina Press, 1930), 68.

87. Revolutionary War operations in the South Carolina Lowcountry are from Carl P. Borick, *A Gallant Defense: the Siege of Charleston, 1780* (Columbia: University of South Carolina Press, 2003), 1–70, except where otherwise noted.

88. Benson J. Lossing, *The Pictorial Field-Book of the Revolution*, vol. II (New York: Harper & Brothers, 1860), 555.

89. Walter Edgar, *Partisans and Redcoats: The Southern Conflict that Turned the Tide of the American Revolution* (New York: HarperCollins, 2001), 46–48.

90. Borick, *Gallant Defense*, 61.

91. Ibid., 81–82, 219, 245.

92. "1775 Muster Roll [transcription]," on Colleton County, South Carolina History and Genealogy website (http://www.oldplaces.org/colleton/1775muster.htm), Pat Sabin, coordinator, downloaded March 26, 2004.

93. *South Carolina History and Genealogy Magazine* 2 (1901).

94. The Edisto company may have been present with a brigade of "country militia" under Brigadier General Lachlan MacIntosh with the batteries on South Bay, Charleston, or another group of militia under Lieutenant Colonel William Scott at Fort Moultrie, Sullivan's Island, during the British siege of 1780. See Borick, *Gallant Defense*, 252.

95. The oral tradition was first written down in 1886 by James Murray's great-granddaughter, Josephine Gabriella Seabrook Waring, "The Murray Family and the Meggett Family of Edisto Island, S.C.," manuscript, 1886, in a Waring plantation journal, 1847–1883 (photocopy and transcription in the personal collection of the author). Josephine was born in the early 1800s, so she could have learned about her ancestors from older family members who personally remembered the Revolutionary War.

96. SCDAH, Index of Legislative Papers 1782–1866, Series 165015, Items 39, 193, 214, 240. A James Clark also suffered for Loyalist sympathies after the Revolution, but he probably was not from Edisto Island. The only adult James Clark on Edisto Island at the time served in both the first (1775) and second (1776) Edisto Patriot companies. Mary Clark Brockman, "Clarks of Edisto Island, S.C., and Clark Family in America," unpublished typescript, n.d. (circa 1950), copy in the author's personal collection, 24.

CHAPTER 3

97. Peter H. Wood, *Black Majority: Negroes in Colonial South Carolina from 1670 through the Stono Rebellion* (New York: Knopf, 1974), 37–42.

98. This is an inference from general statements on labor supply by historians. See, for example, Wood, *Black Majority*, 43–47, and Jordan and Stringfellow, *A Place Called St. John's*, 30.

99. The 1685 date is the author's surmise. The first documented presence of African slaves on Edisto Island was during the Spanish raid in 1686 (below).

100. Wood, *Black Majority*, 47.

101. Ibid., 43–46.

102. Philip D. Curtin, *The Atlantic Slave Trade: A Census* (Madison: University of Wisconsin Press, 1969), 145.

103. Wood, *Black Majority*, 144.

104. Ibid., 63–91.

105. The following summary of the American and the South Carolina slave trade is from Curtin, *Atlantic Slave Trade*, 72–93, 127–62, except as otherwise noted.

106. Slave survival and population growth rates were much higher in the United States than in the Caribbean and Brazil, due in part, probably, to climate, but also to other factors not yet explained. Curtin, *Atlantic Slave Trade*, 92–93.

107. The figure of 150,000 is the author's calculation, based on inferences from Curtin's account.

108. K.W. Stetson, "A Quantitative Approach to Britain's American Slave Trade" (master's thesis, University of Wisconsin, 1967), quoted in Curtin, *Atlantic Slave Trade*, 136–37.

109. Curtin, *Atlantic Slave Trade*, 154, 231.

110. Ibid., 157 (citing earlier research by Elizabeth Donnan, who in turn drew on work by W.S. Pollitzer).

111. David H. Fischer, *Albion's Seed: Four British Folkways in America* (New York: Oxford University Press, 1989), 817. Other possible origins of "Gullah" are in Lorenzo Dow Turner, *Africanisms in the Gullah Dialect* (first published in 1949, Columbia: University of South Carolina Press, 2002), 194.

112. One such scholar is Wood, *Black Majority*, cited in Daniel C. Littlefield, *Rice and Slaves: Ethnicity and the Slave Trade in Colonial South Carolina* (Baton Rouge: Louisiana State University Press, 1981), 76.

113. Littlefield, *Rice and Slaves*, 74–109; quotations, 113–14.

114. Ibid., 89–90.

115. Ibid., 92–98.

116. Wood, *Black Majority*, 144.

117. Ibid., 146–47.

118. Each of the thirty-nine heads of household in 1732 is named in *Documents on Edisto Island History*.

119. National Archives and Records Service, RG 29, Bureau of the Census, Second Population Census of the U.S. (1800), M32, Reel 48. Unfortunately, precise figures are not available from the 1790 Census because the enumerator mingled Edisto with the rest of St. John's Colleton district. See "Edisto Island Censuses from 1790 to 1860" in *Documents on Edisto Island History*.

120. 1800 Census, Reel 48, page 184. The category was "All other free persons, except Indians not taxed." There is little doubt that Robert Mason was African American.

121. Curtin, *Atlantic Slave Trade*, 73–75; Johnson, *Social History*, 35.

122. Lindsay, *And I'm Glad*, 48–50.

123. Sam Gadsden told Nick Lindsay his ancestors were Ibos from Nigeria, but he told African American students at the Penn Center on St. Helena Island that they were from "the Kongo," and he died soon thereafter. Betty Kuyk is the expert who has analyzed both stories in detail and concludes, from multiple clues within the story and the storytelling environments, that the second version is more likely authentic. It is also Kuyk who believes the Vili of Loango Bay, Congo Republic, most closely match internal clues in the story of Kwibo Tom. Betty M. Kuyk, *African Voices in the African-American Heritage* (Bloomington: Indiana University Press, 2003), 4–6, 27–40.


## Chapter 4

124. John Sandford wrote in 1666 that while on Edisto Island, "Wee crossed one Meadowe of not lesse then a thousand Acres." Sandford, "Relation of a Voyage," 300–01.

125. Letter from Governor James Glen to the Lords Commissioners for Trade and Plantations, March 1751, reprinted in *The Colonial South Carolina Scene: Contemporary Views, 1697–1774*, ed. H. Roy Merrens (Columbia: University of South Carolina Press, 1977), 181.

126. Peter A. Coclanis, *The Shadow of a Dream: Economic Life and Death in the South Carolina Low Country, 1670–1920* (New York: Oxford University Press, 1989), 81.

127. Wood, *Black Majority*, 28–29.

128. A small peninsula in the marshes between Edisto Island and Edingsville Beach is still called Cowpens today. The name apparently dates from the 1800s, when families resided on the beach all summer and kept a few animals at Cowpens, easily accessible from the beach.

129. In these early days, owners sometimes entrusted a large herd of cattle to a single African slave with almost no supervision. A black adult herdsman was sometimes called a "cow boy" in the condescending sense of "house boy" or "yard boy." Wood, *Black Majority*, 31 and notes 55–58.

130. Mark Catesby, "The Natural History of Carolina…" [1747], reprinted in *The Colonial South Carolina Scene: Contemporary Views, 1697–1774*, ed. H. Roy Merrens (Columbia: University of South Carolina Press, 1977), 108.

131. Ibid., 108.

132. Ibid., 109.

133. Wood, *Black Majority*, 32–33; Glen letter, 1751, 180–81; Coclanis, *Shadow of a Dream*, 81.

134. Edward Ball, *Slaves in the Family* (New York: Farrar, Straus and Giroux, 1998), 102–05, 248–51.

135. Hilda Black David, "The African-American Women of Edisto Island: 1850–1920" (PhD diss., Emory University, 1990), 83.

136. Jordan and Stringfellow, *A Place Called St. John's*, 65; Edgar, *South Carolina*, 140.

137. Edgar, *South Carolina*, 140.

138. Ibid., 141.

139. Coclanis, *Shadow of a Dream*, 106.

140. Ibid., 82.

141. Jack Leland, "Indigo in America" (pamphlet, 1976), reprinted by Edisto Island Historic Preservation Society, 1994, 8–15; Edgar, *South Carolina*, 146.

142. One such "indigo pit" is documented in Charles S. Spencer, "The History of Cypress Trees Plantation on Edisto Island, SC," unpublished monograph, 1995 (copy in "Murray Family," EIHPS research collection), 10.

143. "The Introduction of a New Staple Crop [three documents from 1747, 1755 and 1785]," in *The Colonial South Carolina Scene: Contemporary Views, 1697–1774*, ed. Roy H. Merrens (Columbia: University of South Carolina Press, 1977), 159–63.

144. These and the following details of indigo processing are from "New Staple Crop," 156–59, except as otherwise noted.

145. Edgar, *South Carolina*, 149.

146. Ibid., 148.

147. Coclanis, *Shadow of a Dream*, 80, 84, 107.

148. Jordan and Stringfellow, *A Place Called St. John's*, 61–62 and note 17.

149. Porcher and Fick, *Story of Sea Island Cotton*, 79–80, 187.

150. Ibid., 187.

151. This summary of the origin of the plant is drawn from Porcher and Fick, *Story of Sea Island Cotton*, 89–100, except as otherwise noted.

152. The full story is, of course, much more complex. See Porcher and Fick, *Story of Sea Island Cotton*, chapter 5.

153. Ibid., 95–96. Figures are rounded, and each represents twelve months beginning the preceding October 1.

154. Ibid., page 96.

155. The following summary of cotton cultivation is from Porcher and Fick, *Story of Sea Island Cotton*, 133–74.

156. Johnson, *Social History*, 55.

157. "Parts of the sea islands were under water in 1804 and 1824," and a third hurricane came ashore on September 8, 1854. These records refer to the entire sea island coasts of Georgia and South Carolina, but Edisto Island crops probably suffered significantly in each of these years. Johnson, *Social History*, 68.

158. Each year the planter chose his single best plant (or two or three), produced perhaps five acres of superior plants from its seed the second year and then saved that seed to plant the entire plantation the third year. Planters who followed this discipline had consistently higher yields per acre and higher-quality fiber than those who did not.

159. "In 1822 there was not a plow or scythe on Edisto, one of the best cultivated of the Sea Islands…At the close of the ante-bellum period, John F. Townsend was the only planter who used plows to any extent." Johnson, *Social History*, 48. See also R.F.W. Allston, *Essay on Sea Coast Crops* (Charleston: A.E. Miller, 1854), 7.

160. Townsend of Edisto Island was also cited favorably for his extensive use of "manures," even if it limited the acreage he could plant: "A very successful planter of Edisto (Mr. Townsend) tends but five acres to the hand. He uses the plow freely, manures well, and makes a good interest [profit]." Allston, *Sea Coast Crops*, 14.

161. This overview of preparing cotton for market is from Porcher and Fick, *Story of Sea Island Cotton*, 173–84, except as otherwise noted.

162. Johnson, *Social History*, 29.

163. The various types of gins are described in Porcher and Fick, *Story of Sea Island Cotton*, 185–237.

164. Allston, *Sea Coast Crops*, 16.

165. H. Houldsworth, "Mr. McCarthy's Cotton Gin," *The Southern Agriculturalist* 4 (New Series), no. 5, 1844.

166. Kovacik and Winberry, *A Geography*, 90–91, provide these statistics, except where otherwise noted.

167. Johnson, *Social History*, 46.


## CHAPTER 5

168. Edgar, *South Carolina*, 254–55.

169. In this book "Golden Age" is always set apart with quotation marks because only the tiny white minority enjoyed the benefits of the unprecedented prosperity.

170. National Archives and Records Administration, RG 29 (Records of the Bureau of Census), First Population Census of the U.S., microfilm publication M637, reel 11, 532–33.

171. The free persons of color in 1860 are named in Chapter 6.

172. National Archives and Records Administration, RG 29 (Records of the Bureau of Census), Eighth Population Census of the U.S., microfilm publication M653, reel 1218, 229–39 (free); reel 1234, 1–66 (slave). The seventeen Edisto planters, with numbers of slaves each, are named in *Documents on Edisto Island History*.

173. 1860 Census.

174. Johnson, *Social History*, 40.

175. Ibid., 74–81.

176. Ibid., 82.

177. Ibid., 78–79.

178. Lindsay, *And I'm Glad*, 54–56. The author has independently verified several circumstantial details of this story and believes it to be essentially true. Sam Gadsden told Nick Lindsay that the overseer's real name was Moosehead. The author believes that was an unintentional shift in oral transmission of the story down three generations, and has changed the name to Muirhead, based on other sources. See Whitmarsh Seabrook Murray, "History of the Murray Family in South Carolina" (unpublished manuscript in collection of the author, n.d., circa 1901), 3.

179. When this incident actually happened is a puzzle. Sam Gadsden in Lindsay, *And I'm Glad*, 56, says Charles was taught to read and write before it became illegal as a result of the Denmark Vesey plot in Charleston (1822). But Kwibo Tom and his family did not arrive on Edisto Island until about 1820 (Chapter 3); Lydia Clark did not marry Major Murray until 1825 (Lindsay, *And I'm Glad*, 50); and she died in 1845. The author thinks it more likely the incident occurred between 1825 and 1845, and that "Miss Liddy" simply ignored the slave code.

180. Johnson, *Social History*, 79–81.

181. Ibid., 81–82.

182. Ibid.

183. Ibid., 87–88, 101–02. Johnson reports that, in 1844, a typical sea-island cotton planter paid seventeen to twenty dollars a year to feed and clothe a slave. Housing, medical care and incidentals brought the total cost close to fifty dollars. If the number of taskable hands (those actually producing income) was half the total number of slaves (and often it was fewer), then the planter's real labor cost was perhaps one hundred dollars per taskable hand.

184. Ibid., 68–70.

185. Ibid., 82–84.

186. Listing is a job done with a hoe and is described in Chapter 4, "Growing Sea-island Cotton."

187. Sam Gadsden in Lindsay, *And I'm Glad*, 55–56.

188. Johnson, *Social History*, 85.

189. Ibid., 86–87; David, "African-American Women," 55–56.

190. Johnson, *Social History*, 86, 142.

191. Tyson Gibbs, et. al., "Nutrition in a Slave Population: An Anthropological Examination," *Medical Anthropology* (Spring 1980), 236, quoted in David, "African-American Women," 55–56.

192. Johnson, *Social History*, 87–88.

193. The English visitor was Captain Basil Hall, quoted in Johnson, *Social History*, 88–90.

194. Ibid., 96–97.

195. On a large, well-managed plantation near Georgetown, South Carolina, in the five-year period ending in 1860, 103 slaves of all ages died of all causes, including old age, but 75 percent of the dead were children younger than age 6. See Johnson, *Social History*, 98–100.

196. Ibid., 91–93; David, "African-American Women," 50.

197. The medical contracts described in this source were near Savannah, Georgia. See Johnson, *Social History*, 93–94.

198. Ibid., 93–95.

199. David, "African-American Women," 43–50.

200. Helen C. Kenner, *Historical Records of Trinity Episcopal Church, Edisto Island, South Carolina* (Edisto Island: Trinity Episcopal Church, 1975), 3–12. The 1841 church building that accommodated slaves is not the one standing today. See Chapter 6.

201. Henry Ashworth Diary, entry for April 16, 1857, at the South Caroliniana Library, quoted in David, "African-American Women," 101.

202. David, "African-American Women," 90, 99.

203. Isaac Jenkins Mikell [Jr.], *Rumbling of the Chariot Wheels* (Columbia: The State Company, 1923), 238–39; David, "African-American Women," 89.

204. Lorenzo Dow Turner, *Africanisms in the Gullah Dialect* (Columbia: University of South Carolina Press, 2002), xi–xlix, note 2; Muriel Miller Branch, *The Water Brought Us: The Story of the Gullah-Speaking People* (Orangeburg, SC: Sandlapper Publishing Co., 1995), 62.

205. Turner, *Africanisms*, xii.

206. David, "African-American Women," 21.

207. Letter, Adams to Clayton, July 29, 1976, in Hephzibah Townsend Papers, Baptist Collection, Furman University, Greenville, SC, quoted in David, "African-American Women," 96–97.

208. David, "African-American Women," 22.

CHAPTER 6

209. "Sea Island cotton was the basis of wealth for a plantation aristocracy that focused on Edisto Island and especially the town of Beaufort." Kovacik and Winberry, *A Geography*, 91.

210. National Archives and Records Administration, RG 29 (Records of the Bureau of Census), Agricultural Census of 1860, South Carolina, St. John's Colleton. All figures are rounded.

211. National Archives and Records Administration, RG 29 (Records of the Bureau of Census), Eighth Population Census of the U.S., South Carolina, St. John's Colleton, microfilm publication M653, reel 1234, 1–66 (slaves).

212. Three Edisto landowners grew no cotton: William Aiken, the rice planter; M.A. Jenkins, a widow; and Thomas Dawson, the Baptist minister.

213. "Losses Claimed by Sea Island Landowners, 1862," in the collection of the South Carolina Historical Society, Charleston. All entries pertaining to Edisto Island plantations are transcribed in *Documents on Edisto Island History*.

214. Only Old House and the Brick House ruin are clearly older. Prospect Hill is arguably older; Sunnyside and Windsor are younger.

215. By 1821 the beach community was already well established. See "Sketch of the History of the Presbyterian Church of Edisto Island From 1821 to 1858 by Rev. Wm. S. Lee, The Pastor," typed transcription by E.M.S.C. [Esther Marion Seabrook Connor] circa 1930, in Presbyterian Church on Edisto Island, Session Books excerpts, 1816–1901, South Carolina Historical Society (43, 97).

216. Fifty-one houses are shown on the 1852 U.S. Coast Survey map of Edingsville (text, Figure 24). The later "Map of the Village of Edingsville, Edisto Island, S.C., Surveyed for J.E. Edings, July 1866, by White E. Gourdin, CE," at the South Carolina Historical Society shows fifty-two lots but only thirty-eight houses. Some may have burned during the Civil War, or been washed away by early hurricanes.

217. List from Gourdin, "Map," alphabetized and edited by the author. Obvious misspellings are corrected, first names are provided for some initials. Gourdin's list almost certainly omits several earlier owners.

218. C.S. Murray, "Edingsville, Edisto Island, S.C.," *Charleston News and Courier*, November 2, 1930; Chalmers S. Murray, "Life in Lost Village of Edingsville," *Charleston News and Courier*, December 25, 1955.

219. Cecil Wescott, son of cotton planter Jabez J.R. Westcoat (Chapter 7), was an Edisto Island postmaster and painter whose life overlapped the nineteenth and twentieth centuries. He changed the spelling of his name from Westcoat to Wescott.

220. Lee, "Presbyterian Church," 2.

221. Albert Sidney Thomas, DD, "The Episcopal Church on Edisto Island…A Sketch… Delivered in Trinity Church, October 10, 1948…" (mimeo, Charleston: The Dalcho Historical Society, 1953), 8–9.

222. The following summary is from Sid Miller, "Edisto's Marvelous Line," *South Carolina Wildlife*, September–October 1995, 34–36.

223. "U.S. Coast Survey, A.D. Bache, Superintendent, Sketch E, No. 3, Showing the progress of the Survey at North & South Edisto River and St. Helena Sound, South Carolina, 1851," Map Division, Library of Congress, Washington, D.C.

224. The U.S. Coast Survey published the three sections of Edisto Island as separate maps, never as a single, merged map of the island. Modern historians and cartographers can easily merge them, but the degree of detail on the original maps is very valuable, and much is lost when they are reduced. The complete Edisto Island 1850s plantations map, far too large for this book, is available as a wall map from the Edisto Island Historic Preservation Society.

225. The ministries of Donald McLeod and William States Lee are summarized in [Marion Seabrook Connor?], "A Brief History of The Presbyterian Church of Edisto Island" (no date, circa 1935, with a Postscript, 1963, Edisto Island: privately printed, 1963); C.F. Klotzberger, "The Presbyterian Pastors of Edisto Island (A Paper in Progress)," unpublished manuscript, 1999, copy in the historical archive of the Presbyterian Church on Edisto Island.

226. The personal life of Donald McLeod is drawn, except as otherwise noted, from Rivers, *Seven South Carolina Low Country Families*, C8; 1790, 1800, 1810 and 1820 Censuses; Spencer, "Cypress Trees Plantation," 33.

227. It may or may not be a coincidence that this issue arose in the Reverend Donald McLeod's life and ministry less than six months after his second wife died. In the absence of more historical details, one has to wonder if he was involved in a misunderstanding about his relations with a woman.

228. This summary of Reverend Lee's ministry is from his own pen, Lee, "Presbyterian Church," except as otherwise noted.

229. Architect Robert Mills was working in Charleston about 1830. He is the documented architect of First Baptist Church in Charleston. The builder of First Baptist Church in the 1820s was a Mr. Curtis, probably the same person who was contracted to repair the Presbyterian Church on Edisto Island in 1836. Mills had drawn a proposal for the interior of St. John's Episcopal Church on Johns Island that was not used by that church, but still exists in the collections of the Charleston Library Society. Mills's proposal for St. John's is remarkably similar to the original interior of the Presbyterian Church on Edisto Island, as reconstructed from architectural evidence in 2002. And Mills was an acquaintance of at least one member of the 1830 PCEI building committee, William Seabrook Jr., of Oak Island Plantation. Author interview with David Lybrand, June 18, 2003.

230. Presbyterian Church on Edisto Island (PCEI), Corporation Minutes, entry for November 15, 1852; Jennifer Ries (office of architect Joseph K. Oppermann, Charleston), Memorandum of Conversation (Telephone Report), January 26, 2001, with attachments. Both documents in Sanctuary Restoration 2002 File, archive of PCEI, Edisto Island.

231. George Howe, DD, *History of the Presbyterian Church in South Carolina* (Columbia: W.J. Duffie, 1883), reprinted (Columbia: The State Printing Company, 1966), vol. II, 556–57.

232. Lee, "Presbyterian Church."

233. The following history of Trinity Church is summarized, except where otherwise noted, from Thomas, "Episcopal Church," 5–8, and from *Historical Records*, 1–12. The parish registers of St. Helena Parish (Beaufort) for the early 1700s also contain a few birth, baptism and

marriage records of Edisto Episcopalians. (E-mail letter, Gary Rake to the author, July 25, 2004.)

234. Thomas A. Osborne papers, 1816–1827, South Carolina Historical Society (43/0820), Charleston.

235. W. Curtis Worthington, "Some Highlights from the History of Trinity Episcopal Church on Edisto Island" (text of a lecture, Edisto Island: Trinity Episcopal Church, 2000), 4.

236. Trinity's first parsonage farm is located and described in Chapter 7 under "Miss Betsy Seabrook."

237. Jack Leland, "Edisto Island's Trinity Episcopal Church Has Long History," *Charleston News and Courier*, March 26, 2001.

238. "Proceedings of the Meeting in Charleston, S.C., May 13–15, 1845, on the Religious Instruction of the Negroes…" (pamphlet), Charleston: B. Jenkins, 1845, 17, in *From Slavery to Freedom: The African-American Pamphlet Collection, 1824–1909*, Library of Congress (LC), Washington, D.C. Accessed online in full digital text, February 2003, as part of LC's American Memory Project (http://memory.loc.gov/).

239. Worthington, "Trinity Episcopal Church," 5.

240. These facts about the Baptist Church, unless otherwise noted, are from Sherrie L. McIntosh, "The Old Edisto Island Baptist Church: Hephzibah Jenkins Townsend: 1780–1847, and the Inheritance of Stewardship and Spiritual Gifts" (master's thesis, West Virginia University, 1998), 31–54.

241. South Carolina Department of Archives and History (Martha Walker Fullington), "Edisto Island Baptist Church" (National Register of Historic Places Inventory–Nomination Form), 1981, section 7: Description.

242. The 1829 date is from National Register Nomination, "Edisto Island Baptist Church," section 8: Significance. The last two named ministers are from the U.S. Censuses of 1850 and 1860.

243. McIntosh, "Hephzibah."

244. Homer L.F. Shuler, "Methodism in Charleston and the Low Country," *Journal of the South Carolina Annual Conference*, 1947, 148–49.

245. F.A. Mood, *Methodism in Charleston: A Narrative…* (Nashville, TN: Methodist Episcopal Church, South, 1856), 60–64. The crime Allen was accused of is not named, but the degree of horrified outrage it prompted was usually reserved, at that time, for homosexuality or incest.

246. Shuler, "Methodism," 151.

247. 1850 Census and 1860 Census; "Meeting on Religious Instruction of Negroes," 17.

248. 1850 Census and 1860 Census. In 1850, four out of six overseers were over forty. None of the six were still there in 1860, and seven out of eight new men were under forty.

249. Johnson, *Social History*, 191.

250. The 1860 Census lists each of these men as "manager," but except for the last two, who owned slaves, the author believes that title was a euphemism for overseer.

251. 1860 Census.

252. The 1860 Census lists the three Irish women as "nurse," but their role in the household was almost certainly what today we call a nanny.

253. The 1860 Census describes all four of these free persons as "mulatto" rather than black.

CHAPTER 7

254. Bleak Hall/Sea Cloud, Point of Pines/Charles Bailey, Sunnyside/Orange Grove, Bailey's Island and Windsor/Ash's were counted as two plantations each. The Presbyterian parsonage, Whooping Island and Betsy Seabrook's Farm were not counted as working plantations. Raccoon Island was counted as part of Laurel Hill, and Dill Farm was counted as part of the Woods Plantation.

255. For the origins of the Townsend plantations, the author relies heavily on earlier, unpublished research by Agnes Baldwin. See "Bleak Hall" file in Agnes Baldwin's Edisto Island research collection (circa 1990) in the EIHPS archive.

256. SCDAH, Colonial Plats, vol. 3, 409, August 2, 1749.

257. SCDAH, Memorials, vol. 7, 62, May 28, 1754.

258. SCDAH, Proprietary Grants, vol. 39, 361, January 13, 1710; SCDAH, Memorials, vol. 3, 305, April 21, 1733.

259. Charleston County Register of Mesne Conveyance (RMC), book X9, 450, November 1707.

260. SCDAH, Proprietary Grants, vol. 38, 279–80, January 10, 1695; SCDAH, Memorials, vol. 5, 229, May 2, 1733 (memorial of Paul Hamilton).

261. SCDAH, Grant book C, 57, March 14, 1695; SCDAH, Memorials, vol. 7, 505, July 27, 1748.

262. Baldwin, "Sea Cloud" file.

263. Rivers, *Seven South Carolina Low Country Families*, C8; Baldwin, "Bleak Hall" file.

264. SCDAH, Royal Grants, vol. 39, 106, January 13, 1710.

265. SCDAH, Royal Grants, vol. 39, 371, August 9, 1711; SDCAH, Memorials, vol. 3, 305, April 21, 1733. This memorial covers Pockoy Island as well as Botany Bay Beach.

266. SCDAH, Memorials, vol. 3, 339, July 23, 1711.

267. Watch Island, commanding the entrance to Edisto's deep harbor, the North Edisto River, may have been where lookouts were posted to watch for enemy ships after the devastating Spanish raid of 1686. Later it was called Clark's Bay [Beach] for an old Edisto family, and now it is Botany Bay Island. Where did that name come from? Chalmers Murray believed that planter John F. Townsend II named his private beach Botany Bay "because he sent his fractious horses and cattle there." (British criminals were sent as settlers to Botany Bay, Australia, in the 1700s and early 1800s.) See Chalmers S. Murray, "Edisto Island and Its Place Names," *Names in South Carolina* (published sporadically by the Department of English, University of South Carolina), Winter 1960, 73–74.

268. SCDAH, Colonial Plats, vol. 4, 266, February 4, 1752.

269. SCDAH, Royal Grants, vol. 1, 640, August 7, 1735; SCDAH, Memorials, vol. 7, 505, July 27, 1748.

270. SCDAH, Colonial Plats, vol. 3, 504, August 19, 1734; "Plan of Sea Cloud and Bleak Hall, John Townsend's Plantation on Edisto Island…by L. Seib in 1855," copy in Baldwin, "Bleak Hall" file.

271. SCDAH, State Plats, vol. 37, 43, January 28, 1800.

272. Kate McChesney Bolls, *The Daniel Townsends of the South Carolina Islands: Their Forbears and Descendants* (Verona, VA: McClure Printing Co., 1975), 13–19. Some descendants assume Townsend named his great house Bleak Hall as an adaptation of *Bleak House*, a popular novel by Charles Dickens. But *Bleak House* was published in 1853, some time after the house was built.

273. Ibid.

274. The ownership and size of the plantation are from National Archives and Records Administration. Record Group 105, Records of the Bureau of Refugees, Freedmen and Abandoned Lands. Assistant Commissioner for South Carolina. Entry 2942: Register of Applications for Restoration of Property, August 1865 to May 1866, application of William E. Seabrook.

275. The details of the house site, gardens and approach road are easily readable in miniature on the 1851 U.S. Coast Survey map of Edisto Island.

276. Rivers, *Seven South Carolina Low Country Families*, S17.

277. The 1851 date is from the U.S. Coast Survey map. The 1856 date is from Rivers, *Seven South Carolina Low Country Families*.

278. SCDAH, Memorials, vol. 7, 529, April 11, 1751; Plat, Charleston County RMC, 1789.

279. SCDAH, Memorials, vol. 3, 339, July 23, 1711.

280. Freedmen's Bureau Applications for Restoration, Joseph Whaley.

281. U.S. Coast Survey map. A jackdaw is a handsome black and white bird, related to the raven, common in the British Isles.

282. SCDAH, Royal Grants, vol. 39, 84, September 24, 1710; SCDAH, Memorials, vol. 4, 274–75, November 4, 1710.

283. Letter to the author from David Lybrand, July 30, 1999; McCrady Plat No. 5639 ("Hon. Jenkins Land," April 1744).

284. McCrady Plat No. 5633 ("Plantation on Edisto Island…," 1870); Freedmen's Bureau Applications for Restoration, William M. Murray.

285. Murray, "History of the Murray Family"; Josephine Waring Manuscript, 2–3.

286. "Wreck of the Steamship *Pulaski*," Wilmington (NC) *Advertiser*, June 18, 1838; Rebecca J. McLeod, "Wreck of the *Pulaski*" unpublished first-person account, circa 1888, edited for Internet distribution by Mary DeLashmit, 2003, copy in the author's files. All the Edisto white people who perished in this disaster are listed on a monument beside the Presbyterian Church on Edisto Island.

287. Manuscript, "History of the Murray Family," 2.

288. Charles S. Spencer, "Ten Generations of the Murray Family of Edisto Island, S.C.," family genealogy chart, privately printed, 1988, copy in the author's personal collection.

289. The "bay" in the 1850s meant the entire barrier island of Edingsville. The "beach" denoted only the narrow tidal strand.

290. SCDAH, Memorials, vol. 3, 278, May 22, 1733; Memorials, vol. 8, 484–85, September 8, 1769.

291. U.S. Coast Survey map.

292. SCDAH, Memorials, vol. 8, 485, September 8, 1769.

293. U.S. Coast Survey map.

294. Rivers, *Seven South Carolina Low Country Families*, S21.

295. U.S. Coast Survey map.

296. Ibid.

297. Ibid. Both Red House and the Seabrook Tract were accessible by farm roads from Baynard's Shell House, Baynard's Seaside and Peter's Point Road. Freedmen's Bureau Applications for Restoration, I. Jenkins Mikell, says Mikell owned a "John Seabrook's" plantation, otherwise unidentified.

298. SCDAH, Royal Grants, vol. 30, 511, January 12, 1705; Memorials, vol. 3, 437.

299. U.S. Coast Survey map.

300. Physical characteristics are from U.S. Coast Survey map.

301. Albergotti, *Abigail's Story*, 24.

302. There is circumstantial evidence it may have been owned just before the Civil War by S. Hamilton Jenkins. See Volume 2, Chapter 3 of this history.

303. U.S. Coast Survey map; Freedmen's Bureau Applications for Restoration, Jabez J.R. Westcoat; "Losses Claimed," entry for J.J.R. Westcoat.

304. Porcher and Fick, *Story of Sea Island Cotton*, 407.

305. In 1866, J. Evans Edings recovered possession of a "Tract containing about 3,000 acres, Known as Edingsville." Since that is many times the size of Edingsville Beach, the tract probably included this Edings plantation. Freedmen's Bureau Applications for Restoration, Entry 2943, Unregistered Applications, J. Evans Edings, 1866.

306. Chalmers Gaston Davidson, *The Last Foray: The South Carolina Planters of 1860: A Sociological Study* (Columbia: University of South Carolina Press, 1971), 194.

307. Physical characteristics are from the U.S. Coast Survey map, acreages from Freedmen's Bureau Applications for Restoration, William Whaley.

308. Porcher and Fick, *Story of Sea Island Cotton*, 465–66.

309. U.S. Coast Survey map.

310. Ibid. Shergould was not the same place as Shargould, the name given in some documents to a property where Hephzibah Jenkins Townsend reportedly lived when she separated temporarily from her husband. Shargould may have been a house at Public Landing on Frampton's Inlet Creek. A tabby ruin at that place is reputed to be the remains of Hephzibah's baking oven.

311. Ibid.

312. There is a Beckett head of household and slave owner in every federal census from 1790 to 1860.

313. U.S. Coast Survey map; Freedmen's Bureau Applications for Restoration, Ephraim Baynard.

314. U.S. Coast Survey map.

315. SCDAH, Royal Grants, vol. 39, 19, May 14, 1707; State (Colleton County) Plats, book A, 286; Townsend Mikell, "The Mikell Genealogy of South Carolina" (Charleston: Walker, Evans and Cogswell, 1910, with 1997 addendum by Sarah Mikell Belser Eggleston), 21.

316. Details of the Peter's Point house are from a state architectural survey in the 1980s, excerpted in Baldwin, "Peter's Point" file.

317. Davidson, *Last Foray*, 230; Mikell, "Mikell Genealogy," 23.

318. Herb Frazier and Jack McCray, "Family gathers to explore lineage; Hutchinson clan's history a common one around the South," *Charleston Post and Courier*, July 17, 2004, 1B.

319. Lawrence Dennis grant: SCDAH, Memorials, vol. 9, 238–39, September 14, 1703. Whaley's purchase from Jenkins: Plat by Charles Vignoles "from Surveys made in March 1821," South Carolina Historical Society (30-08-67), Charleston.

320. The 1806 date is from the Freedmen's Bureau Applications for Restoration, Joseph Whaley.

321. Rivers, *Seven South Carolina Low Country Families*, S7–S11, W7–W8.

322. SCDAH, Royal Grants, vol. 38, 282, March 14, 1695, and vol. 38, 379–80, December 1, 1700; U.S. Coast Survey map.

323. Caroline T. Moore and Agatha A. Simmons, *Abstracts of the Wills of the State of South Carolina, 1670–1740*, 3 volumes (Columbia: The R.L. Bryan Co., 1960), 59, 84; SCDAH, Land Memorials, vol. 5, 272–73; Webber, "Grimball," 39; Stephen B. Barnwell, *The Story of An American Family* (Marquette, IN: Marquette, 1969), 22–23.

324. Webber, "Grimball," 95; Charleston County RMC Office, Book R-6, 93–96; William Garnett Chisolm, "Edings of Edisto Island" (unpublished manuscript, Leesburg, VA, 1943), 16. (Copy in archives of EIHPS.)

325. Chisolm, "Edings of Edisto Island," 16; author interview with John H. Boineau, July 21, 2004; NARA, 1860 Population Census; 1786 plat "of a Tract of Land…late the property of Paul Grimball deceased" by William Norton, Charleston County RMC Office, Book R6, 93–96; 1855 plat of "Plantation of O.H. Middleton" by John Seib, original in possession of Caroline Pope Clarkson Boineau, Edisto Island.

326. The Middletons probably built the present house between their marriage in 1827 and the birth of their first child in 1830. Samuel G. Stoney, *Plantations of the Carolina Low Country* (New York: Dover, and Charleston: Carolina Art Association, 1989, republication of seventh edition, 1977), 83. Architectural historian Gene Waddell later wrote that "The Launch can safely be attributed to Mills." Letter, Waddell to John H. Boineau, March 28, 2001.

327. SCDAH, Grants, vol. 38, 218, October 26, 1683.

328. SCDAH, Memorials, vol. 1, 62–63, March 31, 1722; Memorials, vol. 7, 529, March 22, 1751; Colonial Plats, vol. 1, 439.

329. Plat, Charleston County RMC, vol. B-6, 557, September 14, 1789.

330. Rivers, *Seven South Carolina Low Country Families*, B12–B23; Freedmen's Bureau Applications for Restoration, Estate of Charles J. Bailey.

331. Rivers, *Seven Low Country Families*, S17; 1820 Census.

332. SCDAH, Memorials, vol. 3, 305, April 21, 1733. Joseph Russell sold this land to John Frampton on October 11, 1728.

333. U.S. Coast Survey map.

334. Puckette, *Sea Island Principality*, 11–12, suggests early 1820s as the most likely date. Stoney, *Plantations*, 78, places the construction "not long after 1810," but cites no authority.

335. Rivers, *Seven South Carolina Low Country Families*, S1–S21.

336. General Lafayette's visit to Edisto Island is summarized from Puckette, *Sea Island Principality*, 12; Rivers, *Seven South Carolina Low Country Families*, 21; Jordan and Stringfellow, *A Place Called St. John's*, 95.

337. Bartholomew R. Carroll, ed., "The Late William Seabrook," *The Southern Agriculturalist* 5, no. 2 (February 1837): 57–65.

338. John Berwick Legare inherited Chaplin's Gardens when his wife died in 1852, but he died in 1856. (Rivers, *Seven South Carolina Low Country Families*, S-21.) Chaplin's Gardens had an interesting story after the Civil War: see volume two of this history.

339. Annie Baynard Simons Hasell, *Baynard: An Ancient Family Bearing Arms* (Columbia: R.L. Bryan, 1972), 143–45.

340. Freedmen's Bureau Applications for Restoration, Estate of John Berwick Legare.

341. Rivers, *Seven South Carolina Low Country Families*, S17.

342. W. Jeffrey Bolster and Hilary Anderson, *Soldiers, Sailors, Slaves and Ships: The Civil War Photographs of Henry P. Moore* (Concord: New Hampshire Historical Society, 1999), 70–77.

343. Rivers, *Seven South Carolina Low Country Families*, S17–S18.

344. Esther Marion Seabrook Connor, "Seabrook" (unpublished manuscript, undated, circa 1937), original in possession of Marion M. Seabrook (Mrs. Ben K.) Norwood, Greenville, SC.

345. Puckette, *Sea Island Principality*, 24; Rivers, *Seven South Carolina Low Country Families*, S21.

346. Plat of Point of Pines Plantation, Charleston County RMC, vol. B-6, 557, September 14, 1789; U.S. Coast Survey map.

347. Rivers, *Seven South Carolina Low Country Families*, C3–C6.

348. Ibid.; Freedmen's Bureau Applications for Restoration, Josephine F. Clark. The latter documents show that Clark's was also called, at times, Shell House. This narrative omits that name to avoid confusion with Baynard's Shell House on the seaside of Edisto Island.

349. Ibid.

350. Maria Adelaide Whaley (b. 1849), "The Story of Marie A. Whaley," unpublished memoir, South Carolina Historical Society (43/95), Charleston.

351. Brockman, "Clarks of Edisto Island"; Murray, "Edisto Island and Its Place Names," 74. A full discussion of the location of Joseph Morton's first house is in *Documents on Edisto Island History*.

352. SCDAH, Royal Grants, vol. 39, 20, May 14, 1707; SCDAH Memorials, vol. 4, 310–11, March 5, 1733.

353. Thomas, "Episcopal Church," 5; Rivers, *Seven South Carolina Low Country Families*, B10; 1803 plat by John Diamond, surveyor of Cypress Trees Plantation, original in possession of James C. Murray of Edisto Island, reproduced in the text as Figure 52.

354. Rivers, *Seven South Carolina Low Country Families*, B10, T8; Mikell, "Mikell Genealogy," 20–22. Ephraim Mikell willed to "Daughter Mary plantation bought of Mrs. Elizabeth Mikell." That plantation almost certainly was Governor's Bluff.

355. Freedmen's Bureau applications for restoration, Eliza Y. Mikell.

356. Rivers, *Seven South Carolina Low Country Families* J30–J32.

357. James J. Baldwin III, *The Struck Eagle: Brigadier General Micah Jenkins* (Shippensburg, PA: Burd Street Press, 1996), 1–5.

358. Ibid., 1–5; Rivers, *Seven South Carolina Low Country Families*, 32–33.

359. The original grant for Cypress Trees has not been found, but is cited in detail in two later documents: the 1803 Plat of Cypress Trees and SCDAH, Memorials, vol. 3, 205, April 24, 1733. The adjacent creek already bore Palmenter's name when he got his grant, so he probably was present, even using the land, for several years before 1697.

360. "Sketch of…Lands of A.J. Clark, Esqr." by John A. Michel, March 5 and 7, 1859, original in the possession of James C. Murray, Edisto Island. One more land purchase from Baynard in the nineteenth century expanded Cypress Trees all the way to the Manse Road, with about four hundred acres of high land. For burials in the Clark family cemetery and other details, see Spencer, "Cypress Trees Plantation."

361. Spencer, "Cypress Trees Plantation," 15–20.

362. SCDAH, Royal Grants, vol. 39, 358–59, August 10, 1705; SCDAH, Memorials, 1732; SCDAH, Royal Grants, vol. 38, 357–58, December 1, 1697. The grant that became Ravenswood was bounded "to the Eastward on lands laid out for a Parsonage." Use of the term "parsonage" seems to have favored a nonconformist minister. Both Baptists and Presbyterians are known to have been worshiping together on Edisto Island in the 1690s. This property is known as the manse today, but all documents from the nineteenth century and earlier refer to it as the parsonage.

363. These details are from the U.S. Coast Survey map.

364. Lindsay, *And I'm Glad*, 57–58.

365. Physical description is from the U.S. Coast Survey map.

366. This John Raven Mathewes (1788–1867) was the fourth in a line with that name. Elizabeth Brener, comp., "John Raven Mathewes" (unpublished manuscript, n.d., circa 1990), copy in author's files.

367. U.S. Coast Survey map; Rivers, *Seven South Carolina Low Country Families*, G5.

368. Rivers, *Seven South Carolina Low Country Families*, S21; U.S. Coast Survey map.

369. SCDAH, Memorials, vol. 4, 437.

370. Rivers, *Seven South Carolina Low Country Families*, A1, S7, S17–S21.

371. U.S. Coast Survey map.

372. Rivers, *Seven South Carolina Low Country Families*, C8, J6-7.

373. SCDAH, Memorials, vol. 3, 305, April 24, 1733.

374. Freedmen's Bureau Applications for Restoration, Constantine Bailey.

375. Rivers, *Seven South Carolina Low Country Families*, B12–B28; 1850 and 1860 Censuses.

376. Davidson, *Last Foray*, 174. For Bailey's Confederate service see *Documents on Edisto Island History*.

377. Freedmen's Bureau Applications for Restoration, Ephraim Baynard.

378. SCDAH, Royal Grants, vol. 38, 358, December 1, 1697.

379. 300 hundred acres, Bower to Jenkins, November 22/23, 1753; Jenkins to May, November 23/24, 1753; in SCDAH, Memorials, vol. 7, 61, May 16, 1754. 300 hundred acres, Bower to Burd, June 18, 1754; in SCDAH, Memorials, vol. 7, 83, March 26, 1755. Apparently, 100 to 150 acres were outsold at some point and became the eastern section of Maxcy Plantation (below), leaving about 500 acres in Rabbit Point.

380. U.S. Coast Survey map.

381. In 1865 an Edistonian wrote, "Eph. M. Baynard…was the largest Sea Isld Planter & wealthiest citizen of the St. Johns Colleton Parish…He was worth not far from two millions of Dollars…Mr. Baynard was a Batchellor, and an ultra States Rights Man." See "Subscriptions of Crop for defence of the Confederate States," May 20, 1861, in John Jenkins Papers (P900151, Box 1, Folder 1861) at SCDAH. The handwriting on the document is not that of John Jenkins; it may be that of Edisto planter and Charleston attorney Benjamin Whaley.

382. "This applicant [Ephraim M. Baynard] was an old man (75) years of age [at his death in 1865] and for thirty [years] in feeble health." Freedmen's Bureau Applications for Restoration, Ephraim Baynard.

383. Lindsay, *And I'm Glad*, 52.

384. Acreage is from the Freedmen's Bureau Applications for Restoration, William M. Bailey. Physical description is from U.S. Coast Survey map.

385. SCDAH, Memorials, vol. 7, 61, May 16, 1754; U.S. Coast Survey map.

386. Shape and measurements of Cedar Hall are from U.S. Coast Survey map; acreage is from Freedmen's Bureau Applications for Restoration, James E. Whaley.

387. Rivers, *Seven South Carolina Low Country Families*, W10.

388. U.S. Coast Survey map.

389. Rivers, *Seven South Carolina Low Country Families*, 11–13; Freedmen's Bureau Applications for Restoration, Edward Whaley.

390. U.S. Coast Survey map. The two larger constituent islands are Little Edisto and Jehossee.

391. 802 acres was a considerable underestimate. Twentieth-century surveys show Bailey's Island has about 1,000 acres of high land.

392. SCDAH, Memorials, vol. 4, 40.

393. Baldwin, "Bailey's Island" file, provides the chain of ownership in considerably more detail than recounted here.

394. SCDAH, Memorials, vol. 6, 369–70.

395. SCDAH, State Plats, vol. 16, 3, 5, 6; State Grants, vol. 22, 11–13.

396. McCrady Plat No. 5600, n.d., "Bailey's Island" by John Diamond, circa 1799.

397. U.S. Coast Survey map.

398. Ibid.

399. Acreage is from Freedmen's Bureau Applications for Restoration, Edward W. Seabrook. John Stewart's name is from the plat of a neighboring plantation: SCDAH, McCrady Plat No. 2337.

400. Rivers, *Seven South Carolina Low Country Families*, S6–S18; Davidson, *Last Foray*, 247.

401. U.S. Coast Survey map.

402. SCDAH, Royal Grants, vol. 38, 361, July 15, 1698; Memorials, vol. 9, 238–39, May 18, 1767.

403. U.S. Coast Survey map.

404. SCDAH, Royal Grants, vol. 38, 536, January 12, 1705.

405. SCDAH, Memorials, vol. 3, 480, May 3, 1733.

406. U.S. Coast Survey map; Freedmen's Bureau Applications for Restoration, Joseph James Murray.

407. SCDAH, McCrady Plat No. 2337 (1733); Freedmen's Bureau Applications for Restoration, Henry Seabrook. There are three white graves at Brookland: Joseph Jenkins (1753–1789); his first wife, Martha Grimball (1764–1785); and Joseph Jenkins (1789–1792), his youngest child by his second wife, Elizabeth Bailey Clark.

408. Rivers, *Seven South Carolina Low Country Families*, S9–S17; Porcher and Fick, *Story of Sea Island Cotton*, 452.

409. Chalmers S. Murray, "Brooklands Plantation: Relic of a Gracious Era Long Passed Into History" (four-page illustrated sales brochure) (Charleston: McLeod Creighton, Realtor, n.d., circa 1950), in Chalmers Murray Papers, South Carolina Historical Society, Charleston. Murray cites Samuel G. Stoney as authority for Brookland's probable 1840s construction.

410. Henry Bailey's grants on South Edisto River were: SCDAH, Royal Grants, vol. 38, 169–70, October 21, 1695, 100 acres; vol. 38, 275, January 10, 1694/5, 200 acres; vol. 38, 361, July 15, 1698, 180 acres; and vol. 38, 392, January 11, 1700, 100 acres.

411. U.S. Coast Survey map.

412. Davidson, *Last Foray*, 175; Freedmen's Bureau Applications for Restoration, William M. Bailey.

413. Davidson, *Last Foray*, 174–75.

414. Affidavit of J.W. and Frank Rice, October 19, 1865, Barnwell District, SC, in Freedmen's Bureau Applications for Restoration, William M. Bailey.

415. "William M. Bailey" in Walter B. Edgar, et al. *Biographical Directory of the South Carolina House of Representatives* (Columbia: USC Press, 1974).

416. Freedman's Bureau Applications for Restoration, William Baynard.

417. Prospect Hill was measured at 453 acres in a 1910 survey. That apparently included the planting fields reclaimed from marsh, as well as a small amount of marsh. (SCDAH, McCrady Plat No. 876). The other dimensions and physical features are from the U.S. Coast Survey map.

418. Interview July 26, 2004, with Richard D. Porcher.

419. Puckette, *Sea Island Principality*, 14; Johnson, *Social History*, 109n.

420. Davidson, *Last Foray*, 177; Freedmen's Bureau Applications for Restoration, William G. Baynard.

421. U.S. Coast Survey map.

422. Freedmen's Bureau Applications for Restoration, Ephraim C. Bailey; U.S. Coast Survey map.

423. Rivers, *Seven South Carolina Low Country Families*, B12–B28; Davidson, *Last Foray*, 174.

424. Freedmen's Bureau Applications for Restoration, William M. Bailey; U.S. Coast Survey map.

425. SCDAH, Royal Grants, vol. 38, 361, July 15, 1698; Memorials, vol. 9, 238–39, May 18, 1767.

426. Nell S. Graydon, *Tales of Edisto* (Columbia: The R.L. Bryan Co., 1955), 27.

427. Rivers, *Seven South Carolina Low Country Families*, W8–W10; Freedmen's Bureau Applications for Restoration. For five Whaley children's plantations, see Old House, Cedar Hall and Tom Seabrook's (above), Home Place and Ash's (below). The oldest son, Joseph, died in 1846 at age twenty-five. The seventh child, Thomas B. Whaley, did not have an Edisto plantation, and perhaps did not want one.

428. U.S. Coast Survey map.

429. Ibid.; Davidson, *Last Foray*, 174.

430. SCDAH, Royal Grants, vol. 38, 444, December 1, 1700; Memorials, vol. 5, 90, February 20, 1732.

431. SCDAH, Conveyance Book H7, 271.

432. U.S. Coast Survey map; Rivers, *Seven South Carolina Low Country Families*, W8–W9. The Whaley family circumstances are the author's guesses.

433. Porcher and Fick, *Story of Sea Island Cotton*, 425. Part of Frogmore apparently came from a 1711 grant of 150 acres to Ralph Bailey: SCDAH, Memorials, vol. 4, 330, August 9, 1733.

434. Porcher and Fick, *Story of Sea Island Cotton*, 426–27; Freedmen's Bureau Applications for Restoration, William J. Whaley; U.S. Coast Survey map.

435. Freedmen's Bureau Applications for Restoration, William J. Whaley.

436. Freedmen's Bureau Applications for Restoration, Elizabeth A. Seabrook. The original spelling of her name, Eliza Ann Seabrook, is from Rivers, *Seven South Carolina Low Country Families*, S7.

437. 1860 Agricultural Census. Most likely Betsy Seabrook's cotton acreage was planted on shares by a neighbor, such as Dr. Mitchell of Frogmore or William Edings of Gun Bluff.

438. U.S. Coast Survey map; Freedmen's Bureau Applications for Restoration, Joseph Edings.

439. Puckette, *Sea Island Principality*, 13, tells the story of the rediscovery of Governor Seabrook's grave in the twentieth century.

440. U.S Coast Survey map.

441. SCDAH, Royal Grants, vol. 38, 418, August 14, 1702; U.S. Coast Survey map; Freedmen's Bureau Applications for Restoration, Edward M. Baynard.

442. Hasell, *Baynard*, 154–79. J.C. Baynard, the former owner, has not been further identified.

443. SCDAH, Royal Grants, vol. 39, 441, May 10, 1703; Memorials, vol. 5, 228–30, May 2, 1733; vol. 12, 165, April 28, 1773.

444. Rivers, *Seven South Carolina Low Country Families*, J29; Albergotti, *Abigail's Story*, 20–21.

445. The 1725 date is from Graydon, *Tales of Edisto*, 44–45, and Puckette, *Sea Island Principality*, 4. For an alternative hypothesis, see Chapter 2.

446. Rivers, *Seven South Carolina Low Country Families*, J30–J31; Albergotti, *Abigail's Story*, 71.

447. Rivers, *Seven South Carolina Low Country Families*, J30.

448. Reverend John E. Cornish, "Diary, 1833–1877," in Southern History Collection, University of North Carolina, Chapel Hill (excerpts transcribed by Nancy Peeples, 1990), entries for October 19, 1853, and December 20, 1869; Freedmen's Bureau Applications for Restoration, Joseph E. Jenkins. Roxbury is spelled Rockburg in some Freedmen's Bureau documents, but Colonel Jenkins's spelling was Roxbury.

449. SCDAH, Royal Grants, vol. 39, 295, n.d. (1698); and vol. 38, 376, May 11, 1699; Charleston County RMC, "J.T. Kollock's Property Map of Charleston County Compiled 1932–1933–1934."

450. U.S. Coast Survey map.

451. Ibid.; Freedmen's Bureau Applications for Restoration, E. Mikell Whaley.

452. Porcher and Fick, *Story of Sea Island Cotton*, 426–27.

453. Rivers, *Seven South Carolina Low Country Families*, B9, W9; Hasell, *Baynard*, 166, 189; Porcher and Fick, *Story of Sea Island Cotton*, 482; Freedmen's Bureau Applications for Restoration, E. Mikell Whaley. Mikell and Abigail Whaley did not actually own either Mitchell's or Ash's; their fathers gave them a "life interest" in the two plantations, with title passing to their children.

454. SCDAH, Royal Grants, vol. 39, 86, January 13, 1710; SCDAH Memorials, vol. 9, 302–03, August 22, 1767; Porcher and Fick, *Story of Sea Island Cotton*, 481.

455. U.S. Coast Survey map.

456. SCDAH, Royal Grants, vol. 38, 350, August 16, 1697; Memorials, vol. 2, 94–95, July 11, 1733; U.S. Coast Survey map.

457. U.S. Coast Survey map.

458. Freedmen's Bureau Applications for Restoration, Ephraim Baynard.

459. SCDAH, Royal Grants, vol. 38, 445, May 10, 1700; vol. 39, 295, March 5, 1699, and April 11, 1702; vol. 39, 295–96, August 8, [1702?].

460. U.S. Coast Survey map.

461. SCDAH, Royal Grants, vol. 38, 280, March 14, 1695, and 444, May 10, 1700; SCDAH Memorials, vol. 9, 238–39, May 18, 1767; Freedmen's Bureau Application for Restoration, R.B. Hanahan.

462. U.S. Coast Survey map.

463. Freedmen's Bureau Applications for Restoration, R.B. Hanahan; Rivers, *Seven South Carolina Low Country Families*, B18–B19, C8.

464. SCDAH, Royal Grants, vol. 38, 444, May 10, 1700; Memorials, vol. 9, 301, August 22, 1767.

465. Murray, "Edisto Island and Its Place Names." Older Edistonians all know and agree on this story.

466. U.S. Coast Survey map.

467. The 1696 map has a house symbol and a label "Chehasah" at the precise location of the later Jehossee Plantation headquarters, strongly suggesting some sort of earlier settlement. See Figure 11.

468. SCDAH, Memorials, vol. 3, 166, May 12, 1733. Cedar Island, forty acres just across Fish Creek from Jehossee, has never been considered part of Jehossee, and thus is excluded from this history of Edisto Island.

469. Georgia Colony was chartered in 1732. See Edgar, *South Carolina*, 3.

470. *South-Carolina Gazette*, issue of May 26 to June 2, 1833, at SCDAH. Note that the newspaper spelled Cockran's name Cochran. All other documents have Cockran.

471. SCDAH, Royal Grants, vol. 43, 489–91; H. Exo Hilton, hand-drawn and certified replica of a 1741 Plat of Jehossee Plantation for the Jenys heirs, October 7, 1979, copy in the author's files. Baldwin, "Jehossee Island" file documents the multiple transactions from 1741 to 1830.

472. U.S. Coast Survey map.

473. Nathaniel H. Bishop, *Voyage of the Paper Canoe* (Boston: Lee and Shepard, 1878), republished on the Internet by Eldritchpress.org, c. 2001, Chapter 12, 2.

474. Davidson, *Last Foray*, 171.

475. Visitor, "A Great Plantation," *Charleston Courier*, July 19, 1844, reprinted in *News and Courier*, 1925 (copy in author's files).

## POSTSCRIPT

476. Puckette, *A Sea Island Principality*, 28.

477. Ibid., 26. Another Edistonian with strong doubts was state Senator Edward C. Whaley. "My father…was not for <u>secession</u> but his constituents were, and when it came up in the Senate he voted yes, and [later] said he felt like a coward that he did not get up with Perry of Abbeville and vote no." Whaley, "Story of Marie A. Whaley," 1–2.

478. Shelby Foote, *The Civil War: A Narrative. Volume 1, Fort Sumter to Perryville*, 1, 18.

479. Ibid., 48–50.

# Selected Bibliography

## Published Sources

Albergotti, William G., III. *Abigail's Story: Tides at the Doorstep: The Mackays, LaRoches, Jenkinses, and Chisolms of Low Country South Carolina, 1671–1897.* Spartanburg, SC: The Reprint Company, 1999.

Bolls, Kate McChesney. *The Daniel Townsends of the South Carolina Islands: Their Forbears and Descendants.* Verona, VA: McClure Printing Co., 1975.

Bolster, W. Jeffrey, and Hilary Anderson. *Soldiers, Sailors, Slaves and Ships: The Civil War Photographs of Henry P. Moore.* Concord: New Hampshire Historical Society, 1999.

Borick, Carl P. *A Gallant Defense: The Siege of Charleston, 1780.* Columbia: University of South Carolina Press, 2003.

Catesby, Mark. "The Natural History of Carolina…" [1747] and "The Introduction of a New Staple Crop" [three documents from 1747, 1755 and 1785]. In *The Colonial South Carolina Scene: Contemporary Views, 1697–1774,* edited by H. Roy Merrens. Columbia: University of South Carolina Press, 1977.

Coclanis, Peter A. *The Shadow of a Dream: Economic Life and Death in the South Carolina Low Country, 1670–1920.* New York: Oxford University Press, 1989.

Curtin, Philip D. *The Atlantic Slave Trade: A Census.* Madison: University of Wisconsin Press, 1969.

David, Hilda B. "The African-American Women of Edisto Island: 1850–1920." PhD diss., Emory University, 1990.

# SELECTED BIBLIOGRAPHY

Davidson, Chalmers G. *The Last Foray: The South Carolina Planters of 1860: A Sociological Study.* Columbia: University of South Carolina Press, 1971.

Edgar, Walter B. *Partisans and Redcoats: The Southern Conflict that Turned the Tide of the American Revolution.* New York: HarperCollins, 2001.

————. *South Carolina: A History.* Columbia: University of South Carolina Press, 1998.

Hasell, Annie Baynard Simons. *Baynard: An Ancient Family Bearing Arms.* Columbia: R.L. Bryan, 1972.

Howe, George, DD. *History of the Presbyterian Church in South Carolina.* 2 vols. Columbia: The State Printing Company, 1966. Originally published at Columbia: W.J. Duffie, 1883.

Johnson, Guion G. *A Social History of the Sea Islands; With Special Reference to St. Helena Island, South Carolina.* Chapel Hill: University of North Carolina Press, 1930.

Jordan, Laylon W., and Elizabeth H. Stringfellow. *A Place Called St. John's.* Spartanburg, SC: The Reprint Company, 1998.

Kenner, Helen C. *Historical Records of Trinity Episcopal Church, Edisto Island, South Carolina.* Edisto Island: Trinity Episcopal Church, 1975.

Kovacik, Charles F., and John J. Winberry. *South Carolina: A Geography.* Boulder, CO: Westview Press, 1987.

Leiding, Harriet K. *Historic Houses of South Carolina.* New York: Lippincott, 1921.

Leland, Jack. "Indigo in America" (pamphlet). Edisto Island: Edisto Island Historic Preservation Society, 1994. Originally published at Parsippany, NJ: BASF Wyandotte Corp., 1976.

Lesser, Charles H. "Secretary Paul Grimball, the Sothell Coup D'etat, and the William Dunlop Papers." In *South Carolina Begins: The Records of a Proprietary Colony, 1663–1721.* Columbia: South Carolina Department of Archives and History, 1995.

Lindsay, Nicholas C., ed. *And I'm Glad: An Oral History of Edisto Island.* Charleston: Tempus Publishing, 2000.

Littlefield, Daniel C. *Rice and Slaves: Ethnicity and the Slave Trade in Colonial South Carolina,* Baton Rouge: Louisiana State University Press, 1981.

McAmis, Herb. "Indian People of the Edisto River: A Brief History of the Kusso-Natchez Indians, Often Called 'Edistos'" (pamphlet). Ridgeville(?), SC: Edisto Tribal Council, Inc., n.d. (circa 1990).

McCrady, Edward. *The History of South Carolina under the Proprietary Government, 1670–1719.* New York: Russell & Russell, 1969. Originally published, New York: McMillan, 1901.

McIntosh, Sherrie L. "The Old Edisto Island Baptist Church: Hephzibah Jenkins Townsend, 1780–1847, and the Inheritance of Stewardship and Spiritual Gifts." Master's thesis, West Virginia University, 1998.

Mikell, Isaac Jenkins, [Jr.]. *Rumbling of the Chariot Wheels.* Columbia: The State Company, 1923.

Mikell, Townsend. "The Mikell Genealogy of South Carolina." Charleston: Walker, Evans and Cogswell, 1910. With 1997 addendum by Sarah Mikell Belser Eggleston.

Miller, Sid. "Edisto's Marvelous Line." *South Carolina Wildlife*, September–October 1995.

Mood, F.A. *Methodism in Charleston: A Narrative…* Nashville, TN: Methodist Episcopal Church, South, 1856.

Murray, Chalmers S. "Edisto Island and Its Place Names." *Names in South Carolina.* Columbia: Department of English, University of South Carolina.

———. "Life in Lost Village of Edingsville." *Charleston News and Courier*, December 25, 1955.

Murray, John G., MD. "The Murray Family of Edisto Island" (booklet). Greenville, SC: privately printed, 1958. Copy in the author's personal collection.

Porcher, Richard D., and Sarah Fick. *The Story of Sea Island Cotton.* Charleston: Wyrick and Company, 2005.

Puckette, Clara C., with Clara C. Mackenzie. *Edisto: A Sea Island Principality.* Cleveland, OH: Seaforth, 1978.

Rivers, Joseph L. *Seven South Carolina Low Country Families: Bailey, Clark, Grimball, Jenkins, Seabrook, Townsend, and Whaley.* Charleston: privately printed, revised edition, 1999.

# Selected Bibliography

Rowland, Lawrence S., Alexander Moore and George C. Rogers Jr. *The History of Beaufort County, South Carolina: Volume I, 1514–1861*. Columbia: University of South Carolina Press, 1996.

Sandford, Robert. "A Relation of a Voyage on the Coast of the Province of Carolina, 1666." In *Narratives of Early Carolina, 1650–1708*, edited by Alexander S. Salley. New York: C. Scribner's Sons, 1911.

Shuler, Homer L.F. "Methodism in Charleston and the Low Country." *Journal of the South Carolina Annual Conference*, 1947.

Smith, Henry A.M. "The Baronies of South Carolina." *The South Carolina Historical and Genealogical Magazine* 11, no. 2 (April 1910).

Spencer, Charles S., comp. *Documents on Edisto Island History*. Edisto Island: Edisto Island Historic Preservation Society, forthcoming (2008).

Stoney, Samuel G. *Plantations of the Carolina Low Country*. New York, Dover, and Charleston: Carolina Art Association, 1989. (Seventh edition, originally published in 1977.)

Thomas, Albert S., DD. "The Episcopal Church on Edisto Island…A Sketch… Delivered in Trinity Church, October 10, 1948…" (mimeo). Charleston: The Dalcho Historical Society, 1953.

Turner, Lorenzo Dow. *Africanisms in the Gullah Dialect*. Columbia: University of South Carolina Press, 2002. Originally published in 1949.

Webber, Mabel L. "Grimball of Edisto Island." *The South Carolina Historical and Genealogical Magazine* 23 (1922) in three parts: no. 1, 1–7; no. 2, 39–45; no. 3, 94–110.

Wood, Peter H. *Black Majority: Negroes in Colonial South Carolina from 1670 through the Stono Rebellion*. New York: Knopf, 1974.

## Unpublished and Digital Sources

"1775 Muster Roll." On the Colleton County, South Carolina History and Genealogy Website (http://www.oldplaces.org/colleton/1775muster.htm), Pat Sabin, coordinator. (Accessed March 26, 2004.)

"Assessments on Edisto Island in St. Paul's Parish, according to Law." Unpublished document, April 20, 1732. South Carolina Department of Archives and History, Private Papers, Box 8.

Baldwin, Agnes. Edisto Island land research files, approx. 1 cubic foot, circa 1990. Edisto Island Historic Preservation Society.

"A Brief History of the Presbyterian Church of Edisto Island." Pamphlet, n.d. (circa 1935), with a postscript, 1963. No author (Esther M. Seabrook Connor?) Privately printed, Edisto Island, 1963. Copy in the archive of the Presbyterian Church on Edisto Island.

Brockman, Mary Clark. "Clarks of Edisto Island, S.C., and Clark Family in America." Unpublished typescript, n.d. (circa 1950), copy in the author's personal collection.

Chisolm, William G. "Edings of Edisto Island." Unpublished manuscript, 1943. South Caroliniana Library, University of South Carolina, Columbia.

Connor, Esther M. Seabrook. "Seabrook." Unpublished manuscript, n.d. (circa 1937), original in possession of Marion C. Norwood, Greenville, SC.

Cornish, Reverend John E. "Diary, 1833–1877." Southern History Collection, University of North Carolina, Chapel Hill. Excerpts transcribed by Nancy Peeples, 1990. Copy in the author's personal collection.

"Edisto Island Baptist Church." South Carolina Department of Archives and History. National Register of Historic Places Inventory Nomination Form, 1981.

Fickling, William A., III, comp., et. al. "The First Ficklings in America" and "George Fickling of South Carolina [and descendants]." On the Fickling family website, http://www.ficklin-fickling.org/. (Accessed August 19, 2001.)

Gourdin, White E., C.E. "Map of the Village of Edingsville, Edisto Island, S.C." Surveyed for J.E. Edings, July 1866. South Carolina Historical Society, Charleston.

Lee, Reverend W. States. "Sketch of the History of the Presbyterian Church of Edisto Island from 1821 to 1858." Unpublished manuscript in Church Session Books, originals on deposit at South Caroliniana Library, University of South Carolina, Columbia. Typed transcription by E.M.S.C. [Esther M. Seabrook Connor], circa 1930. Archive of the Presbyterian Church on Edisto Island.

"Losses Claimed by Sea Island Landowners, 1862." Manuscripts in the collection of the South Carolina Historical Society, Charleston. Excerpts transcribed by Nancy Peeples, digitally merged and edited by Blanchard Smith, 2001. Copy in the author's collection.

# Selected Bibliography

McLeod, Rebecca Lamar. "Wreck of the *Pulaski*" (detailed, first-person account, circa 1888). Digitally transcribed and edited by Mary DeLashmit for internet access at http://members.aol.com/eleanorcol/WreckPulaski.html. (Accessed November 20, 2003.)

Murray, Chalmers S. "Side Tour of Edisto Island." Unpublished Federal Writers Project manuscript, circa 1936. Chalmers Murray Papers (1178). South Carolina Historical Society, Charleston.

Murray, Whitmarsh S. "History of the Murray Family in South Carolina." Unpublished manuscript, circa 1901. Typescript, 1958, by Charles Spencer. Edisto Island Historic Preservation Society, "Murray Family."

National Archives and Records Administration, Record Group 29, Records of the Bureau of Census. Agricultural Census of 1860, South Carolina, Parish of St. John's Colleton.

———, Record Group 29, Records of the Bureau of Census. First (1790) through Eighth (1860) Population Censuses of the U.S. South Carolina, Parish of St. John's Colleton. Microfilm publications: M367, Reel 11 (1790); M32, Reel 48 (1800); M252, Reel 60 (1810); M33, Reel 11 (1820); M19, Reel 170 (1830); M704, Reel 510 (1840); M432, Reel 850 (free persons, 1850) and Reel 863 (slaves, 1850); M653, Reel 1218 (free persons, 1860) and Reel 1234 (slaves, 1860).

———, Record Group 105, Records of the Bureau of Refugees, Freedmen and Abandoned Lands. Assistant Commissioner for South Carolina. Entry 2942: Register of Applications for Restoration of Property, August 1865 to May 1866. Entry 2943: Applications for Restoration of Property.

"Proceedings of the Meeting in Charleston, S.C., May 13–15, 1845, on the Religious Instruction of the Negroes, together with the Report of the Committee, and the Address to the Public." Pamphlet, Charleston: B. Jenkins, 1845. In "From Slavery to Freedom: The African-American Pamphlet Collection, 1824–1909," Library of Congress, Washington, D.C. Digital text available online in Library of Congress's American Memory Project: http://memory.loc.gov/ammem/aapchtml/aapchome.html. (Accessed in February 2003.)

South Carolina Department of Archives and History. Land Memorials, volumes 1–12.

———. Proprietary Grants and Royal Grants.

Thomas, Edward. "Private Register of Rev. Edward Thomas While Rector of Trinity Church, Edisto." Unpublished typescript, circa 1954, in the library of Trinity Episcopal Church.

U.S. Coast Survey, A.D. Bache, superintendent. "Sketch E, No. 3, Showing the Progress of the Survey at North & South Edisto River and St. Helena Sound, South Carolina, 1851." Map Division, Library of Congress, Washington, D.C.

Worthington, W. Curtis. "Some Highlights from the History of Trinity Episcopal Church on Edisto Island." Unpublished lecture text, 2000, in the Library of Trinity Episcopal Church.

# INDEX

# Index